i

Printed in U.S.A.

First Published 2013

ISBN – 978-0-9891677-1-0

MassMedia.mobi Press
2809 Mount Vernon Ave., Suite 201
Alexandria, Virginia 22301
Website www.TheFirstApple.com

Contents

We've chosen to let interviewees speak in their own voices, and we defer to them in terms of their recollections and how accurately they express tech concepts.

Footnotes are provided for terms that recur throughout the text. They are in the back of the book on page 367, in alphabetical order, and sometimes listed with the name of an interviewee.

Cast of Characters:

Allen Baum – Met Wozniak in high school. He and his dad lent money to start Apple.

Mario Boglioni – Italian fashion mogul. Apple collector.

Joey Copson – Atari game programmer. Original owner of Apple-1 from Byte Shop.

Rick Crandall – Former technology CEO, currently on various corporate boards.

Bill Fernandez – Childhood neighbor of Wozniak. High school classmate of Jobs. Apple employee # 4.

Elizabeth Holmes – Reed College classmate of Jobs. Apple Computer's first bookkeeper.

Dick Huston – Apple employee, with his brother Cliff, starting in 1977.

Federico Ini – Broadcast personality and technology reporter in Argentina.

Sellam Ismail – Computer collector, show organizer, technology recycler.

Steve Jobs – Apple Computer co-founder in 1976. *Editorial note: Mr. Jobs died during the course of work on* The First Apple. *Some interviews refer to him in the present tense.*

Dan Kottke – Friends with Jobs at Reed College, Apple employee # 12.

Dave Larsen – Vintage computer collector, entrepreneur in Floyd, Virginia.

Liza Loop – Educational activist, met Wozniak at Homebrew Club meeting.

Lonnie Mimms – Atlanta based computer collector, in commercial real estate.

Neil Goldberg – 1960's singer/songwriter, owned a used computer store.

Owen O'Mahony – British citizen and retired Royal Air Force pilot.

Jef Raskin – Apple employee # 31. Innovative engineering designer.

Charles Ricketts – Original owner of the Apple-1 computer that inspired the investigation detailed in this book.

Wendell Sander – RAM chip designer for Fairchild Semiconductor, Apple employee # 16.

Risley Sams – Former auctioneer LaSalle Gallery, San Francisco.

Adam Schoolsky – Was a Los Angeles based boyhood friend of Wozniak.

Mike Scott – Apple Computer President '77 to '81, employee # 7.

Dan Sokol – Silicon Valley veteran, longtime friend of Wozniak.

Craig Solomonson – Educational software background, eclectic collector.

Paul Terrell – Founded Byte Shop chain of computer stores. 1st retailer to sell Apples.

Bruce Waldack – Serial entrepreneur in Washington, D.C. during dot com boom.

David Waldack – Brother and co-worker of Bruce Waldack.

Ron Wayne – Third co-founder of Apple Computer. Designed original Apple logo.

Randy Wigginton – High school-age attendee of Homebrew Computer Club and protégé of Wozniak. Apple employee # 6.

Mike Willegal – Curator of the Apple-1 Registry.

Steve Wozniak – Co-founder of Apple Computer. Designed Apple-1 and the Apple][.

Introduction

In 2009, five years after finding my Apple-1, I decided to write the story of my auction purchase. I was toying with the idea of selling my Apple, and wondering how to go about it. Consigning to an auction seemed risky, even one of the major auction companies, because there wasn't an established market. I figured if I wrote up my story, and got it published, that might lead to a buyer. For me to even consider selling this museum-piece, I needed to feel I was getting a very good price for it. I felt confident I was in possession of something highly desirable, and I needed to figure out a way to find the optimum purchaser.

So, I sat down to write my story for publication. I imagined the story ending up in *Vanity Fair* or *The Wall Street Journal*. When I'd finished my article, I contacted the *WSJ*. I was put in touch with one of their journalists who'd written a book about *MySpace*, but she never responded after I'd sent her my article.

The finished article was much longer than I'd anticipated. By detailing the whole sequence of events, and the twists and turns of the auction I attended, my article expanded to over five thousand words. '*Wow*, I thought, I wonder how long it would need to be for it to be a book?' So, I Googled, "number of words in a book," and I learned that it should be from fifty thousand to one hundred thousand words. Well, I'd pretty much told my whole story, so what else could I say to make it a book? That was a tall order. But the more I thought about it, I figured if the story of my Apple-1 was interesting, maybe the story of *all* the Apple-1's would be compelling.

I needed to further investigate my own machine's history, so maybe I could collect stories about the Apple-1 computer in general. And, as time passed, the ongoing story of Apple and Steve Jobs got better and better. The value of these machines might appreciate, since the Apple-1 was the cornerstone of a company with a track record of introducing one smash hit product after another. Steve Jobs wasn't just involved with Apple; he also owned Pixar animation studio. For a long time, it seemed he could do no wrong.

There were hints and leads related to the history of my machine, but also many unanswered questions. Who really was Charles Ricketts, the original owner of my machine? Was he simply a hobbyist who lived four miles from Steve Jobs, who'd heard about the first Apple computers, and wanted one for himself? Did he personally know Jobs or Wozniak from the Homebrew Computer Club meetings? Or was Ricketts more than that; an engineer, or a possible investor in Apple? The fact that he'd purchased his machine directly from Jobs' garage, and not from a Byte Shop computer store, was intriguing. Also, knowing the exact date of his purchase indicated a *very early* purchase in terms of Apple Computer history. I wondered, could the Ricketts' machine have been the first sale of an Apple product directly to an individual? I figured if I were able to talk to the people involved at the time, someone might know.

I engaged the help of an intern, and we found that most everybody we reached out to was willing to talk with us. They often referred the names of others we should speak with. They'd give us people's contact information, or volunteer to email an introduction for us. So we've been able to find many of the first people associated with early Apple history, folks who were friends of Steve Jobs and Steve Wozniak, and even the people who'd worked in the Jobs' house and garage during that crucial first summer of the company's existence. We were interested in hearing their stories, and of course we also wanted to know what they knew, if anything, about Charles Ricketts.

So how could I tell if my computer might actually be the first one sold directly to a consumer by Apple? The Apple-1 computers didn't have serial numbers, so you can't say that 'this is number such and such.' We knew the actual 'first sale' by Apple was when they originally landed a bulk sale of fifty units to a computer retail store chain called the Byte Shop. Those fifty computers would not have been retailed by Apple, so payment for any one of them would have been made to the Byte Shop. The cancelled checks for my machine are made out to Apple Computer.

So here's what I did:

I met Steve Wozniak at a conference where he was giving a speech, and showed him pictures of my Apple-1.

I found an article in the National Enquirer about the third Apple founder, Ron Wayne. I called and interviewed Ron, and subsequently met with him in-person.

I read that an Apple-1 sold for over two hundred thousand dollars at auction in London in November 2010, and I interviewed the Italian collector who'd purchased it.

I tried to track down the LaSalle Gallery people, where I knew my Apple-1 had been auctioned off in 1999. Eventually I was able to interview the auctioneer. I wanted to confirm what I'd read, that the family of Charles Ricketts had consigned the computer. It was published that it sold for eighteen thousand dollars, and I wanted to confirm that price. I was interested in finding the winning bidder, and maybe the auction house could help me.

I hired Sarah Hutton as a summer intern to help me do interviews and track down anyone associated with the Apple-1. Sarah had just graduated with a degree in Public Relations from Temple University in Philadelphia, so she seemed well-qualified to help gather the stories. We found and interviewed people who were involved with building the machines over thirty years ago. Often, they were also friends with Steve Jobs or Steve Wozniak, so that made it even more interesting. Then, we tracked down and interviewed some of today's collectors who own an Apple-1. Neither Sarah or I are *techies*; we focused on collecting the human interest stories behind the technology. She interviewed some brilliant engineers from the beginning of the personal computer revolution, and she held her own with them.

As the project moved forward, Sarah moved on in her career. After a time, I recruited another experienced editor and writer, Larry Rodman. Larry's done a first-class job of locating people, interviewing them, research and editing.

I traveled to Southern Virginia to meet with a former Christmas tree farmer, who owns a computer collection that includes more Apple-1's than anybody else in the world.

In Northern California, I checked out the apartment community where Charles Ricketts lived in 1976. In Santa Cruz, I met with a 1960s pop music veteran, and Saturday morning cartoon songwriter, who had a hand in our story. He invited my son Cameron and I to go to the top of a mountain and meet his yogi. On the same journey, we visited the man who's brokered the sale of more Apple-1 computers than anyone else, in Livermore, California, at his computer recycling business. He then took us on a journey of many miles to his remote warehouse, where he houses what he claims is the largest privately-held vintage computer collection in the world.

As we interviewed more and more people, we began to uncover the true story about my Apple-1. Its history reminds me of the Hope Diamond legend. The Hope Diamond has a marvelous history, but it's said to be cursed. I haven't been able to find out all of the answers regarding my machine, but read on and I'll share what I know.

Chapter 1

The Backpack

Dan Sokol, a longtime friend of Apple co-founder Steve Wozniak, told me this story:

"Apple co-founder Steve Wozniak gave a speech back in the '90s at MacWorld Japan. Steve and I got there a day before. There's this huge conference center. We walked over from the hotel and figured we'd walk through and take a look at it a day in advance. As we're walking around this big empty place, there were a couple security guards, and people building booths and stuff. Nobody paid much attention to us. I noticed every time we'd go into a new area, there would be some younger individual with a walkie-talkie, and they would turn their back to us every time I'd have eye contact with them. I mentioned it to Steve, and he said,

'Yeah, I saw one or two people like that. I wonder what's going on?' I said, 'I don't know, but keep your eyes out. Maybe we're being spied on.' And we were. It was a local computer club who'd heard he was coming, and they thought if they showed up a day early, they might find him and talk to him.

We entered this one hall, and these kids came running from six different directions at once. And I mean running. One of them stopped in front of us, 'Mr. Wozniak,' you know, broken English, all starry-eyed. But this one kid—I use the word kid, but he must have been thirty to thirty-five years old—he's panting. He has this backpack, and in the backpack is an Apple-1, and all the original manuals and stuff in plastic bags. He asked Steve if he would sign it for him. We're talking about someone who's seriously hyperventilating. I'm looking at this kid and wondering if I'm going to have to perform CPR on him.

We couldn't communicate with him, 'It's alright, we're not going anywhere. Take your time.' He was having a hard time getting his message out. I was wondering if he had asthma, too. It's like, 'Wow, what's going on here?' Anyway, Steve signed it and they talked for a while. He told Steve how he got it, from a friend who had it in his garage. He bought it years ago, and never built it up. Then he asked Steve if he would sign his Apple][. That computer was also in the backpack! So Steve signed his Apple][and two disk drives. He had this stuff in his backpack all day while they were looking for him. That was perhaps the weirdest thing that ever happened to us."

Chapter 2

The First Cell Phone

My dad always liked cars and gadgets. *Cool* cars and *neat* gadgets. Pretty much his whole career was in sales for IBM, in the Washington D.C. area. Being on a sales force in the '60s and '70s was similar to the show *Mad Men*. The guys (in those days, it was *all* guys) had to strike a balance between being family men, and being cool guys on a competitive sales force. Part of being a cool guy was to drive a nice car. If you were an IBM sales rep at that time, you could afford a spiffy car. One salesman would touch off a trend, and the car buying would happen in waves. When one rep showed up at work with a brand new 1966 Buick Riviera, you can bet there were going to be others in the office who got Rivieras. After that phase, it was the 1969 Pontiac Grand Prix. Then there'd be a switch to something different, like foreign cars. One guy bought a Mercedes in the then popular Tobacco Brown, and soon everyone in the office was out looking at new or used Mercedes.

In the late 1970s, Dad had a portable telephone in a briefcase, which he carried in his car. So it was a car phone. Only it wasn't, because that type of phone was really a type of radio. He couldn't directly dial another phone. He had to call an operator. She (and they were *all* women) would make the call and 'patch' him in through his radio phone. Even if it didn't work very well, it didn't matter, because he really didn't

3

actually need a portable phone. It was just a cool gadget for him to show off. He wasn't one to brag, but instead was an enthusiast. He'd get people excited about a subject because of his own enthusiasm.

I have five siblings, so Dad had to watch his spending. He was the breadwinner for a large family. One day in 1980, he received in the mail an offer for a new portable phone. It was *really* new, and it was going to cost two hundred dollars per month. That was a huge amount for him. He mentioned it to me, but he wasn't going to spring for it. The mailer made it sound really neat, and I figured I could afford it. I was a young single guy living at home and making pretty good money, so I had disposable income. Dad and I shared the same first name, so I took his invitation and responded as if it had been sent to me.

I signed on to the program and soon had my Motorola DynaTAC cell phone, affectionately known as the 'brick phone' to gadget historians. This was 1981, and I later learned I was one of the first one hundred fifty people *in the world* to have a cell phone, as part of this Motorola test program.

It was a great novelty and conversation piece; nobody I knew had ever seen one before. Also, it worked very well. Reception wasn't great inside a solid brick or concrete building, but otherwise it was as clear as cell phones are today.

Once in a while, the DynaTAC had a maintenance issue. In those instances, I just had to get to the Motorola office in downtown D.C., and they'd give me a replacement phone. As the years have passed, I've often thought how I wish I'd been able to keep that very first original phone. Being one of the first one hundred fifty, it probably had a low serial number and might be quite valuable today. But any time I had a problem with a particular phone, I swapped it. So after a couple of years of use, due to the replacement cycle, I probably no longer had a low serial number unit. Of course, at the time, I didn't realize that it was historic. I just thought it was cool.

4

Chapter 3

Sheriff's Sale

In December 2004, I was reading my local newspaper, *The Washington Post*, and I noticed a tiny classified ad for an auction. It was a sheriff's sale. They were holding an auction of goods that had been seized by the Fairfax County, Virginia, Sheriff's Department. There was a short list of items, including what was described as "2 Segway Scooters (1 of which was the 1st Segway ever offered)," and "1st Apple Computer ever sold (one of a kind item, Cert.)."

I thought back to my original Motorola cell phone. That was twenty-four years ago, but it always bothered me that I'd not been able to hang onto that first phone. Given the opportunity for another *first*, I would not let it slip through my fingers.

I called the phone number in the ad to get more information. It was the office of an attorney. He told me he represented GE Capital, and GE had a client who'd stopped making lease payments on his private jet. On behalf of GE, the attorney had obtained a judgment against the man. To collect on the judgment, he arranged for the sheriff to seize items of value from the home of the fellow who'd been leasing the jet. I asked the attorney for the man's name, and he said he couldn't disclose that information. So I asked, "How about if I guess his name?" and he replied, "Sure." "Bruce Waldack," I said. Sounding surprised, he said, "You're correct. How did you know that?"

I went on to tell him that I remembered reading, sometime in late 1999, or early 2000, that Segway was auctioning the first three scooters they built. The auction was going to be on Amazon.com. The Segway was new to the marketplace at the time, and Amazon was experimenting with auctions, in direct competition with *eBay*. The auction would serve to generate publicity for Segway and Amazon. All proceeds would go to charity, and each of the three Segways ended up selling at auction for about one hundred thousand dollars, about twenty times the list price of a standard Segway. I read at the time that one of the three was purchased by Bruce Waldack, a successful local entrepreneur.

At a very young age, Bruce founded one of the first Internet Service Providers, or ISP's, by the name of DigitalNation. Bruce sold out to Vario, a Japanese company, at the height of the dot com boom. Bruce's take on the deal was a hundred million dollars. Verio didn't acquire DigitalNation with stock, it was an all-cash deal.

At some point after Bruce bought the Segway, he also received some unflattering publicity. He contributed to the campaign of a local politician who was running for office. News leaked that Bruce's new start-up business, an online advertising firm, relied on the porn industry for a large amount of its income. Bruce had to publicly distance himself from the candidate.

I asked the attorney about the Segway. The "first Apple" also caught my interest. Steve Jobs was back at Apple and had introduced the iPod, which was a huge success. Having started Apple, and now introducing the iPod and starting to completely change the business and distribution of music, I figured Jobs had a brighter future still; maybe his first computer would be a smart investment. "How do you know it is the *first* Apple computer?" I asked the attorney. He told me that he had proof, and described two cancelled checks from 1976 that were used to purchase the computer. I asked what a vintage Apple looked like, because at the time I had no clue. He said that I might find a picture of it on *eBay*. The owner listed it on *eBay* in an attempt to sell it. When the sheriff seized the computer, the *eBay* listing was terminated. The auction was going to happen in about ten days, and so I started to do some homework.

I was able to find the old article about the Segway auction. The Segway is a profoundly unique and brilliant creation. As a lifelong collector of various objects, including vintage cars, I thought it would be neat to own the very first one built. If the Segway became a wildly popular conveyance over time, it would be highly desirable to own one of the first three ever built. It would be similar to owning the first Mustang from 1964, or maybe Henry Ford's very first Model T Ford.

I knew *eBay* listings stayed up as an archive for a limited period of time, so I searched for the Apple computer listing. No luck. I sat at the desk in my basement, researching late into the night. After doing a little bit of basic research on Apple, I now knew I was looking for a listing for an Apple-1. It's pronounced *apple one*.

The next evening I sat down at my home computer again. I'd always been good at finding things, so I decided to give it another shot. No luck on *eBay*, but I found myself doing online searches and any kind of drilling down to try to find some other evidence. I came across a blog. It may have been the very first blog I'd ever seen. It came up during a search that was something like 'Apple-1 computer *eBay*.' The blog mentioned someone selling an old machine on *eBay*, and I clicked on a hyperlink. *Bingo!* I was now looking at a cancelled *eBay* listing, including pictures, for the Apple-1 computer. Wow, this was a rudimentary looking machine. The seller stated that he was now "Moving off to the sea," and so he couldn't take his most prized possession with him. The phrase about going to sea seemed to be like something straight out of a ship captain's journal from the 1800s! The machine certainly looked real to me, and the documentation was impressive.

The *eBay* listing was from September 25th, 2004, and was titled "Holy Grail of Collectible Computers - Apple-1 CPU." It also said, "Bidding has ended for this item," which would have been the case once the sheriff showed up at the Waldack home. The seller had an *eBay* rating of 128, and a 97.8 percent positive feedback rating, but was also shown as "Not a registered user." How someone could sell one hundred twenty-eight items on *eBay* and still be "unregistered" was a mystery to me! The location was in Alexandria, Virginia. The *eBay* listing copy read:

"OWN A PIECE OF HISTORY. THIS COMPUTER WAS IN THE TIME/NEWSWEEK MILLENNIUM ISSUE. LISTED AS ONE OF THE 100 MOST IMPORTANT INVENTIONS OF THE MILLENNIUM.

Over five years ago, I bought this Apple-1 computer for over $30,000.00 I am now moving off to the sea and can't bear the thought of the salt and sea air destroying this valuable piece of computer history. There are several sites dedicated to this computer, which will all document and show my computer to be correct. There are said to be less than 30 Apple-1's still in existence.

This computer, as is documented, was bought from Steve Jobs' parents' garage. The checks for the purchase and original manual are included. The checks are in fact made out to and endorsed by Apple Computer Company. They (Apple) were not yet incorporated.

This is a true, and real opportunity to purchase a computer that also resides in the Smithsonian Museum.

These are rarely if ever offered, and never at this price, with this kind of documentation.

Included are.

The CPU

The Keyboard

The Original manual

The checks that were used to buy the computer in 1976."

As I looked over the *eBay* listing, I wondered what else this guy was selling on *eBay* before the sheriff raided his home? So I hit the link for "Other Items From This Seller." *Bingo*, there were pages of items listed. I dove in and started checking out the listings, which started to paint quite a picture of Bruce...

There were many listings for authentic, antique Tiffany vases. He mentioned in some of his listings that he'd been a major success in the technology world, and had made a lot of money, so he was able to collect the best examples of anything that he was interested in. Clearly, Bruce was a collector extraordinaire of fine Tiffany glass. In the photos, you could tell that all the Tiffany was displayed in his office. It was strange, however, that the photos were often blurry. These items were selling for several thousand dollars each, and yet the photos were horrible. I figured that a knowledgeable Tiffany collector would be able to discern, despite the blurry photos, that this was authentic Tiffany. But, at the same time, I suspected that the bidders were staying cautious. They didn't know this guy; he was just some stranger selling stuff on *eBay*. A blurry photo of a colored vase could hide the fact that there might be a few chips in the glass, so to be safe, they'd probably only bid it up to about half of market value.

At the same time, I knew how deep this guy's pockets were. I was starting to get an idea of his tastes. I suspected that he hadn't collected vases that were chipped. No, he undoubtedly collected the good stuff, only the finest examples of a particular item. So, why was he now dumping it all on *eBay*? And doing it in a sloppy fashion, blurry photos and minimal descriptions? I was starting to guess that this guy had a problem. I didn't know what, but it looked like he might be desperate for cash. It occurred to me that he'd listed items that he could see without having to get up from the desk chair in his office! He was selling everything in sight. But *why*?

9

There were a few neat guitars in the *eBay* listings. That made sense, because the little classified ad mentioned that a large number of electric guitars would be in the auction. So he also liked guitars. I was able to see about forty items that he'd bought or sold on *eBay*. The majority of items were the Tiffany, and the handful of guitars, and the Apple-1. There were four other items, and those seemed to tell more of the story.

All of the *eBay* listings were for items that he was selling, except for three items he'd bought on *eBay*. He'd purchased a gold and diamond woman's bracelet, an airline ticket voucher for First-Class seats for two to Las Vegas, and a couple of nights stay at the Palms Hotel & Casino. It seemed strange. When you see someone just dumping things that they've carefully collected, there's probably good reason for their desperation. Oh, and he was without his jet.

The last *eBay* listing may have been the most interesting. It was for a Lincoln Continental Limousine that the seller described in detail. He explained in the description that he was a huge Jimmy Buffet fan, and that he'd spent over one hundred thousand dollars to have this car customized exclusively to attend Jimmy Buffet concerts. The roof had been mostly removed, making the limousine into a convertible. There was some sort of bamboo trellis over the back passenger seat. All the trim decor was island-themed. And to top it off, protruding out of the front grill was a large shark's head, jutting out between the headlights, and a large shark tailfin was sticking up quite high from the back trunk. It sold at 'no reserve' on *eBay*, just like he had sold every other item else he'd listed. The car only brought about six thousand dollars. And clearly, if the sheriff's department had not entered Bruce's home during the *eBay* listing, the Apple-1 would have also gone to the highest bidder.

I knew the basics of Apple's history, and I'd kept up on articles about Steve Jobs over the years. I'd read John Scully's book about his tenure running Apple after Jobs was fired. But I knew nothing about the actual computers, or about the first version. So I did some reading and learned the Apple-1 was the first computer built by Jobs and Wozniak, and they made about two hundred of them. Jobs had struck a deal with a local computer store for an initial bulk sale of fifty units. When the Apple][came along—the model that was a quantum leap in improvement—the owners of Apple-1 computers were offered a generous trade-in. Evidently many owners took advantage of the offer. The traded-in units were said to have been destroyed by Apple.

Now that I was learning a little bit about the Apple-1, and the auction day was approaching, I had a few questions for the attorney. I phoned him. It was the Friday before the auction, which was scheduled for Tuesday. His assistant said he was out of town. So I asked when he was due to return, and was told it wasn't going to be soon. "He won't be attending the auction?" I asked. No, she said, he would not. *Wow*, I thought that was strange. I figured part of his job would be to attend and observe the auction, but that was evidently not the case.

The classified ad indicated there'd be forty Gibson guitars slated to be sold at the auction, which was intriguing. I didn't know much about guitars, so I called my friend Bill, a collector and sometime vintage guitar dealer. I told him about the auction, and asked if he'd like to attend with me. I also warned him that the classified ad for the auction said "cash only," and the sheriff was likely to stick to that rule, so to come prepared. We agreed to meet at eight a.m. on Tuesday at the self-storage facility in Chantilly, Virginia where the auction was to be held. The auction wasn't scheduled to start until ten, but I wanted to be nice and early so that we had ample time to carefully preview and look over the merchandise on offer.

Chapter 4

Classified Ads

In the 1960s, my grandparents lived in a stately old home in Paoli, Pennsylvania. Paoli is not far from Valley Forge, best known for its part in the Revolutionary War. The original rooms of their house dated back to that time, and were said to have been occupied by troops trying to stay warm during the winter of 1777. Grand dad and Grani Catherine had a trove of American antiques, and that was my first exposure to collections of neat old stuff. I was hooked. What appealed to me was the history, and the mystery conveyed by the wonderful patina of items that were a hundred years old. Also, there was a profit incentive. If you were to find something old and get it cheap, you might make some money reselling it. One way of finding old stuff was to attend auctions, which I started to do when I was fifteen. After having attended many auctions over the years, I have my own auction rules of thumb.

Most auctions turn out to be a disappointment. The ads make them sound great, but when you arrive, there's just a bunch of junk. Or, sometimes the prices are sky high for the few good items. But if you go to enough auctions, the law of averages determines that you'll find something good. Once in a while, you'll hit the mother lode, an auction that's just a bonanza of great finds or true bargains. At an auction like this, you can almost buy with abandon, and later be glad you did. In the stock market, if an analyst finds a compelling stock to buy, he'll say, "Back up the truck!" This means you should load up while the 'gettin's good.' The opportunity doesn't come along very often, so make the most of it.

At a lousy auction, you may not buy anything, and it ends up being a waste of time. But at a good auction, when the deals are happening, it's time to take advantage. If you're really buying *right*, go for it! I've been to a number of auctions where I felt instinctively, 'this is a good one, take full advantage.' I've never regretted buying lots of items during a really a good sale.

How high to bid? When you're bidding, when do you stop? My own policy is never to have a definite stopping point. Yes, admittedly, that can be dangerous. But, in most instances, I find I've developed a gut feeling for the approximate price limit. That comfort level is usually based on research, due diligence, and comparative price-checking. Let's say there's an item at auction that you really want. And, in a disciplined fashion, you set a stopping-point for the bidding. Then, when the bidding starts, you reach your pre-set limit, and you stop bidding. Often, I've found at that point the bidding has narrowed down to one other bidder and me. When either one of us drops out, the rival wins the item with one more bid. If I stop bidding prematurely, the other guy gets the item for a small amount over my limit. If it was a really good item, and something I planned on keeping for a long time, what difference would it have made if I'd bid just a little bit more? Maybe one more bid is what it would've taken for the *other* bidder to drop out. If I'm buying a pricey collectible, or some sort of appreciating asset, wouldn't the increase in value over time make up for the fact that I paid a bit more? All I can say is that it's worked for me.

The last rule of thumb isn't really original to me. It's based on the old adage that you can't buy a bad example cheap enough, and you can't pay too much for the best example. This doesn't apply to new stuff; it's a rule for buying something unique at auction. You probably shouldn't buy a lousy example of *anything*, no matter how low the price or how cheap it seems. In that case, there's no price that really makes sense. On the other hand, if you are buying the best of the best, it may be okay to pay whatever it takes. Part of the reason for that is that there will always be someone later on who'll lust for it, and value it even higher. Just ask any auctioneer how often they know of items selling after an auction has ended. People think, 'I should have bought that, darn it!' And then, they're willing to pay more than they would have gotten it for in the auction.

When I was a teen, I was a classified ad fanatic. I discovered there were deals to be found in the newspaper ads. Often, it meant you had to be the first to get to someone's front door, but that was part of the fun. Sometimes it would be like attending an auction and being the only bidder. Once, I went to look at a 1963 Jaguar E-Type Roadster, in British Racing Green. It was in the garage of a man who told me that he was an heir of a well-known American company. The problem was that I had a rival show up to see the car at the same time, a fellow with only one arm. (Later, I came to know this fellow, Ace Rosner, a well-known car collector.) The car was priced a little high, but the seller was probably negotiable. I figured I could work out a deal with the owner, but not with another bidder present. So, I figured I had to wait him out, and stay on until the other prospect left, no matter how long it took, which was *forever*. This guy eyeballed that car from end to end. Finally, the one-armed man told the seller that he'd think about it, and get back to him with an offer. *Wow*. As soon as he was gone, we were negotiating. I made sure that I walked out of there with a solid contract. I didn't have all of the money in my pocket to pay for it on the spot, but I gave him a deposit and he signed a bill of sale. That baby was sold!

Seven years ago, my son and I went to look at a 1962 Volkswagen Beetle Convertible we'd found in a classified ad in *The Sunday Washington Post*. It was priced at ten thousand dollars. As soon as we walked up to his garage, I knew from giving it the once over this car was

14

well worth the price. I needed to buy it before another prospect showed up. I immediately asked if he was willing to negotiate (you gotta at least ask!). The seller said, "No," and so I said, "I'll take it." He seemed a little taken aback that I wanted to wrap up the deal without even thoroughly checking the car over, but he went along with it. I told him that I had some cash for a deposit, and a check I'd write for the balance. He could hold that personal check, and at the time I returned to pick up the car, I'd replace the check with a Cashier's Check. We wrote up a bill of sale. It started with "Sold, to ____." It was a solid contract.

Good thing, too. It so happened that I'd agreed to take my son to a nearby toy store afterwards, and on the return trip we had to drive back by the VW seller's house. Sure enough, the seller was out in the driveway, showing the car to someone else. I said to my son, "Don't worry, it's sold." I explained that the seller could not change his mind even if he got a higher bid, since we had a solid contract. A few hours later, I got a call from the seller. Seems the next guy really wanted the car, and was willing to pay me a three thousand dollar profit. *Wow*; that would have been a fast deal. But my son and I loved the car, and we wanted to keep it.

Back in 1979, the infamous Hunt Brothers of Texas had cornered the silver market, which ran up the price. I was a twenty-one-year-old car salesman at the time, at Dick Stevens Chevrolet in Wheaton, Maryland. Another salesman, Mark Allen, shared that he was visiting the coin department at a venerable Washington, D.C. department store, and buying silver coins. Woodward & Lothrop had been an institution for shoppers in the Nation's Capital since 1887. In the 1970s, Woodies had a coin department, which catered to collectors. Mark, who was smart as a whip, realized that their pricing of coins was not keeping up with the increase in the value of the silver content of the coins. So he was cleaning up by buying old coins cheap and reselling them for their silver content, for a nice profit.

15

I was jealous. Mark had a good thing going. So I watched the classifieds ads even closer than usual, looking for an opportunity. I came across an ad, which read "Silver bullion from the U.S. Mint," and I phoned the seller. He explained that at one time the mint had sold off excess silver, and he'd bought some as a retirement investment. He priced it at about the going rate for silver, and it was ten thousand dollars for all he had. It wasn't really that great a deal, except that the price of silver was going up every day. I figured that if I bought it, and the price continued up at such a steep rate, it would be a good investment.

The silver was in granular form, so I had to arrange to have a knowledgeable jeweler check it to make sure that I was actually getting what it was represented to be. The seller said that it was 99.9 percent pure. I called a local jewelry shop that my parents had used over the years and arranged for them to test the silver.

I had to work at the time that it was convenient for the seller and the jeweler, so I asked my dad to stand in for me. Dad said the seller and his wife showed up. The jewelry shop was in a shopping mall, and the seller said that he'd take his wife shopping while the silver was being looked at. And off they went.

The jeweler worked for a while and then informed my dad that the purity was fine, but that the quantity was substantially more than the seller had represented. He guessed that the man had weighed it using the standard measurements. With precious metals, you use troy ounces. Somehow that meant there was more there then the seller had figured.

When he and his wife returned from shopping, my dad shared that the purity had checked out fine. He also told him that there was more quantity then he had calculated. Dad told me that he said, "It's okay, he seems like a nice young man. The price we agreed on is fine." Dad gave him my check and we were set.

When I caught up with Dad, he had this metal box to pass to me. It was about the size of a small briefcase, but square. The silver bullion was incredibly heavy. It was really difficult to lift.

So I was already ahead on my investment, because of the measuring difference. Silver continued to rise in value, and one week later an ad that I placed in the *Wall Street Journal* brought me a purchaser. He was an attorney and looking to get in on the silver craze. Because of the measurement error and the increase in the value over the week, he was glad to pay me twenty-five thousand dollars for the silver. One lesson was it showed me that you can never predict how a deal might turn in your favor. A deal can start off as just an okay deal, but it might end up a really good deal.

In 1991, I was dealing in vintage cars and attended an auction held at the Charlotte Motor Speedway, a NASCAR track in North Carolina. In addition to a hundred or so antique and classic cars that were set to cross the auction block, there were hundreds of items of clothing to be sold. These items were hanging on movable clothing racks, outdoors next to where the auction cars were on display. They were costumes from the making of the Tom Cruise film *Days of Thunder*. The rows of racks were filled with bright combination-colored jackets that had a similar look to motorcycle jackets. The variety of colors had to do with the several NASCAR teams portrayed in the film, and each team had its own colors.

The team that Cruise drove for used the colors of its sponsor, Mellow Yellow soda. Those colors were fluorescent yellow on a black background. Another team had pink and black as their color combination. I remember that the auctioning off of all this clothing seemed to take forever, with one jacket selling after another. There were also pants, helmets, and even a few beat up NASCAR cars that had been props in the film. I toyed with the idea of buying a pink and black jacket for my sister, but wondered if she'd actually wear it. I wasn't sure she

17

would, so I didn't bid on any of the clothing. Among the offerings were a racing suit worn by Tom Cruise in the film. They also offered a helmet, and separately, his racing shoes.

After they'd finished selling all the clothing and got back to the vintage cars, which I'd come for, I started kicking myself. Here I was, wondering whether to buy a jacket for my sister, and as I'm thinking about that, the auctioneer's selling items actually worn in a film by Tom Cruise. Why didn't I think to bid on those? Tom Cruise was a big success and seemed to have a bright future, so an authentic movie prop/costume might be a good investment. But I was too late.

Everyone at the auction was invited back that evening to the racetrack owner's suite for cocktail hour. I was there on my own, and didn't feel very social, as I hadn't bought any cars at the auction. But the offer of a cocktail hour appealed to me, so I went. As I entered the room, I saw that chairs were set up as if someone were to give a talk at the front of the room. There was an announcement that after we all had a chance to get refreshments, they were going to have a brief auction of choice items that hadn't been offered during the day. On the impromptu mimeographed list handed out was "Tom Cruise's character Cole Trickle full racing outfit and helmet." Then and there I made up my mind. I'd neglected to buy any of the Cruise items earlier, and I wasn't going to miss my second chance. I intended to buy this item, no matter what it took. I waited. They got to the item, the actual Nomex racing suit worn by Cruise in the movie. The package also included his helmet, racing gloves and shoes. I started bidding. Finally I was the high bidder at just under two thousand dollars. Everyone else in the room might have thought that I'd paid too much. My perspective was that I had now bet on Tom Cruise's career. If he continued to have a successful film career, I figured it was a good investment.

18

Chapter 5

The Auction

On December 14, 2004, I rose early and drove the half hour to Chantilly, a bedroom community in Northern Virginia. It would go on to be one of the coldest days I'd ever experienced. I found the storage facility in a typical light industrial area, and my guitar enthusiast friend Bill showed up to meet me. We were early, so it wasn't surprising that there was no one else around. I walked over to the storage facility office and asked the fellow behind the desk about the auction. 'Was this the right place? Where would they be setting up? Why wasn't there a tent or some sort of structure for the auction?' He seemed to have no clue. So we waited.

Finally, an unmarked car showed up, and then another one. I approached a deputy to ask a few questions about the auction. Mainly, when would they be bringing the merchandise out for a preview? I was told there wasn't going to be a preview. Auctions always have a preview of some sort, so prospective bidders can eye the merchandise ahead of time. More and more sheriff's staff showed up, and a small crowd began to materialize. Finally there was an announcement from one of the deputies present.

Items would be brought out from the storage unit in groups of ten lots at a time. They would spread them out on the pavement, and sell the ten items immediately. If you were a successful bidder, you were then expected to walk over to a card table they'd set up, and pay your cash due on the spot. I'd been to many auctions in my lifetime, but never one like this. If you purchased one item from a group of ten, then you'd probably end up in the cashier's line waiting to settle up, and would likely miss the next ten items. This was going to be tricky.

Besides, selling valuable goods this way was not usually how a seller managed to get good prices. At the least, auction-goers expect a little time to preview items prior to bidding. That wasn't going to happen here. And it wasn't junk that was going to be sold, either. There was a lot of top of the line Bang & Olufsen stereo equipment, some extremely large Apple monitors, many high-end guitars, the Segway, the Apple-1, and lord knows what else...

So they brought out the first ten lots. The Apple monitors came up early. Someone was clearly getting good buys on them, but I really did not know how much something like that sold for. The stereo equipment was probably also a deal. This merchandise was all top of the line, the best money could buy. It was what you'd buy if you'd sold a company for a hundred million dollars.

It was absolutely freezing cold standing out there. I don't think anyone in attendance thought they'd be exposed to the elements for five or six hours. We all assumed that they'd hold the auction indoors, protected from the wind and the cold. But this was one of those storage places that has a tiny little office, and rows of storage locker buildings. There was no place to do this inside, so the deputies were going to get the job done outdoors. There were about fifty people in attendance. Deputies would set ten lots of merchandise out onto the pavement. The crowd would form a circle around the lot, and a few of the deputies would stay inside the circle, one of them acting as auctioneer.

Finally, they brought out two of Waldack's Segway scooters. Now the question was, which one was the unit that he had paid over one hundred thousand dollars for? Which machine was one of the very first made, and therefore could someday be quite valuable? They offered up

20

the first one, and I yelled out in the direction of the deputies within the circle with the merchandise, "Can you read off the serial number?" A deputy looked down at the unit, and said, "It ends in 007." *Wow*, I thought, that one must be the Amazon auction Segway. I'm a vintage car enthusiast, and I know that the first few of anything off the line aren't necessarily serial numbered 1, 2, and 3. The very first prototypes or production units of anything may be used for testing, and some could be crash-tested. So it was logical that serial number 007 might be one of the first three ever built. The bidding started, and I bid, and kept bidding.

I won the Segway! And for one of the first three built, it was cheap! My winning bid was fifteen hundred dollars. Immediately the second Segway was put up for auction. Even though I had the one I wanted, I had to ask. I had to check. I yelled out the question, "What is the serial number?" The deputy crouched down and read the number, "Zero...zero...seven." Wait, this can't be! Instantly, someone in the crowd yelled, "That's the *model* number!"

Oh, my gosh! I was instantly dejected. I thought I'd made a fabulous buy: one of the first three Segways built, probably by hand, by its famous inventor, Dean Kamen. Instead of a motorized contraption that would someday be worth a small fortune, I realized that, in fact, I'd just bought a *used* Segway. Nothing more. *Drat!*

Later, I still held out hope that it might actually be one of the first. I contacted Segway, and eventually I found that Bruce had bought three more Segways at a much later date than his Amazon auction purchase. I was also told that the first three built had some special gold trim, and that you'd know right away if you were looking at one of those first-built special units. So the auction had included two of Bruce's three standard Segways.

My Segway was missing one part, the charger cord. But I was told that it used the same standard cord that you use to plug a personal computer into any electrical outlet. So that night I borrowed one off my

21

home computer, plugged it in, and started charging the Segway. I was a little anxious to give it a try. After midnight that evening, I was padding around the house in my bedroom slippers, and walked by the charging Segway. The little light indicated that it was now fully charged.

I had to give it a try. My wife and kids were asleep. I wheeled it from the screened-in porch out to the driveway. It was dark, but I couldn't wait until the morning. I looked it over and thought that, ideally, I'd climb up on the rider's mount, lean forward, and off I'd go. But I needed some way to hold the contraption up, while I boosted myself up on something to get to the right level. The best method I could think of was to open up my Camry's front door, step up on the door sill—which precariously wedged me in between the door and the car—and step over onto the Segway platform. The problem was that if I fell I might get hurt. How embarrassing it would be to get hurt doing something like this, alone, late at night, in my pajamas and bedroom slippers. But I was really anxious to try it. I climbed up on the sill, stepped onto the Segway while leaning my upper body against the door of my car, and then leaned forward and kind of pushed off from the car. Down the driveway the Segway and I went. I drove around in the dark, on the driveway, for a few minutes. It was neat to actually try it. Then I got off, feeling lucky that I didn't have to deal with the embarrassment of having to tell my wife that I'd fallen down in our driveway in the middle of the night.

Of the forty electric guitars in the auction, many were Gibsons that had been issued in limited editions and had 'themes,' some of which had little to do with music or guitars. One was a 1957 Chevrolet commemorative electric guitar. It was done in period Chevrolet colors, turquoise and white, and had decorative styling aspects that were similar to the vintage Chevy. Evidently, Gibson found that issuing these limited edition versions was a good way to sell a bunch of guitars, and Bruce apparently bought one of every edition.

The crowd was fairly big for a bitter cold weekday, standing outside at what was effectively a storage unit auction. As the guitars started selling, I realized it was largely a guitar enthusiast crowd. Place an ad that says that forty guitars are going to be selling at a sheriff's sale, and the word's going to get around. At one point, I was in line for the cashier and overheard a couple of guitar store owners chatting. Clearly, they were there to buy up some choice inventory, and some of them literally had wads of cash. I encouraged my friend Bill to bid on some guitars, but he wasn't interested in aggressively bidding. Since it seemed the buying was being done by dealers with the objective of recouping their investment and then some, I suggested that Bill take action; the prices were probably pretty low. I was itching to buy a guitar myself; the colors and finishes were beautiful. Finally, one came up for auction that made sense to me; I thought they were *all* neat, but I really wasn't interested in taking guitar lessons. It was a special-edition Yahoo guitar, celebrating the Yahoo.com website. It was truly resplendent in its brand colors of purple and yellow. It was pretty enough to just be a striking decoration on a wall, so I bought it.

The deputies brought out some leather furniture, and I was kicking myself for not having bought a couch and chair set in handsome beige leather, because it sold for only a few hundred dollars. A little later in the auction, they brought out a couple of dark blue leather chairs. Not bad, I thought. But then, they announced that they were part of a set with a couch, and ended up bringing that out too. Much of the furniture was in shrink wrap; the sheriff's department had done a nice job of protecting the items they'd seized. They tore some of the wrap off the couch and chairs so the crowd could see what they were bidding on. *Ugh!* The couch wasn't just blue; it also had large black leather panels.

Black and blue! The colors of a *black eye*. What a horrible combination for a family room! I started bidding anyway. I figured that if I was able to buy the set cheaply enough, I could keep the chairs and discard the ugly sofa. Like most of all the items in the auction, the furniture looked absolutely brand new. No wear and tear whatsoever. I ended up winning the lot for six hundred dollars. I knew that had to be a steal, even if it only for the chairs, so I was happy. I figured that when the auction ended, I'd offer the sofa to one of the other bidders for a few hundred dollars. Then, I could just cart my two chairs home.

Why were the prices low? I think one reason is that we had now spent a few hours outside in the bitter cold. Most people hadn't come prepared; I didn't see that many hats or gloves being worn in the crowd. But people were choosing to let their extremities get numb from the cold rather than walking away from such a good auction.

At the end of the day, I found a pick-up truck to rent nearby. Bill helped me load the couch and chairs in the back. I'd decided that I would haul the couch home, so my wife could help decide whether we should keep it. It would be just as easy to get rid of it from our house, if we decided to go that route. The surprise was that the couch and chairs were incredibly heavy. What was the deal with that? On the bottom of the chairs, you could see their beautiful metal tubular frame construction. Maybe that's why they were so heavy. As my friend and I were ready to go our separate ways at the end of the day, standing next to the pick-up, I saw a small metal tag on one of the chairs. It had an 'S' on it. I looked a little closer and saw the name "de Sede" imprinted in the liner material under the chair. I'd check that out once I got home.

Later, I did a search online for de Sede furniture. I found that de Sede is fifty year-old manufacturer of exclusive luxury furniture from Klingnau, Switzerland. Only cowhides from Switzerland and southern Germany are used for the leather. Each piece of furniture that I bought had originally listed for over fifteen thousand dollars. So my six hundred dollar purchase bought me close to fifty thousand dollars' worth of furniture. The chairs were designed to mimic the seats from a 1930s racing car. That awful black and blue couch was starting to grow on me!

24

As the auction day wore on, I was getting into a bind. Sixty days before, I'd borrowed some money from my 401K account at Schwab. Today was the day I needed to pay it back, or I'd have to pay a ten percent penalty, plus income taxes. I'd brought the check with me, so that I could leave the auction and proceed to the local Schwab office, and now it was time. I knew the Reston, Virginia Schwab office closed at five p.m. But the Apple-1 had still not come up for auction. All this waiting in the cold, my research, and now it might all be a waste of time. I approached one of the deputies, and asked him if I could request that they bring up an item. I told him that I had a predicament, and needed to leave, but I was very interested in the Apple, and could they bring it up to sell soon? They'd earlier handed out a five-page listing of the auction items, and it was scheduled to be the last item offered.

Well, bring it out they did. It wasn't much to look at, just a big blue metal box with a sheet of Plexiglas attached to the top, so you could see inside the box. I wasn't surprised by the appearance, because I'd seen photos on the cancelled *eBay* listing. The keyboard was a separate wooden box, but was shrink wrapped and had a sheriff's seizure sticker on it.

The bidding started. I knew that a lot of the crowd was there for the guitars, so I didn't expect many bidders on the Apple. But somewhere in the crowd, someone was consistently bidding against me. I couldn't actually see who it was; the crowd that circled the sheriff's auctioneer was just big enough so it was hard to see everybody. I didn't want to move out from the middle of the little crowd of people that I was in and call attention to myself. Better to just keep bidding as anonymously as possible and hope the other bidder would drop out of the bidding soon.

I really didn't have a pre-planned maximum bid. I never have bid that way. I figure if you really want something, it's better to leave it a little vague as to when you'll stop bidding. If you set a limit, do you just stop when you reach that limit? What if one hundred dollars more would have won the bidding? For a hundred bucks, would it make sense to stop bidding, and not get what you wanted? So I bid and bid, on and on. I kept hoping that each bid of his or hers would be their last. Finally we reached a point where there was no other bid coming from the other side of the crowd. I'd won the Apple-1 for seven thousand six hundred dollars. I was very excited. At the time, I think that many in the crowd thought that I might be crazy to pay thousands of dollars for this old blue box, but I felt that the historical significance of this machine, combined with what seemed like an ever-brighter future for Steve Jobs, might make this a good investment.

The sheriff's deputy immediately handed the blue box to me, and I cradled it in my arms on the way to the cash-only card table. I paid up, and turned to carry my new prize directly to the trunk of my nearby old gold Camry. Besides the keyboard, it also came with its original owner's manual and the set of cancelled checks used for the purchase in 1976. The original owner's manual is a small format booklet with a sketch on the cover of Isaac Newton sitting under an apple tree. It's a nice traditional-looking design, and nothing like the graphic 'apple with a bite taken' that we see so much today.

There are two cancelled checks, mounted in a clear page protector. The first is from Charles Ricketts and is made out to *Apple Computer*, and is dated July 27, 1976. It's for six hundred dollars, *even*. I'd read that Steve Jobs priced the computers at $666.66, but evidently not this one. I later Google Mapped the original owner's address on the check, and then compared it to the address of the Jobs' family home. Charles Ricketts lived in an apartment on Continental Circle, in Mountain View, California. He lived four miles from Steve Jobs.

The second check from Ricketts is from August 5th, 1976. It's for $193.00, and there's a label that indicates it was for software programmed by Steve Jobs in August of 1976.

Chapter 6

Aged Apples

After I purchased the Apple-1, I figured I'd just put it away. I didn't know if I'd hang on to it for a long time, or if I might sell it at some point down the road. Maybe it was so special that someday I'd want to pass it on to my kids, but I had two kids and only one Apple-1. It wasn't something you could cut in half.

Since the original purchaser, Charles Ricketts, lived only four miles from Steve Jobs in Los Altos, I wondered if he was a friend of Jobs or somehow involved with Apple Computer.

The only history I could find on my Apple were two articles that came up in an online search. One was dated June 1999 and was from *Wired Magazine*. I knew it was about my machine because there were some accompanying photos. And from the photos, it was clearly mine. Blue box and all. And a photo of the two cancelled checks. The article, entitled "Icon for Sale: The First Apple-1," said it been put up for auction in San Francisco. This article was written prior to the auction.

It started off with "The very first Apple computer—the original Apple-1 assembled by Steve Wozniak and Steve Jobs—is going on the auction block." It said the La Salle Gallery had expected it to bring over forty thousand dollars.

Owen Linzmayer, author of *Apple Confidential*, was quoted saying, "If the item up for auction can be proven to be the first Apple-1 ever sold, it deserves to be preserved in a museum. But, given the technical nature of the item, and the awesome disposable incomes in Silicon Valley, I wouldn't be surprised to see two stock option-rich geeks bid the price up to astronomical levels."

La Salle Auctioneer Risley Sams stated, "It's the first Apple-1 built and sold by Apple. We offered it to Steve Jobs, but he said he had such a hard time selling it in the first place that he didn't really want it. He made a small offer, but we have better ones." Sams also said the Apple came with documentation proving its authenticity, including two checks from the buyer written in July and August 1976. According to Sams, one check was for the machine and the other for software. The sale also included the original owner's manual. The article also stated that Sams said the machine was being sold by a relative of the original owner.

The Apple-1 wasn't the only vintage Apple being offered. Also being auctioned was an Apple prototype called the GLM, a machine Sams said preceded the Macintosh, and a LISA. Some other vintage Apple computers were offered by Jef Raskin, a well-known former Apple employee.

Linzmayer suggested the first Apple-1 had probably originally been sold to a member of the Homebrew Computer Club. He said the Apple-1 was assembled by hand in the garage of Jobs' parents by the company's two founders, and customers had to add their own keyboard and case, as well as wire the machine to a monitor.

Sellam Ismail, the producer of the annual Vintage Computer Festival, said Apple-1's are probably the most sought-after antique PCs on the market. They rarely go on sale. Ismail noted that a friend of his had bought an Apple-1 for two thousand dollars in cash at the previous year's festival. He said, "The buyer definitely got the deal of the century. The person who sold it probably had no idea what it was worth. I guess he needed the money."

Ismail concluded by saying, "There's a decent chance someone will pay forty thousand dollars for it. Is it worth that? I don't know. They're highly sought after, of course. I want one." He said interest in collecting old computers had risen dramatically in the last few years. Like all collectibles, it's driven largely by waves of nostalgia.

The other article was on a website called The Mac Geek and was titled "Few Buyers for Aged Apples" and was written after the auction had concluded. The buyer of my Apple-1 was reported to be a retired officer of the British Royal Air Force, who bid by phone. Purchaser "Captain Owen O'Mahoney" won the bidding with a high bid of eighteen thousand dollars.

This article quoted Jack Sacks, an auction employee who handled O'Mahoney's bid, and who said the winning bidder was delighted at his purchase. He said the bidder was prepared to pay up to twenty five thousand dollars. When the bidder could not be reached for comment, Sacks said he'd gone out to dinner to celebrate.

Chapter 7

SteveJobs.com

In late 2007, I was looking around online and I thought to do a search for Bruce Waldack. I was very surprised to learn he'd passed away. He had died on June 23rd, while living in Buenos Aires. It had been about two and a half years since he fled the U.S., and since the sheriff's auction.

I found several websites with tributes to Bruce. He was only forty-four years old. One article said his death was due to complications from a fall earlier in the year.

The stories and tributes described a man that lived life to the fullest, was loyal to his friends, and never left a party or a bar without getting to know everyone there. That might be because he bought drinks for everyone in the house, or he impressed them all with his bar tricks. And he was a practical joker. Bruce seemed to have quite an effect on everybody he knew. Or maybe on everybody he met. There were stories and comments from former employees, friends, and even brief casual acquaintances. Someone who chauffeured him around when he was in Los Angeles described how knowing Bruce had changed his life.

My favorite story was written by a former employee. Shortly after joining Bruce's company, he was invited out for a weekend afternoon on Bruce's boat. Traveling down the Potomac, south of Washington D.C., Bruce stopped the boat at a waterside restaurant. Bruce ordered rounds of vodka shots and the new guy felt it necessary to do as his workmates were, so he drank a number of shots. He was amazed at how Bruce could down those shots. Only later did he learn that Bruce had prearranged with the bartender to serve water to all the others. It was a setup! There are many stories that involve Bruce drinking and partying, but in this case, he was pulling a fast one and 'breaking in' a new employee.

There was a televised interview, from 2005, of Bruce Waldack that could be found online. He was a guest on the Tekno Show in Argentina, and it lasted for close to an hour. The interviewer was Federico Ini. The full interview seems to have been lost, but a two minute clip of it is still online today. Bruce talked about his business career and told stories. He'd owned many domain names, including SteveJobs.com. Bruce greatly admired Jobs, and he offered to sell Jobs the domain name for a dollar. Bruce's brother David told me that the payment check Bruce received from Jobs was never to be cashed.

Bruce - I remember one day, I said, there's nothing on the Internet (that I haven't seen.) I had seen everything. I'd seen every site there was. Now, it's not possible for me to see the sites that were put up this hour.

We were the first company—if not the first company, the second company—to ever offer dedicated hosting and hosting.

I still have still several thousand domain names.

I had Vagina dot com, and I sold that for twenty-seven thousand dollars.

Federico - It's a good business.

Bruce - Right. And I also had Saving Private Ryan dot com, and I registered it before Dreamworks registered the trademark.

Now, in the end I lost money, because I saw the movie. The movie affected me so much, that I gave them the domain name, and then I donated fifty thousand dollars to the war memorial. So it was a negative. I also had Steve Jobs dot com.

Federico - You have it, or you had it?

Bruce - I had it. I said the only way I'll sell it is if Steve gives me his personal check. Because, that alone was worth the story.

At the conclusion of the interview:
Bruce - Well, I'd like to tell you that I was brilliant, but it was more luck and the right place and the right time.

In early 2013, I finally was able to reach Federico Ini by phone.
Federico - Bruce was a very unorthodox man. He was a real character with many sides, depending on the day you could get to know.
Bob - How did you come to meet him?
Federico - It was totally random thing. Because a girl I was seeing told me to go to some house over the downtown of the city. There were two famous rockers, and there was some billionaire or millionaire janky character. We didn't really care about that, but we were kind of bored. So I went to the house in a very nice, very aristocratic part of the city. And there was this guy that was having a cigar and there was a lot of booze and good alcohol there. So we started just having some drinks.

Here in Argentina, we go out really late. It was three a.m. or something like that. The rock stars were gone when I got there, and we started chatting. This guy Bruce told me he worked on the Internet and that he had some big websites. I was one of the only persons there that was speaking fluent English, and he said "Just Google me." And we're talking about the year...it was around 2005. It wasn't a common expression at the time. He gave me a card and I say, who's this guy? He was really generous, and, you could smoke a cigar and hang out in his house. I really liked the connection we had talking about technology.

I was then working as a tech journalist and I'd done some investigative journalism. He gave me his card and I sent him an email, thanking him and that I really enjoyed myself. So he said, "Okay, why don't you come to another barbeque?" And he made a barbeque.

32

Sometimes friends of his cooked, and some of the time this big huge rock star in Argentina cooked. It was kind of weird. Imagine that you're there in the States, and let me find something similar to what I'm going to say, and Bruce Springsteen makes your barbeque. At the time, that rock star's a very well-known person here. And he says, "Uh, how do you want your barbeque, well-done or rare?" He starts serving. And I say, 'What the fuck's going on?'

I enjoyed more my conversation with Bruce. He talked about DigitalNation and how he made that, he was a pioneer. How he started selling computers, and he made his first million. How he dealt with Steve Jobs. I read somewhere that he was selling NeXT Computers at some point. Bruce was like a bit of a showoff, but very generous at the same time. You never knew if what he said was entirely true. He had a bodyguard. You couldn't tell, is this guy for real?

So then he started showing us pictures, and he was saying, 'I had those cars over there. And I used to have a guy that was in charge of the house. I had three Ferraris.' He liked to talk about and show the pictures of his kids, and also to show pictures of Pamela Anderson and Kid Rock.

In Argentina, he had an old BMW M5 series. It was previously from some embassy or important person, and the car was bulletproof. And that was kind of funny because it was a very powerful car, kind of a little bit old, but it wasn't the latest model.

Bob - Did he live in a house or an apartment?

Federico - He rented a penthouse at the plaza, the San Martin Plaza. He told me it was rented.

Bob - Was it nice inside?

Federico - Yeah, really beautiful. It was spacious, it had at least two floors, plus a terrace. It was a really big place and it was very luxurious. I don't know if it was luxurious... Pretentious, but was really nice; it was all furnished and it was a nice spot to be in.

Bob - I guess the dollar goes farther than in the U.S.

Federico - Yeah, of course. Properties here are not that expensive. With the same house in some areas like New York or San Francisco, it might be half a million or seven hundred fifty thousand dollars. And here with that money, you can get really nice places. That has changed over time, but when he was here, the difference between the dollars and the pesos was much more convenient that it is now. So Argentina was not an expensive country to be in. Sometimes we went out to eat, and for Bruce seventy or eighty dollars was like a joke.

Because this guy was connected to everything, but most of all he was connected to a lot of historic things. He said, "Okay, I've got this site DigitalNation, it sold for a hundred million dollars. That was the best deal I've done." I got to know him really well. We were never really clear on the reasons he was here. He started telling me that he was here because he didn't want to get served a summons. Because, even though he had a prenup, there was some mess with his divorce.

Well, it was pretty neat that I got to be friends with someone who introduced me to Apple Computers. He was a huge fan of everything Apple-related. Bruce was really a fan of Apple products, and he had all the products. I'm a very careful guy with my electronics. I don't like to scratch them. I don't like to do anything that might jeopardize the value they have when I want to switch for something newer. Bruce apparently didn't have that concern. He had like three or four iPods, and he had two iMacs, and he scratched everything. I said, "Bruce, you're crazy. How can you do this? You have a new iPod, just take care of it." He said, "For me it's just a tool."

Bob - Yeah, a utility.

Federico - Yeah, things had to serve him, instead of him being careful about his possessions. But he was an Apple fan.

Bruce became very good friends with this guy Andreas Calamaro, this huge rock star in Argentina. Calamaro was supposed to be going through a bad time, and he was coming back to Argentina from Spain.

And they met on the plane. Bruce introduced Calamaro to the Apple Computer, too. Calamaro has been interviewed and said that Bruce gave him this computer, and he got into blogging, and he got into composing things again or using it really heavily and he introduced him to this '2.0 life'. He attributes a lot of his success to Bruce.

This was also the work of Bruce; he was evangelist in this sense where you could see he had this love for computers that he thought were something apart from the others. So, in that sense, he was surrounded by Macs, even though at that time he didn't have this computer we're talking about, the Apple-1.

Bob - The rock stars that you referred to originally that were at Bruce's penthouse before you got there, were they Argentinian?

Federico - Yeah, they were.

Bob - And the fellow who was doing the cooking, was that Calamaro?

Federico - Calamaro. Yeah. Andeas Calamaro.

Bruce has a lot of stories about being first, or pioneering, things. And he told me he had a first-edition Segway, one of the five samples, I guess.

Bob - Yes, one of three.

Federico - There was a metal thing on it that said, "This is one of the prototypes of Segway," and he spoke really highly of the inventor of Segway, and of him being a really interesting person that had a lot of patents. He took the Segway to a beach. Argentina is next to Uruguay, which is a small country, and there's a very famous beach area called *Puentes de Lente*. So we were driving this Segway, and at some point he told us how much he had paid for it. He had bought it in an auction, for a hundred thousand dollars?

Bob - Correct. It was for charity.

Federico - So Bruce rented a house and he brought the Segway over there with a private jet, and we were using the Segway on the street. I don't think he really cared about it too much. He just wanted to have fun, and to have that special thing because he saw the value on the pioneer part of that.

Even though I guess he told me a few times about the Apple-1, I wasn't that familiar with it, or the history then. Or I didn't really measure that, so today with all the things I've read, I'm amazed that we were talking about this computer.

Bob - You remember him mentioning it?

Federico - Yeah, yeah, because he liked to talk about the things that he had collected that were important.

Bob - When you went to Uruguay, he had a jet take you?

Federico - We came back on a private jet. And he went there, if I'm not mistaken, on a private jet. We're on this house near the beach. I'm used to being at the airport on time, because if the plane leaves, and if you don't get to the airport on time, you lose. I was really worried then, "Bruce, we have to go. The flight is at ten". He said, "I don't fucking care." He used to talk like that. "We go when we want to go. That's why we rent my plane, because if not, I have to go on time." I said, "Okay, you suit yourself. I'm just telling you we're getting late."

He had two Vertu phones from Nokia.

Bob - The real fancy phone, yeah.

Federico - Yeah, so Bruce used to drive with the Segway on Retiro. That was kind of weird, because it was not the aristocratic area where he lived. That area has a lot of bars and a big train station. It goes from nice to not-so-nice really quickly. There are parts where there's a lot of Irish pubs and all that. And a lot of buses go around that area. The streets are not wide, kind of narrow, and that's where Bruce used to drive the Segway.

So, one time he fell from the Segway and he injured himself and someone robbed him of a Vertu. They took advantage of that situation and stole a really special and pricey phone. He told us this was a special phone. You had to get on a waiting list to get one.

36

Bob - I'd heard about that accident. It had gone around that the injury lead to his death, but his brother David said that that wasn't the case.

Federico - No, I don't think that had anything to do. He had a skiing accident that left him with a leg condition. I don't want to say it was from Aspen, I don't remember. He said he slipped going down the stairs and he landed incorrectly and he really hurt his leg.

The other day I was remembering, there's a very known restaurant here called Kansas. And Bruce never wanted to sit at a table, he'd rather be at the bar, because his leg was more comfortable there. Also because he could have four or five vodka tonics, which was his drink.

He dared the cook to drink some gin, which was what the cook liked. He said, "Okay, Motor, (which means 'engine,' the nickname of the guy). We're going to have a round of vodka tonics, and you have to drink gin." He said, "No, Mr. Bruce, I'm working." It was late. And it was "No, you have to have the gin. I say so." So the guy started drinking gin, and of course, most of us ended up wasted. The poor guy having three or four glasses of gin, of just straight gin, while he was cooking, because of the dare. So Bruce really got himself noticed.

Bob - Were you aware of him actually doing business in Argentina? You mentioned that he sponsored your show.

Federico - At the time, I didn't have a show of my own, and he wasn't involved then. There was a girl he was friends with, and she had a wine shop and I guess Bruce was there helping her. Or was taking some part of the business, I guess that was that. When I was doing the show he rounded a few of his friends; this girl with the wine shop, and he was very good friends with a person on a cigar store, so we kind of got them together. The show I had was in peril in that moment, and we needed to raise some sponsors or we were going to be shut down. And he took care of that, he arranged that. I'm not sure if he was doing some other business while he was in Argentina.

Chapter 8

Woz

Four years passed, with the Apple sitting on top of my son's clothes dresser, often under a stack of freshly folded shirts. In January of 2009 I attended a professional conference in Los Angeles. Every year the conference organizers would hire a well-known figure to speak. This year it was going to be Steve Wozniak. I figured this might be my one opportunity to be able to meet him and hopefully ask him about my Apple-1. I signed up for the conference and prepared by taking some photos of my Apple-1 to try and show to Steve. One way or another, I was determined that I'd meet Steve.

At the conference, many of the sessions were in a large ball room with a stage. As the time approached that he was scheduled to speak, I watched the doors to the room and kept an eye on the conference organizers. I figured the organizers would have to greet him outside the room, and that might be my chance. About ten minutes before he was scheduled to go on stage, I saw some commotion with the organizers. They left the ballroom, so I followed them into the hallway of the convention center. Soon, I saw Steve Wozniak being accompanied in, and I followed closely. As he then stood off to the side of the stage waiting for his cue, I approached and quickly introduced myself. I showed him my pictures and asked if he recalled Charles Ricketts and his Apple-1 purchase. I told him that it had been purported to be the first one sold. He was very gracious, even though I was kind of accosting him. He said that Ricketts' name was vaguely familiar, but he couldn't quite remember the details. I asked if he might have been the person who bought the first Apple-1. Steve said, "He might have bought the first one from us. I just can't remember. You should ask Steve (Jobs). Steve would know." And then he was whisked onto the stage.

As he spoke on stage in kind of an interview format, I kept thinking of what I should have asked him when I had the chance. Maybe if I was lucky, I would be able to speak with him afterwards.

His talk finished and there was large applause, and he left the stage. A few minutes later, I looked to the back of the room. Steve had wondered back in, sat down, and was alone in the audience. Amazingly, he was not being mobbed. The lights were dim because there was activity onstage, so maybe others in the audience just didn't realize that this man now sitting down alone was Wozniak. I made my move, walked over and sat down next to him. It was great, because we were able to talk some more, but he did not have much more to add about Ricketts. I did get his autograph, and he simply signed "Woz."

It was only much later that Steve told me that he was not really involved in the sales, and he said that was certainly more Steve Jobs' area. In the early days of the Apple-1, Wozniak would show up to work in the evening at the Jobs house. He had spent the work-day at his job with Hewlett Packard. As he later told me, "I did my engineering and steered out of the way of marketing, operations, accounting, etcetera."

Chapter 9

The Auctioneer

I figured if I contacted the LaSalle Gallery auction house in San Francisco, they might be able to supply information on my Apple and who the seller was. I wanted to know who consigned my computer, and if they could tell me anything about O'Mahoney, the buyer.

I found the gallery was evidently out of business. The phone number was dead, and the listings I found online all led to dead ends. I did have two employee names from the auction article, and one name - Risley Sams, was a fairly uncommon name. It would be easier to track him down online then it would be to find someone with a more common name.

In 2010, he proved hard to find. He was popping up on the social media sites, so I could see his photo. His employment listings and a personal website didn't really give me a good phone number or email address for him. Finally, one of my attempts did get thru and we spoke.

At the time of our talk, I really appreciated that he was willing to spend some time with me, and that he had to reach far back in his memory. But today, when I recall what he said, it sounds like he was being defensive. At the time, I kind of missed that.

Risley - Let me explain to you, I don't know very much, I was kind of a hired gun for those guys. I worked a little bit for them and realized it wasn't a good thing, so I was just auctioning for them because I was a good auctioneer. I was only there for three, maybe four months and I was kind of working as a contractor on the side for them. I wasn't really part of their organization, I didn't have a title there. I was just helping them out.

Bob - I knew you were the auctioneer, because I found an old article where you had talked about the Apple computer, which I subsequently bought.

Risley - They asked me to do it and I actually reluctantly did it, which frustrated me because I had no prep for it. I had no idea what I was talking about. I should never have, but because I was the auctioneer, I was the figurehead. Which was super frustrating. I know nothing, I know very little about it.

So basically, let me tell you what I know. The owners of the auction house said they got this thing on consignment. Obviously the owners of the auction house didn't own it. It sold to an undisclosed bidder from what I understood, and that's all I understood, but I never heard anything more about the transaction from the firm and I still to this day have no idea.

There's articles on the web with my name attached, I know nothing. I felt bad, I'm like I don't want to do this, and you know, *Wired* is talking to me? I kind of like, I was a little nonchalant about it, I don't know, it's something to auction. And it turned into this big hubbub, because it is the Apple-1 and I hadn't really thought about it, and everyone wants to know all this information about it and I just don't know. No one has talked to me in ten years about it.

Bob - In the old articles, it says it was bought at the auction by Captain Owen O'Mahoney, who was from Scotland or Ireland. When I first read that, I figured, 'Okay.' But the more I thought about it, the guy I got it from was a real *character*. I started to wonder if maybe there was no Captain Owen O'Mahoney. Maybe it had really gone to the guy I subsequently got it from, whose name was Bruce Waldack. But it sounds like you don't have a clue about that.

Risley - I don't have a clue. What I do know is it was an undisclosed bidder, and now that you said something about Scotland, it just kind of something reminds me and I couldn't possibly be sure about any of it, but that it might have been a bidder from abroad. I can tell you it was a phone bidder. So there's a good chance that it was someone from abroad. It could have been a phone bidder from anywhere. I think I recall something about a bidder abroad.

Honestly, I just wanted it all to go away. There was all this hubbub and all I wanted to do was auction stuff off. I was used to selling art and you know, stuff where you're like, we have a certificate so this is an authentic chair. It could be one, it could not be one, inspect it, that's your problem. And it was like, ugh, I got riddled with questions after, and I'm just like 'I don't know. I was just the messenger.'

Bob - If you recall, the one that I got, the one you were involved with, sold with cancelled checks, so there was a way to date it based on the cancelled checks.

Risley - That I remember, and yeah, that was the only thing that kind of led us to believe it was what, you know, it said it was.

Bob - They did quote you saying it was the first Apple-1 built and sold by Apple and your auction house said you offered it to Steve Jobs, and he said he had such a hard time selling it in the first place, that he didn't want it. I just was wondering if you recollect if you had any reason to think it was the first one sold.

Risley - What I will tell you is what they told me. All that information was given to me from the owners of the business who actually owned the auction house and they said that this is what the consigner had told them. That is it. And I don't know who the consigner was either. They

42

kept it very, the consigner wanted to be kept secret which is not uncommon in the auction world. And then they asked me a few questions, where I'm like I can't comment on that. There were a few things where I don't really feel comfortable saying something because I'm not sure. In fact, when I made that quote, I remember going, 'Look guys, this is what the consigner told us, so you know you can print it,' but I was kind of hoping that they'd say, 'From what we understand from the consigner...' I have no idea. Like I could quote Steve jobs...

Bob - What about the guy who owned the auction house? Is he someone I could contact?

Risley - The only thing I know about them was they were from South Africa. And they did not do so well, especially after I left, because they didn't really have a good auctioneer. And I think they... I mean, I kind of saw things not doing so well there, so I thought it was better to just disassociate... I didn't need the money that bad, and it was kind of that auction that kind of left a bad taste in my mouth, because they kind of put a lot of stuff on me, and I literally had people calling me like six months later saying, 'I didn't get my check,' from something else. I'm like, 'Look, you can't... I didn't, you know, I didn't work... I don't think you can find them.' I think they got out of Dodge, honestly.

Bob - So good chance they went back to South Africa?

Risley - I think they probably did. Or just left. Because I know I personally got calls saying, "Hey, I never got my..." People were looking for them. They overleveraged themselves. I think the thing was only in business for a year. They basically bought it, although one thing I do know is that an old woman ran LaSalle Gallery for years. She sold the business and died like a month and a half after that. She sold it to these guys; an older couple too, all South Africans. Basically, I had worked for Butterfield and Butterfield Auctioneers and I had left there. I stopped by LaSalle to see what was going on and to see if there was a job opening and they instantly snatched me up. I said I'm only going to work as a consultant. I was going to go back to business school. I had left to kind of study for my GMAT and go back and get my MBA. So it all kind of coincided. So I figured it was some side money. Anyway, long story short, I'm not going to go into too much detail, but the reality was I was in my twenties, making some money, but I actually left not long after that because I was just kind of uncomfortable.

Bob - Well can you give the names of this couple?

Risley - I can't even remember their names. I could try to find it but it was so long ago and I worked there for maybe six months... I mean, I'd love to help you out, but I'm kind of also, I just don't...

Bob - If you recall the name and can email it back to me, I'd appreciate it.

Risley - Yeah, I'll look in my records, all that stuff I have in storage. That must have been thirteen years ago now. I wish I could help you. I'm literally trying to remember the names, I only remember one guy's name, but I really can't remember.

I will look through my stuff and I'd love to help you. I understand how hard it is to establish provenance like that. Your story sounds like so many stories I've heard, 'Oh, I've found this somewhere and now I'm trying to establish provenance, it could be worth 'x' or it could be worth 'y', and 'x' is worth a lot more, etcetera.'

Bob - Well, an Apple-1 just sold in London for two hundred thousand dollars.

Risley - Yeah I can't remember what the number was, but it wasn't very much. It wasn't as much as we thought it might go for. We had a Lisa there and none of the other stuff even sold.

Bob - From what I read, this was the only thing that sold.

Risley - I remember you could hear crickets chirping. People were there, but you could hear crickets. We had a couple bids on the floor and then the phone and that was it.

I mentioned to him that in the past I was involved in a business that was one of the first online auctions which offered live bidding online.

Risley - I remember that at Butterfield, they tried to integrate the Internet and no one was using the Internet yet. You still had tons of people phone bidding, but no one online.

Bob - Yup, my brother's company was called Leftbid.com and they were early in the game.

Risley - I remember them. I'll tell you one funny story and then I have to go. Steve Westly, he's one of the main guys who built *eBay*, he didn't start *eBay*, but he and Meg Whitman built *eBay*. Sharp guy, really smart. When I was in college, my brother was an astrophysicist, so he got me onto the VAX server. So this was early, late '80s early '90s when I was in college. He got me on the VAX server because he was over in Germany and we wanted to talk, but neither of us had money to make phone calls. So I actually had email. I asked the staff for permission to use the VAX server and they gave me an email that was like a mile long. And there were a few bulletin boards out there and I was like, this is a great idea. So for my senior thesis, I came up with *eBay*, or something like *eBay*. I told my dad about it and he was like, you should get into the auction business. That's pretty much how I got involved. I didn't go directly to that, but I came later. I remember when I got to Butterfields, I was like, '*Oh, my God*, you could never put this online. This is difficult, no one could do this.' And after I had been there about two and a half years, Steve Westly comes and he's viewing our company. I'm like, what a mistake, these guys are toast. My mistake. He's now a billionaire and I'm, you know, I had to go back to get an MBA and start a finance business.

Chapter 10

No Corvettes

In May 2011 we started getting in touch with friends of Jobs and Wozniak, and employees from the earliest days of Apple, we lucked into finding several people who were gracious about sharing their stories. One was Dan Sokol, who seems to have often been in the right place at the right time.

Dan Sokol - I went straight from high school into the Air Force. They decided to teach me electronics. When I left, I used the GI Bill and went to college. In 1970, I was just leaving college, and at that time there was price controls. They were trying to control inflation after the Vietnam disaster. I moved to Southern California. I lived in Pomona, and got a job in a defense plant run by General Dynamics. We were working on a training device for the Redeye, which was a missile system. I was working on the swing shift and going to school during the day. I was getting a degree in business administration because my dad had convinced me that, while I was having a lot of fun playing with electronics, there was no future in it.

In the end, I couldn't decide which way to go. I ended up getting a degree in business administration, and then this Nixonomics thing hit. There was no work anywhere. I had gotten laid-off, along with a lot of other people. My roommate Chuck was having the same problem I was.

46

We looked at each other and said, "What do we do now?" What else do you do when you're in your early twenties and you get laid-off? You take a vacation! We hopped into his Jaguar and drove up to northern California where we had an old friend who had a sailboat, and we went sailing for two weeks.

On the way home, we're driving down Highway 101. Remember, this is two guys who have been working in the field of engineering. This is hard to explain to anyone who wasn't there. In the early 1970s, there were places and company names that were mystical, magical to engineers who weren't living in the Bay Area. Places like Palo Alto, Sunnyvale, Mountain View. There were only five semiconductor companies that existed at the time. Our whole future as electronic engineers was tied up to these magical companies that were manufacturing components. Anyway, to work for one of them was my personal dream.

We're driving back to his house in southern California, and we're looking forward to a nice ten-hour drive. You have to remember, in 1970 Highway 5 wasn't done yet. Highway 5 only went about halfway, the bottom half. There was a two hundred eighty-five mile stretch of Highway 5 with no gas stations. This is right after it opened, it wasn't completed and all the sudden you're back to one lane in each direction. The Highway Patrol was so pissed, they had these funny handwritten signs that said things like "No Corvettes past this point," and "The Highway Patrol will not bring gasoline to Corvette owners."

We're coming down and we hit Palo Alto, and we see signs for a company that Chuck had worked for a competitor of. He said, "Maybe we should stop and drop our resumes off." So we did, and they wouldn't let him leave. When they saw him, they wanted him. They didn't even have an opening, but they basically kept passing him around to talk to people. They made him an offer on the spot. So we stayed overnight, and the next day we drove home and made arrangements. They were going to pay for

47

his room, so I moved my stuff too. We both came back, and I started looking for work.

I ended up working for three months at a company called TAB Products. I was really good at the technical stuff, but I hated dealing with customers. During that period of time, I had dropped my resume at all the semiconductor companies I could find, and AMI called me. I took a job there as foreman of a test group second shift. And I did really well. Three months later I was a general foreman of the test group. Because of my background in engineering, I was improving the techniques and working on improving methodologies. Basically making the process work better. Next thing I know, I'm a test engineer. Head of test engineering, product engineer, head of product engineering. I ended up in R&D as a product engineer. From 1970 to 1976, I was in the semiconductor industry and I loved every minute of it.

My computer interest at that point in time was minimal. I had gone through school, and one of the classes we were required to take was Programming 101. In 1969, that meant you wrote your program out in a wonderful language called *FORTRAN*. You punched each line of code into a card, an IBM Hollerith card. And then you put it into a little slot to submit it, and you'd come back the next day. Of course, what you'd get is your card deck back and a pad of paper, a printout that tells you where your bugs were without actually telling you what went wrong.

My personal feeling when I left college was that computers had no future. It took too long to get them to do anything.

Homebrew Computer Club

I was working for American Microsystems, living up in Santa Cruz and commuting with a friend. That friend asked me if I would go to this meeting that he had picked up a flier on. I seem to remember it was a Wednesday. Some guy named Gordon French was holding it at his house, and it was about personal computers. Of course, nobody used that term

48

at the time. It was about building your own computer, or something. I had zero interest, but since he was a friend and we commuted together, I went with him. Since it was my day to drive, I drove.

I have to be honest; at the time what was more interesting was meeting these people. Computers were computers. We got there a little bit late, and we couldn't find a place to park within blocks. There were a hundred people outside in front of this guy's garage, because so many people had shown up. And so I got out and walked around, and I just looked and said, 'Oh, this is interesting.' They were all basically ogling over all the years of computer junk that Gordon had collected. He also had a wife and a very nice house. The computers were all in the garage.

The newest issue of *Popular Electronics* discussed the very first computer that was within a price range that people could afford. I believe it was four hundred dollars for a kit, and everyone was all excited over it. There was a copy of the magazine at the meeting. Gordon had it, and everyone was talking about it, discussing what could it do, and what we could do with it. But mostly the people were talking to each other and finding out that there were like-minded, curious people around.

I wasn't particularly excited over it. I did find the people very interesting, because they came from all different places. I was from the semiconductor industry, but there were engineers from pretty much every industry. The discussions taking place were, 'What do you do?' 'What are you doing with this stuff?' 'Do you know where I can get one of these?' Since this friend of mine was into it, I started going to these meetings. The first meeting was in Gordon's garage and the only thing that actually came out of it was, 'Well, we can't meet here again. We have to find someplace larger.'

I think the second meeting was held in a Montessori school. That was the first time any of us saw any of the hardware. By the third meeting, we ended up in the Stanford Linear Accelerator auditorium. We

49

held all the meetings after that there. It was every other week and it was a lot of fun.

I can remember one meeting early on when we were asked how many people owned computers, and maybe ten hands went up out of four hundred. And then we were asked, "How many of you are planning on getting one?" and every hand in the place goes up.

We were anarchists. You can go through every file you can think of, every place in the world. If you can find a single picture of that club meeting, you will have found the *only* picture of the club meeting. The only people who ever took pictures were the FBI. Really, nobody ever thought to take pictures of us at this club meeting. In fact, anybody who tried would have been accused of being an FBI agent. I'm serious, this was a group of anarchists. We couldn't even agree on a name for the club. There were four hundred people in the room, and we got four hundred different names. When we went to vote, each name got one vote. We couldn't agree on a charter because nobody wanted to join the committee to write the charter. So we never actually became official, at least not for the first couple of years. The guy who used to run the meetings, how did he get to run the meeting? He had the loudest voice. And nobody objected. It was a lot of fun. It was an earlier time and nobody knew that you could actually go and start a company. That was before any of that kind of thing actually happened. Companies came, companies went, and nearly everybody that was at Homebrew at one time or another was part of a start-up. I helped a couple of them get off the ground.

The best part was not the actual meeting, but what took place before. People sat around talking in groups of three or four, about what they were doing and what they were going to do. I guess the word is *swap meet*, but we weren't really swapping. We were just exchanging stuff. If someone needed something and you had one and weren't using it, you'd arrange to get it for them and they'd give you something else. In my bloodied history, a lot of very interesting things happened. At one of

50

these meetings, someone stood up and asked, "Is there anyone here who has access to a high-speed paper tape reader and punch that can make duplicates?" I raised my hand because one of the machines I was responsible for at work had a PA in it, and it was a memory tester. It had a paper tape reader and punch. He said, "Oh, good," and he came over and handed me this paper tape.

It turned out to be Microsoft, or what turned out to be Microsoft *BASIC*. It was the only piece of software that existed for these early machines. He asked me to go make a couple of copies. I took it to work and read it into the machine and saved it to a tape, and printed out, or punched out, oh, about seventy copies. Now, this thing was all rolled-up, it was about three inches in diameter. So we're talking about a fairly substantial box full. So I brought them to the next meeting. I laid them down and stated what they were, and ten seconds later they were all gone. That piece of action caused me to become the world's first software pirate.

I can tell you that it was unintentional. There was no, 'Oh, wait a minute, maybe I shouldn't be doing this.' It never occurred to me. It never occurred to anyone. The first person who becomes a pirate is unaware that what he's doing is piracy because nobody's done it before. People always ask if I got in trouble for that, and the answer is no. And the reason is because in 1974, '75, when this happened, software was neither copyrightable nor patentable. It wasn't until 1978—probably because of what I did—that they changed the copyright laws to protect software for the first time. It's one of those things, you know. I can't avoid it, it's the skeleton in my closet that just will not stay down. Anyway, that's part of my story. I unwittingly became the world's first software pirate.

One day at work, we get called in and there's a rush project. We don't know anything about it. We're not making the chips, we're just testing them. We don't know exactly what they are. It's this new little company in town, and they're paying a fortune for us to test these chips. Here's the test program, here's the test board, go set it up make sure everything works. I was still the general foreman of the test group. I took the stuff out there, gave it to one of the engineers, and helped them set it up. I looked over and saw the word Atari on the top of the chip, and said, "Hmm. I'll be back in a minute."

I went down to the mask group, and asked the guys there to pull me the bonding diagram for the chip. So I got the bonding diagram and I looked down and it had things like 3.5/8. V out. A out. Pad 1 in, pad 2 in. I thought this was very interesting. So, I took one of the chips home and wired it up. With my knowledge of what those words meant, I hooked it up to a monitor, actually put the TV through a modulator and, *boom!*, I had a *Pong* game. And so, three months before Atari even announced the game, I had shown up at the Homebrew Computer Club with a schematic and a PC board layout and fifty of the chips, which I had taken off the production line. Oh, man, did people come for that one. We all had our own *Pong* games running before Atari even had this thing out to the marketplace. And later on I met Al Alcorn, whom had put his name on the disk. That's how I found out he designed it. It said "Designed by Al Alcorn" on the second mask layer. You could see it on the chip with a microscope, along with a picture of Betty Boop. A six micron-sized Betty Boop, I think that was pretty cute. Of course, today you do something like that, you're violating copyrights and God knows what else.

Meeting Steve Wozniak

Like I said, the best part of the meetings was that period of time when people would just sit around and talk. I remember one time I got there early, and I had some stuff with me that I had brought to trade with someone whom had specifically asked for it. I'd mentioned that I worked for AMI as a product engineer and I had access to semiconductors which were rare, expensive and hard to find unless you had connections. And I was that connection. I had these processing chips for him and I didn't want to carry them around, so I put them next to my jacket in the auditorium. I was on my way back outside because there was no one there yet, and there was one guy sitting by himself in the middle of the top row, all alone.

His head was down, and he was writing something on a piece of paper. I walked up behind him, and was thinking, 'What the hell is going on here? Do I know him?' So I walk up behind his shoulder and he's got a typical graph paper-type pad, and he's writing stuff down. On the left column he's writing numonics, the assembly language code for the 6502 processor. He'd write four, five, six lines; and then off to the right he'd write the hex code equivalent to the assembly language that he had just written. *In his head.* He wasn't looking up the numonics and finding out what the hex value was. He *knew* them all. And so he was essentially writing code at assembly level and then assembling it in his head. Complete with jumps and vectors and all the other things that you need to do to assemble code and I just thought, '*Whoa!*'

I sat there and watched him for a minute and thought, '*Whoa, that's impressive.*' I waited until he got to the end of the page and I said "Hi," and he sort of jumped a little bit. I said "I'm Dan, who are you?" He said, "Oh, I'm Steve." I said, "What are you doing?" He said "Oh, I'm writing a *BASIC* interpreter for my personal computer." I said, "Oh, which one do you have?"

He said, "Oh, I haven't built it yet. I'm having some problems getting it built, because I'm having problems getting the components. I'm just a technician at HP. If I were an engineer, I could call Hamilton, or Avnet or one of the other suppliers and could get them."

Bob - Did he stand out at the meetings?

Dan - No, he was very quiet, shy, and wasn't someone who asked questions or provided answers. He just sat and listened.

Bob - Was he the type who people quickly realized was brilliant?

Dan - Yes, he was, but here's your problem. Everyone there was brilliant. You had no stupid people in that audience. You had to want to be there, and you had to go out of your way to show up. Things tend to get foggy over time. They tend to be shinier over time than they were when you were there. But I can tell you, I was pretty much in awe of most of the people who were there. They were all intelligent. Many of them had specific knowledge and capabilities well beyond mine. I had my own area of expertise, but there were no stupid people in the audience.

I met a lot of people that I befriended. There was a lot of trading of equipment and parts. I was in a particularly unique position as an engineer in the semiconductor industry, because not only did I know what was coming, but I had access to parts. I could predict what was coming, based upon just seeing what was selling. Knowing what's going on in the industry, from the inside, means you can pretty well guess what's going to happen next.

Anyway, I took pity on Woz, and gave him a shoebox full of 6800 processor parts, some of which he used to build his first Apple-1 computer. And, of course, he gave me the schematic for his Apple-1. In fact, he gave me one of the Apple-1 boards that he and Jobs had designed, so I could build my first Apple-1 board. Which I did. And then when the Apple][came out, I pulled the components off that board and put them in the Apple][that he arranged to get me.

I remember when he showed off the Apple-1. He gave away the schematics, and he gave away the code for the monitor assembler that he had written. He didn't do the *BASIC* until the Apple][. When he showed off the prototype of the Apple][, you couldn't get near it. Jobs was there with him. Perhaps that 'reality distortion field' that we all have gotten accustomed to may actually have been in effect back then, because I could not get close to the machine itself. It was three or four people deep. I figured, '*Screw it*. It's just another computer. I'll get to see it later.'

We became friends after that. And we've been good friends ever since. I even had an opportunity to be one of the early Apple employees. This's the sad part of the story. I had an opportunity to be one of the first ten employees at Apple. In order to take that position, I would have had to take a fifty percent cut in pay. I was ready to do it. I thought it would be a great thing to do. My girlfriend at the time freaked, and didn't want me to do it, so I didn't. And I don't have her now either. I was making very good money and the money didn't mean that much. But she freaked. She thought it was... Apple was a start-up. And at the time, start-ups didn't have any meaning. I actually had a couple of opportunities, but I never took advantage of them. I wish I had, it would have been a much more interesting story. But I didn't, I'm one of many people who didn't. You know, I look back and I don't have any of the advantages and I don't have that girlfriend anymore.

The Homebrew Computer Club was fantastic. It was a whole bunch of anarchists who couldn't agree on anything, other than the fact that computers were going to be big. But nobody had an answer about what you'd do with them. The person who answered that question was not even a club member. It was Dan Bricklin, who invented *VisiCalc*, the world's first spreadsheet, that ran on the Apple][. And it was the piece of software that made the difference. Not Microsoft *BASIC*. *BASIC* basically allowed you to play games and toys and build little applications, nothing major.

VisiCalc changed the entire game. The term 'paradigm shift'— that's what *VisiCalc* was. I took accounting and finance. I went to business school in the 1970s—late '60, early '70s—in University of California, Fullerton. The 'what if' equations were done on paper, column after column. 'What if the interest rate is changed to this?' 'Lease or buy?' The lease or buy decision, which was ninety percent of what finance guys did in the 1960s and '70s was never done as simply or as excitingly. *VisiCalc* was a *holy shit!* whole new world. You showed that to a finance guy and he came in his pants. I mean, this was the Holy Grail that he didn't know existed. And, how much did that little machine cost? Two grand? With all the pieces, three? *I want one!* Throw in the printer! This is what kept the Byte Shops and the small computer stores alive, was this sudden demand.

You had a pencil and at the other end of the pencil was this thing called an eraser. That's what life was like before the spreadsheet. You can do so much with spreadsheets, and I know some people who are geniuses with them, but you don't have to be. Most of the stuff is pretty easy to work out. But Dan Bricklin and *VisiCalc* changed everything. The hardware was the platform, the place to stand, but the software was the element that actually accelerated the change. We didn't have to answer that question, 'What are you going to do with personal computers?' That got answered for us. As they say, everything else is history.

All in all, I think I came out ahead. As I put it to Steve Wozniak a couple of times, there are six billion people on the planet. I know maybe one hundred of them. And one of them is Steve. How many people can you say you've known for forty-plus years?

Bob - What did you think when you first saw the Apple-1?

Dan - Well, when I first saw it, I went and built one. I said, "Cool, what do you do with it?" Really, you built the computer and then what did you have? You had to have some device to look at the output, and you had to have a keyboard. You know, there's so much you take for granted now. Keyboards, printers. There were no printers. God help us all. What few printers we were had were really bizarre protocols. No two were the same, you had to build everything up yourself. It was a hell of a learning experience.

We'd hold contests at the club and see who could figure out the most efficient way to do something. Then we'd have arguments for hours over the definition of 'efficient.' Is efficiency 'every byte counts?' Or is it 'how fast does it run?' I look back and the computers we were using had

56

top speeds of about 1 megahertz. Not gigahertz, *megahertz*. They were one thousand times *slower*. They were 8-bit machines. Not 32 and 64-bit: *8-bit* machines. Graphics were a joke. No one would have predicted that it'd go the way it went, or that it'd continue to evolve as it has. We were doing it because it was fun. We were all geeks. We were all nerdy types; engineers, technicians, people who were engrossed in the technology industry and worked in it in one form or another and were curious.

Then there were people like Wozniak, who because of his background had interfaces with computers from an early age. He built computers, real computers, and always wanted one even if he couldn't figure out what to do with it, because they were fun to play with. There was a certain—what is the phrase?—I want to describe this right. There was a certain level of perfection and control, something that engineers really liked, that was, you know, we're talking about an era... In the 1970s there was the transition between the analog and digital world. And in the digital world everything is very, very precise. In the analog world... *not so much*. So, when you program a computer, you give it a set of precise instructions. 'Do this, do this, do this, and if this happens, do that.' And the ability to do that, to tell a piece of hardware to do something *specific*, and to have it do exactly what you tell it, there was a certain amount of power and enjoyment out of that. And there still is.

The appeal of programming is that you have control. Of course, when the computer does something unexpected—but you told it not to do it—that's a bug. Life becomes less pleasurable when you have to track down your own mistakes. But usually nobody dies. That's why so few of us design nuclear power plants... Okay, that's the bad joke for the day.

Bob - Even though you didn't work together, you saw Steve often in the early Apple years?

Dan - Oh, I spent many a lunchtime picking Steve up at the Bandley Apple building and going to have lunch with him. I was literally around the corner.

Bob - And what was that atmosphere like?

Dan - Crazy. It was a start-up. It's like all start-ups. And Steve was the kind of guy who practically lived there. He was there all the time. They had more than one building at that time; they were growing like a weed. But Bandley was where Woz was.

They were very successful back then. They were shipping something like ten thousand Apple]['s per week and growing. We're talking right after they were founded, but before they went public. They were growing like a weed and doing really well. The big event that turned them from shipping ten thousand a week to shipping twenty-five thousand a week was right around the corner.

It was a madhouse. A company that was growing. At the speed that Apple was growing then, it was anything but organized. They had some great upper management, and they had control, but you know, it was just a madhouse. They had multiple engineering groups that were focused on doing different things. They hadn't yet reached the point where secrecy was of any importance to them. When you look at the Apple][and the Apple][e—which for many years was their bread and butter—what they were doing from a business standpoint was finding better ways to manufacture it cheaper and more reliably, so there was a lot of focus of QA and sales, and engineering revisions, and software improvements and add-on products that they could make. At that particular time there was a big push into the schools. As the company went forward, the early PCs had not yet arrived, and Microsoft had only provided a single piece of software for the world, and that was Microsoft *BASIC*. But the piece of software that put the Apple][on the map was *VisiCalc*. And the reason was the floppy drive that Woz designed. It was that device that made the difference that took Apple from a small growing company into a very large growing company. *VisiCalc* is what drove the Apple][into business. If you were an accountant in the late 1970s, before the IBM PC came to market, you had to have an Apple][. Because it could do things that the mainframe couldn't.

Your mother used to tell you, 'Money can't buy you happiness.' I watched Woz go from just another engineer to suddenly having a lot of money. For the first time, he had money and a lot of toys. He had a Porsche with "Apple][" as the license plate. He had a beautiful house in Scotts Valley. That house, by the way, fell down the side of the mountain when the earthquake hit. He had sold it, he was long gone. The house did not survive the '89 quake.

Money does change people. Having watched Steve for forty-plus years, I can tell you it changes the way you do things. It changes the way you view the world. In some ways, life is more relaxed and in other ways it's a lot less relaxed.

I can also tell you fame is not everything it's cracked up to be. On the other hand, I get to be part of his entourage. I got to stay at his house, and eat the food, and I had no responsibilities. It was one of the best parties I've ever been to. I've gotten to travel the world with him. And, you know, I've helped him run his computer school stuff. So I have no complaints. To me, it's been the best of both possible worlds. I know if it had been me that had all that money, I never would have survived.

Bob - You said that Woz launched the computer revolution, and was a historical individual, but then you said he stopped engineering after he became famous.

Dan - Engineering isn't something you turn on and off. It's a lot like computer programming. When you're doing it, you disappear. The house could be burning down and until it gets to your fingers or toes, you don't notice it. You don't notice anything going on around you. You're focused on design, you're focused on how the electrons or the logic is moving. You're juggling parameters; you're juggling what happens in time and space in your head. You're laying out schematics and transferring them. These tasks are mentally intensive to the point of blocking out everything that happens around you. You don't stop to take a break, you stop when it's time to stop. You reach a point where you can't do anymore, you go have something to eat, you take a nap, you exercise, then you go back when you're ready. Steve is one of those guys who doesn't need very much sleep. He tends to work two or three days straight, and then fall asleep for twenty-four hours. I don't know if he can do it anymore; I mean he's a lot older now.

I remember one day walking into Woz's office, and on his white board he'd written, "Wozniak's rule: Do it right the second time." He apparently had spent a lot of time trying to get something to work, had it all designed, and then went back and did it again, so he decided to formalize that concept. Which I got a kick out of. I've always remembered that particular quote.

The Crash

You know, Steve's very lucky. He did all the things that new money people do. And almost died. You know, he had a plane crash. He's very, very lucky to have survived the plane crash. In fact, he's lucky to have survived the hospital after the plane crash. At the time I was still working for AMI, and I had just come back from a week in Korea at Korean Microsystems, which was a wholly owned subsidiary of AMI. It's February, 1981, and I remember getting home in the late afternoon exhausted. Just for background noise I turned on the TV, and heard the news about a Silicon Valley executive plane crash, and I turn around and see the picture of his plane, a blue plane upside down, and I'm like, 'Oh, shit!' I immediately got on the phone and called a mutual friend. He said, "Yeah, that was Steve." They had him up at a hospital in Santa Cruz, and I'm like, 'Oh, no.' So the next day we went to see Steve in the hospital. We couldn't find his room. They didn't have it listed. We asked and they told

60

us the room number, and we go off to the room and the door's closed. There's this thing on the door but it's some old lady's name. Steve's in there and he's pretty messed up in the bed. I walk in and pick up the clipboard at the end of the bed, and it doesn't have his name, it has the name of this old lady. She's listed as a diabetic due for an insulin shot. About that time Steve's mom and dad came in. I showed the chart to them, and I said, "Get him out of here, get him to Stanford. Get him out of here before they kill him."

So they did; they moved him to Stanford that afternoon. But the other part of the story is he recovered slowly. He went back to work, and six months after the accident I get a call from him at around eleven one morning. He says, "You're not going to believe this, but I just woke up today." And I'm like, "What?" He said, "This morning I got up, got out of bed, and had breakfast and suddenly looked around and I realized that six months of my life was missing." He'd spent six months half-awake. And he'd just recovered. I suppose the term is 'walking coma.' Anyway, we had lunch that afternoon, and we talked about that and some other things at length. I was just glad to see that he was recovered and had his sense of humor back.

Las Vegas

I moved to Texas in 1980 for business, and so we'd get together in Las Vegas every few months and continue to see each other, until I came back to California in '88. We had a lot of fun, he and I. Thanks to Woz, I have the perfect gambling system. You gamble with someone else's money. He and I would go to Las Vegas, and he'd take ten grand— and that's all he'd take—and then we'd gamble with that money. And if we lost, *wham!*, we had a good time and we'd go home. And if we won, he'd take enough money off of the winnings to recover the ten grand, and whatever was left we'd split fifty-fifty.

I remember one trip, we just came into the casino, and we were walking by one of these poker machines. That was one of his favorite games. And he threw a buck in and he was about to pull the handle, so I said, "That's a five dollar machine, you're going to have to put a little more in." "Oh, okay. Well, I'm committed." So he throws in twenty-five bucks, and pulls the handle down and hits the jackpot for fifty grand. That was a great trip, I remember that one. I came home with like fifteen thousand dollars.

Sometimes we'd play *Craps*, but his favorite game was *Blackjack*. The reason was because he had come up with a system. That was actually very clever and *worked* about, well, one out of every six times. I could explain the system. It was not card-counting; it wasn't based on cards. It was based on the fact that two people were playing and sharing. The way it worked was our bets always had to be identical. And if one of us won and one of us lost, the winner would take the winnings and put it in the loser's circle. So essentially, all of the hands where you had one win and one loss were wipes. It was like we didn't play the hand. Okay, but if we both won, we'd double down. And we'd go to the next level. When we both lost, we'd start over with the smallest chip.

We'd set boundaries, like if we got up to eight chips, regardless of what the chips were we pulled one back, so we got the original bet back. So if we lost, we haven't lost anything. The original idea was to go as long as possible with a hundred dollars each on a five dollar table. And sometimes we'd play all night on that hundred dollars. Every once in a while, if you could do eight doublings, without both of you losing, you can win a lot of money out there. So, we'd set a top end. Usually, it was five grand, which was the table limit. If we hit five grand, we'd just pull everything back and walk away.

Oh, and we wouldn't play by the standard rules for *Blackjack*. Most of the time you played by the standard rules. But let's just say that the dealer had the points showing and we both had thirteen. Okay? It doesn't matter what the bet is. We both have thirteen; the first one of us would take a card, and if he busted, the second one would not take a card. Why bother? If you don't take the card and the dealer busts, we're still in the game. If you take a card and you bust, we're out. And, if you had a bad hand, we would not both take cards. We would necessarily both take a card. If one of us got a good hand, that looked like it might hold, the other one would do nothing. Sometimes it would work and sometimes it didn't. You see where we're coming from? We're playing for the doubling. It's a good strategy, it's a lot of fun. It gives you a lot of time to sit there and talk about other things, meet people from around the country.

Bob - And he came up with that?

Dan - Yeah, he came up with that. He invented it so that he could play with his first wife, who wasn't very good at it. It's just a way of getting the money to last longer. And by the time he had figured out what he had done, we realized we had a system there that actually worked. And he could actually sit there and tell her what to do. Another thing we would do is the slot machines. He liked to play the slots, mostly the poker slots.

Education

     I was Woz's technical assistant in the 1990s for ten years, and it was a lot of fun. I built a lot of things for him I can't talk about, because you know, he's a prankster. He decided it was time to start teaching kids to use computers. First of all, he adopted the Los Gatos school district. He wired up all the schools for Internet, put computer labs in all the schools, and picked an elementary school which just happened to be the one his kids were going to. 'Steve's going to teach a voluntary computer class, come in.' So here's what he'd do, he'd come in, introduce himself to each of you, and then everybody in the class got a brand new portable computer, a printer, a ton of software, and you took the class. He would do this three times a week, and me and two of his friends were his assistants. What's our job? Our job is to repair these computers as fast as the kids could break them.

He'd bring in professionals to teach some of these programs. We discovered very soon afterwards that we had to do a separate class for the teachers. One teacher commented, "I'm amazed at how much better my kids can spell now." And Steve goes, "This teacher doesn't know there's a spell-checker in the computer." We had a good chuckle over it. What we did is set up a professional organization that taught adults to use computers, and we had them come in and teach the teachers so they could be a little ahead of the kids. Good luck on that!

From my perspective, you know, I said to Steve one day, these kids are all eleven, twelve now. They're going to go through high school and they're going to have a computer and know how to use it. They already know typing. I was the only one allowed to be a two-finger typist, under the assumption I was too old to learn. Which worked out to my advantage. Now that we have the iPhone, and iPad, you have to be a two-finger typist.

So I said to Steve, "Try to put yourself in the place of these kids." They're going to go to high school, do all their reports on computers, its second nature to them. Then one day they're going to graduate high school and to college. And they're going to move into the dorm and their roommate is going to look at them and say, 'Oh wow, nice computer.' And they're going to say, 'Oh, yeah, Steve Wozniak got it for me and taught me how to use it.' And it's not going to mean a thing to them. They just don't get who you are. You're just 'that guy Steve' to them. You're not Steve Wozniak, the co-founder of Apple computer, the guy who launched the computer revolution.

It's hard to remember, even for me, since I've known him forty-five years, that this is someone special. A national treasure. On the downside, the country lost one of its best engineers because he stopped doing engineering after he became famous. Sometimes you have to go where demand is.

It cost him on average about two hundred thousand a year to do this. One class; computers for all the kids, software for all the kids, printers for all the kids. You got to keep the stuff if you passed his class. He didn't pick the wealthiest school in the district, he picked the *least* wealthy school in the district. The school up in the mountains, where at least two-thirds of the students come from families at the lower end of the economic scale. Families that don't have thirteen computers in the house, like I do. Don't ask. There's a story about my daughter. One day, right after I met her—which is a story onto it self, a love child from the '60s who'd found me around the year 2000 on the Internet—one of her questions was, "How many computers do you have?" and I had to stop for a minute and ask, "Running? Or in the house?" And she laughed and she said "Running," and I said "Gee, I don't know. Just a minute, I have to go count." And the answer was twelve.

Bob - You said Steve gave you an Apple-1 board, and later you took the components off of that to use on an Apple][. Did you keep that Apple-1 board?

Dan - Everybody who I know who's ever had an Apple-1 who sees one sell for a quarter of a million dollars at a Christie's auction is like, "What the fuck?" Well, what I did with that Apple-1 board is I went to a friend of mine who was an artist, and I had him take that board and put it on a piece of painted wood with a metal silver border around it. Then he put it in a frame with the words "Our Founder" and I gave it to Steve for one of his birthdays as a gag gift. I have a picture of Steve holding it up. Yeah, and you know, I look at that and say, "*Damn*, I want that back!"

Bob - Steve's got a storage unit somewhere. Maybe that's where the frame ended up.

Dan - He had a huge storage area with all this junk, and they dumped it ten years ago. He'd been paying money to store it, the stuff has been collecting dust and spider webs, and they went in there and dumped everything. You know, I would have taken it, but my garage is already full of junk.

Chapter 11
Denny's

Another friend of Steve Wozniak from the '70s, Randy Wigginton joined Apple early on and was a longtime key employee.

Randy Wigginton - When I was a freshman in high school, my typical day started at five-thirty a.m. I'd get up and ride the bus to school. It was an hour bus ride. I was on the swim team, so I'd have a swim before and after school. And then I'd ride the bus back home, and usually be home about five p.m. The bus rides were wonderful for me, because for two months solid, I did nothing but read the 6502 manuals, learning a lot about assembly language, and computer concepts. Because I didn't know anything. I just learned how to program a little bit. The bus rides were wonderful chances to read whatever computer books I could find. And there weren't very many.

Bob - Would it have been unusual for a high schooler to be into computers at that time?

Randy - For the day, certainly unusual. The only way to do computers for a hobby is if you exerted a huge amount of effort. You know it isn't like you could just pull up a Google search on 'how to program.'

Bob - Did you have support within your family for your hobby?

Randy - They had no idea what to make of it. It isn't like anyone else was doing it. But my parents have a lot of trust in me. That was to my benefit. They pretty much allowed me to pursue the interest. There were no computers available, at least for regular people. I called around to various computer companies trying to find a place that would offer free timeshare for a student. And most of them weren't very interested in helping out. A few had programs to offer students free time. One was a company called Call Computer that had a remote terminal.

While I was at Call using their computers, I heard about the Homebrew Computer Club, and I started going. The problem is I couldn't drive, because I was too young. I would get a ride from anyone I could, until I met Woz, and as it turned out he lived only like three blocks from my house. I was able to hitch a ride with him from my house from that point on.

Bob - What was your first impression of him?

Randy - First of all, he was incredibly brilliant. He was really friendly, really kind, and he loved to joke.

Bob - You were lucky to find somebody who was an incredible mentor.

Randy - Oh, absolutely. Woz realized that he could actually make the 'dumb' (or 'remote') terminal into a computer. He did that, and while he was doing it he was giving me rides up and back from the computer club. He drove a terrible car, a Fiat. That car broke down every time you just looked at it. It was so terrible. I remember once after I started driving, I was driving down the freeway one day and I saw his car sitting on the side of the road.

Bob - Always the possibility of ending up on the side of the road with his car?

Randy - No, but we always thought we were going to. There were a number of times where we had trouble starting, etcetera, but we always managed to make it where we were going. He would pick me up from my house, and we'd drive up to SLAC (Stanford Linear Accelerator Center).

Usually it was early, because he wanted to show off the Apple-1, or the Apple][. We'd unpack his car and set up in the entryway, the foyer, and get everything working. He'd sit down and proceed to type in several pages worth of hex codes, because he didn't have any sort of cassette reader/write capability. I would go in, and the meeting would start. At the end of the meeting, I'd help Woz pack up his car, and we'd head back down. Pretty much every night we'd stop at Denny's, and complain about the food. Basically, I'd just ask him question after question on how things worked, how to program such-and-such. That was my computer science class. Homebrew was usually over around nine or so. And then, you know, Woz and I would spend forty-five minutes a day at Denny's, so I'd be home at ten-thirty or eleven.

Bob - In a Denny's, you'd be able to concentrate on what Woz was teaching you?

Randy - So, I would just tune out everything else other than Woz. I mean also, I've always had incredible focus, sometimes too much so. In first grade, for example, I kept on reading right on through a fire alarm. Just because I'm focused.

In those days there were basically two groups of computer people. There were the hobbyists, and those who were trying to figure out how to make money off it. There were interesting intersections between the two. The original terminal got started because there was someone that wanted to make money selling timeshare access. Woz built a terminal, including the modem, and he realized, 'Well, heck, I could just put in this cheap microprocessor that I found and make it into a whole computer.' He did that in no time at all. I mean, he was amazing. He was magic. Woz developed his computer. When he finally finished the design and got one working, immediately of course, I wanted to build one.

Bob - What did you think of the design?

Randy - I thought it was absolutely amazing. I thought it was the greatest thing ever. It was actually the cheapest thing around. There wasn't anything as affordable, as I recall. It was certainly less expensive than the Altair or the IMSAI, and it was much better than those. When you turned it on, something was immediately running. You immediately had some way of going forward. Whereas, with the other computers, you generally had to enter in your bootstrap sequence via the front panel. Which was enormously painful.

Bob - Your involvement with Apple from the beginning is one of those things that turned out to be a good happenstance, in your case.

Randy - Well think about it, I mean most everything is sort of happenstance. Really we don't control much of our own fate.

Bob - How long did you work at Apple?

Randy - Basically up through 1985. For nine years or so.

Bob - Do you have good memories about the Apple-1 or the very early days?

Randy - Oh, God, there were so many. People always say they joined the company in the garage stage. Well, I joined in the couch stage. We weren't big enough for the garage yet. We were on the couch, you know. It eventually moved over to Jobs' garage and building stuff there. My brother built some of the original cases for the Apple-1's. Everything was very mom and pop. When the company became real, we rented office space.

Bob - The third founder, Ron Wayne, was there for a very short time. When you joined, was he already gone?

Randy - Well, I met him. But Apple was incorporated twice. They incorporated once in early '76, and then again at the end of '76. Ron was never part of the second incorporation of Apple. He was still around, but he never really did that much. You know, I mean he drew some diagrams and wrote up some documentation, but that was kind of it.

Bob - And it wasn't necessarily a formal business in the beginning, where everybody would be there nine-to-five?

Randy - Not at all. Everything was out of Jobs' house, and everybody had real full-time jobs. That's the reason Ron Wayne backed out. He'd been involved with several start-ups that didn't work out, and he didn't want to gamble.

Bob - You mentioned that your brother built some of the original cases for the Apple-1.

Randy - He was home from college, and didn't have anything going on. He was trying to figure out what he wanted to do, and liked woodworking. So I said, "Yeah, he can do that." He built some of those original ones.

Bob - Do you remember any metal boxes?

Randy - No, in general people wouldn't have used metal. Metal was too clunky for Steve Jobs.

Bob - I didn't realize you had joined Apple when it first started. What employee number were you?

Randy - Number 6.

Bob - There were two phases. There was one where I was still in school, and another where I had graduated. By this time, I was finally driving. I'd drive in to the office at about five-thirty am or so, work until about eight am, and then drive to school. After school I'd drive back and work at Apple from about four pm 'til seven o'clock at night. Then, once I finished school, I'd usually get in at seven, seven-thirty. Woz would usually arrive about eight thirty, or so. We would always, always, *always* walk down the street to Bob's Big Boy, and have breakfast. And he'd always complain about how awful the coffee was, but he ordered it every single day. We'd talk about computers, and what was going on with Apple.

Bob - Denny's, Bob's Big Boy, did you guys prefer burgers or all-day breakfast?

Randy - It was all-day breakfast.

Bob - I'm assuming Denny's has probably not changed a whole lot in the interim.

70

Randy - No. I don't think the cuisine has improved.

Bob - As to office décor, I read that the Good Earth location featured cubbies equipped with cardboard barriers because of the high incidence of Nerf projectiles.

Randy - There was a lot of Nerf play, yes. Actually, the Mac division moved three times. It started off in Good Earth, and then it went to the Texaco Building, which was on the corner of Steven's Creek and De Anza Blvd. From there, it actually moved back to 10260 Bandley.

Bob - How did the Good Earth location feel, more institutional, scruffy, locker-roomy?

Randy - It was totally scruffy. It's been widely reported, Steve Jobs was not a regular shower-taker in those days. We were just making it up as we were going along. We really had no idea what we were doing, starting a company. All we knew is that we were growing fast. We started off in one little office—which seemed like it had tons of room—and before very long we had another office in the same Good Earth complex.

From there we moved over to Bandley. When we finally got there, it started becoming more like a real company. There wasn't any sort of furniture planning. People would just sort of bring in desks, or order a desk and they'd get it. There was no consistency in the desks or between the desks or the chairs or anything.

Bob - The Bandley location was relatively more formal, then. Can you point to anything there that stood out in terms of the eccentricity of a bunch of people doing design, engineering, what have you?

Randy - Well, yeah, we had the Ping Pong tables out back. At one point—I can't remember who it was—brought in a couple of tennis rackets, and we were playing tennis in back (indoors). It was so huge. When we moved in we didn't have nearly enough people for that building.

Bob - What did you actually do at Apple? What kind of projects did you end up working on during your time there?

Randy - I was programming. I did any and all software. Basically, Woz was more of the hardware guy, and sort of the base-level software. There were things that he needed help with, so that's what I did. From the original Apple][ROM and the Apple][disk routines, and one of the first programs we had for the Apple][was called *Checkbook*. Mike Markkula and I spent a couple months on *Checkbook*, so that people could balance their checkbook with the computer.

Bob - Did you ever envision things moving the direction they did with personal computing?

Randy - Oh, heck no. Absolutely not. Jobs admitted to me that he didn't either. No one ever thought it would get this large. We knew there was a market for it, because we wanted it. But nobody ever thought it would become a multi-billion dollar industry. Possibly Mike Markkula could have foreseen how large it would become. That may be why he invested in Apple. I don't know, though. We were just a bunch of kids having fun.

Bob - My Apple-1 was originally purchased, directly from Apple in July of 1976, by a man named Charles Ricketts. Do you recall him?

Randy - Umm...yeah... You know who would know a lot about that is Steve Jobs. I remember that name being said, so, yes, there is something there. But no one let me near the money. You don't let sixteen-year-olds near the money.

Bob - So you were that young when you started at Apple?

Randy - Yeah.

Bob - Ricketts had bought his Apple-1 directly from Apple in July 1976. You commented that you remembered hearing Ricketts' name, but you can't think of anything more. Why did you recognize the name?

Randy - As I recall, he was owner of a computer store, or something like that. He was definitely a real hustler. He wanted to make a business out of these things. He kept coming up with ideas on how it could be used. I remember Steve Jobs discussing him a whole bunch of times. Steve would probably be the only one who really remembers him.

72

Bob - The second check for $193.00, which says Steve Jobs "programmed" the computer in August, a month later.

Randy - I could be mistaken, but I'm pretty sure that's a program I did for them which I think he wanted to put it into Sears Automotive Centers, so when people had their order number called. Yeah, that's one of the programs I wrote back then. I think that's who he is.

You know, how you wait for your number to get called? Well, they wanted to put them up on a screen.

Bob - Maybe you just pulled a curtain back. You stayed at Apple quite a while. Why did you eventually leave the company?

Randy - I left shortly after Jobs did. I was young and arrogant, and thought I knew everything. I thought I could do it again. I didn't realize how incredibly fortunate that was. Typical child star kind of thing.

Bob - In going through the registry of Apple-1's, there are references to numbers that were put on the back of the boards. Some were written in magic marker and some were on little labels. I was wondering if you remember anything about that.

Randy - No, I don't remember. I know Steve thought they should do that to start keeping track of them at some point.

Bob - Steve *Jobs*, you mean?

Randy - Yeah.

Bob - So, keeping track would be for inventory purposes?

Randy - Just knowing who had which ones.

Bob - Since they didn't have serial numbers, if somebody had a service problem, they could say, 'I have number 13,' or something? Would that be the objective?

Randy - Yes, and there were also three different runs of the boards, so if they knew which run it was, they would know which buttons were on it.

Bob - How did you feel about the Apple-1 in terms of its value as an educational tool?

Randy - The Apple-1 wasn't a very good fit for education. It really wasn't all that easy to use unless you were a real uber-geek like me. What was motivating about Steve Wozniak, and the reason I always loved working with him, was that he always wanted to help people learn. He always cared about helping people to grow. When he drove me to the Homebrew Computer Club, he'd basically spend the whole time teaching me. We'd spend an hour each night at the Denny's, and he'd teach me computer science. He wanted the Apple-1 for education, but it was too hard. Look even now at how much trouble teachers have setting up and administering their own computers. And I look at the Apple-1 and that was not an easy machine.

The thing is that the Apple-1, Steve Jobs was frustrated with it pretty quickly, because it was so hard to use and so limited. When the Apple][came out, which was very shortly thereafter, the Apple-1 was pretty much forgotten. There were all sorts of things that Jobs wanted to do with the Apple-1, but it didn't have any graphics. The slow display was a problem, etcetera.

I actually taught computer classes at my high school for a couple of years, and used the Apple-1. And, yeah, it was painful. You had to spend a whole bunch of time just loading up, for example, *BASIC*, off of cassettes. First, you had to hook it up to a TV. We didn't have monitors in those days that anyone could afford. There would be this fuzzy picture that was bending and tearing, and it was primitive. There weren't a whole lot of choices in those days, so it was the best thing you could get at that time. Now, for hardcore computer classes, I'm sure some of them were able to use it, probably more on the college level than in the high school.

In the early Apple days, we had education discounts almost from day one. As I recall, we donated a fair amount of computers to different schools and stuff like that. Education was one of the fundamental beliefs of the original founders. Jobs and Woz always believed in education. Scotty, the first president, he believed in education too. Everybody

74

wanted to improve the world a little bit. When we built the Mac, Jobs really thought it would shine in education.

Bob - Do you think you succeeded in improving the world a little bit?

Randy - Uh... Sometimes I wonder. But yeah, mostly I'm pretty happy with the way things have turned out. Mostly, we were just busy managing the growth and riding the rocket.

Chapter 12

Christie's

A major truing point in the valuation of Apple-1 computers came on November 23rd, 2010, when Christie's sold an Apple-1 at auction in London for $212,267. It was said to have been consigned by a private collector. The sale also included the original box, instruction manual and a period signed letter from Steve Jobs. The return address on the box was his parent's house. Apple co-founder Steve Wozniak attended the auction. Wozniak said, "I gave them (the plans) away for free. It was really just an attempt to help people move the world forward". The buyer was Marco Boglione, a private Italian collector, bidding by phone.

Christie's Julian Wilson said, "At today's auction, we saw people studying the sale catalogue on their iPads using the Christie's app while the auctioneer took online bids through Christie's LIVE; it is a fitting illustration of how computers have revolutionized the world to have sold an Apple-1 computer as an historic relic in Christie's salerooms. This is the first time that an Apple-1 has been sold at a major international auction, and we are thrilled with the global interest and enthusiasm that we saw leading up to the sale, and with the price realized by this rare and exceptional piece of computing history."

The computer was described as number 82 of the two hundred.

The catalog description:

"The first Apple computer, and the first personal computer with a fully assembled motherboard, heralding the home computer revolution. Introduced in July 1976, the Apple-1 was sold without a casing, power supply, keyboard or monitor. However, because the motherboard was completely pre-assembled, it represented a major step forward in comparison with the competing self-assembly kits of the day."

It's always interesting to read peoples' comments online, such as, "It was the start of a revolution." Another called it "The cherry on top of any historical computing collection."

Chapter 13

Freelance Teacher

I'd heard that a woman who was a school teacher owned the first Apple. It turned out that Liza Loop lived north of San Francisco, and we first spoke in March of 2011. She had received her Apple-1 directly from Steve Wozniak.

Liza Loop - To start early, I came from a very privileged background. I'm one of those WASPs who grew up in the suburbs of Boston and had highly educated parents, and so I've had all the advantages. My mission is to share those advantages as widely as I can.

Both my parents were very intellectual, they were both practicing scientists. They were both entrepreneurial. So even though they didn't get along, they had a lot in common, and I think I have a lot of similar traits.

My mom grew up as a chicken farmer. She majored in Zoology in college, she was born in 1913. She graduated from college in The Depression. She met my father when she worked as a technician at the medical school for the College of Physicians and Surgeons, in New York. She continued to do biological research after they married. She was going to go on for a Master's degree, but then she had three kids. At that time, she was just furious because Wellesley College wouldn't let her pursue her Master's degree part-time. And she wasn't willing to leave her children that long.

My maiden name is Straus. My father's family owned Macy's Department Store. He always wanted to be an engineer, and his mom made him go to medical school. So he got his medical degree, but he never practiced medicine. I know that he wanted to go to MIT, and his mother considered it a trade school and wouldn't let him go.

He started in the Army around 1941, and stayed through '45. He studied pilots—as a doctor—Oxygen Narcosis, and did a lot of—I'm kind of filling in here because I haven't read this, but what I think happened was—that the way they knew about what was going on with the pilots was by studying their radio communications. And so he got very interested in radio communications and acoustics. And that got him from medicine into engineering. I didn't know him very well, because my parents were split up essentially before I was born. He was a logician, as well. When you study Linguistics... I don't know how much you know about Linguistics. It sounds like it's about language. You could think about its about English and literature. But it's not. It's about the systems and the structures of language. So, it's what's behind the spoken word, and highly analytical. So, what I think probably happened is in his work in the Army, in studying radio transmissions, a lot of that radio transmission was in code. As well as spoken. In studying Oxygen Narcosis and people not being able to process, what happens when the brain can't process these signals? That got him into Linguistics. During the war, there was a huge amount of work to try and decode the German secret codes. That's what Alan Turing was doing that got him into computing.

He also invested in Radio Shack. I remember being in Radio Shack when it was literally a shack. It was not really retail at the time. It was audio and acoustic research. He was an audiophile and a technologist. I just sort of visited him up until I was twelve. We had a split when I was twelve, I didn't see him until I was eighteen. I saw him twice when I was eighteen. And I never saw him again.

I went to highly academically advanced private schools. I figure I got what most people get their first two years of college in my last two years of high school. I went to Cornell University in Upstate New York for two years, and what I discovered then—which I was able to put a name on many years later—is that I have a real problem with depression. So, during my junior year, my two best friends moved on—one of them flunked out and the other one graduated—and without that support system I couldn't continue school. So I dropped out, went to work, and worked for two years.

I met my boyfriend through the first computer dating service. It was Operation Match at MIT. I dropped out of Cornell in 1965, so that would have been '66. We used mark-sense cards, which was just a paper form where you fill in with a number 2 pencil in a circle. Then they batch process them at MIT. It was run by MIT, there weren't any women at MIT. And I got thirteen responses.

And my then boyfriend said, "Let's go to California." So I came to California and decided I was ready to go back to school. We arrived in California in 1967, the Summer of Love, and I was pretty conservative. We landed in a nonstudent household in Berkeley, and they were flying helicopters over our house, and dropping tear gas on demonstrators in the streets. And that, itself, was a tremendous education.

The thing that greatly influenced my thinking was being introduced to the work of Abraham Maslow in humanistic psychology. And Montessori. I saw a demonstration of Montessori methods in high school, so I was exposed to it early on.

When I get introduced to something that impresses me, it gestates for a while. It was a real privilege for me to be able to do that. So for me, Montessori keeps re-emerging. My children went to Montessori nursery schools, and I helped start one. Educational philosophy and practice and humanistic psychology, such as self-actualization, learner-centered practice keeps reemerging in my life.

I went to Sonoma State, which was the only place I could get in that fall, having made my decision to go back to school late. Classes had already started. It turned out that Sonoma State was very much involved with humanistic psychology, and I got to meet a lot of really wonderful practitioners in that field. I graduated from Sonoma State by '71, I think, no, earlier than that, 1970.

I've never been a full classroom teacher, I'm a 'freelance teacher.' Which means I serve as a guest teacher, or I do after-school projects. I really admire people who can show up in the classroom day after day and do that job. If I had young students, I'd have them hanging off the ceiling. But I can come in and have students for a short time. I consider everything that I do to be teaching. In conversation with someone, they're teaching me who they are, what they do and know. And I'm reciprocating. I learn a huge amount when I'm interacting with someone, even if it's an infant.

When I was in graduate school, I started LO*OP Center, which is my nonprofit. And we were taking computers into schools. We'd be a guest. I'd contact teachers and say, 'Do you want to do a unit on computers? I can bring these computers to you.' I was going to lots of different institutions, and also writing. Freelance writing is a common term, so I just applied it to teaching. I'd always been interested in teaching; my mother and our boarder at our household were both teachers, so it was a really easy direction for me to go in. And my father was a scientist and an entrepreneur, so all that background was available.

As for getting into computing, I was married, and pregnant with my first child, and living in Santa Rosa. I'd gotten my undergraduate degree from Sonoma State. I took a course in Montessori education in 1971. My husband and I were both hippies at that time. I knew that it might be difficult for my children to conform to a normal public education. I took parenting very seriously. I studied parenting techniques worldwide, as well as education. I knew I was going to have to face some

80

decisions about how to educate my own kids, and I wanted to have options. And any option that I have, I can offer to the rest of the world. For the first sessions of our Montessori course, our instructor kept saying "Wait till Dr. Brown gets here. He'll wow you. He's doing wonderful stuff." Within the first five minutes of Dr. Dean Brown speaking, I said 'That's my career. That's where I'm going, that's what I'm going to do.'

It was all about working with computers in the field. He was just inspirational. He's passed away now. I'd kind of been casting around, I wasn't particularly worried because I knew I was going to have more than one job as well as being a stay-at-home mom, so this just set a direction for me. So Dean was having the students in the Montessori school, even at five and six years old, program a mainframe computer that they contacted over the telephone using a teletype machine. They programmed their lessons so that other kids could use them as games. And that was 1971.

I've kept all of the correspondence, the literature, the magazines, the software, and some of the machines that I've used since 1971. I'm creating a virtual museum on the history of computing in education. Some of today's folks going into the field—whether it's into teaching or computing or software development or instructional design—rarely have access to this material. There's an awful lot of reinventing of the wheel going on because people don't know the history.

Bob - You always believed computers would become pervasive in our society. Did meeting Dean influence your thinking?

Liza - Certainly meeting Dean brought that to the fore, because he also believed that. But actually, my dad in the early '50s was at MIT, and he was working with the development of the very first computers. I grew up in that context. I want to give due credit to my parents for being very avant-garde in philosophy, in technological development, and in the crossing of disciplines. And I've just carried that on.

81

Bob - How do you think—either in context of computers or not—the educational system here compares to other places in the world?

Liza - Well, I want to kind of go underneath that question. I've also studied a little bit of anthropology and how human societies have passed on their culture. Didactic teaching is a relatively new phenomenon. People learn by modeling and observation. All of our culture, all of the ways we behave, are learned. I crusade against the idea of formal education as opposed to holistic learning. Starting from smiling, eating, and how to hug someone, and going on to walking and talking, and then social cues, then you can get into formal education. But half of what we learn is learned before we ever think of going to school. So, in that context, I think that formal education puts young children into sensory deprivation tanks. Formal education teaches them what they wouldn't learn and absorb spontaneously. And I think it's the wrong way to go about bringing someone up.

Computers are just one more tool. They happen to be a particularly powerful tool, on par with the invention of writing, the printing press, the invention of the telegraph, and all of the distance communication devices that have come after. So, that really opens up possibilities for how we can transmit learning content *or* lessons. And it means what we used to have to deliver physically into a classroom setting, can suddenly now be accessed anywhere in the world.

There's a project called *The Hole in The Wall*, in India. This guy had a monitor and keyboard connected to the Internet, and installed it literally in a wall where a bunch of the street kids gather, and just watched what happened. There was no teaching or instruction. The kids mostly taught themselves to use it. Of course, they taught each other English, because a lot of the language of the Internet is English. And then, they began teaching each other. That project is worth looking at. Google "Hole In the Wall" and "TED" and you'll find the lecture on it.

Well, see, now I'm freelance teaching. In my teaching, I share resources that I know about with you. I'm not going to drill you, or give you any credit for this, but I'm going to try to enable your learning and then be available so if you get to a point where you want to talk about it, you can call me. It's teaching on-demand. You, as the learner, are in control. I'll stay available as long as you're willing, able, and interested. It's a whole different process than what's done in classrooms.

So, you asked me about U.S. education versus education around the world. What I think is that the early Northern European model for schooling has been exported around the world. And there are people who thrive with that approach, and who find that's really the ideal way to learn. But I don't think that's true of the majority of people, and I think we do a tremendous disservice to all those for whom it isn't the best way to learn.

I've written an article which I call the *Trojan Horse*, that deals with computer applications in the classroom. So, that was the vision I was working with when Woz developed the Apple-1. When microcomputers came into existence, I immediately jumped on them. And that's a good segue perhaps to how I met Steve and why I have Apple-1 *number one.*

While I was sitting in that Montessori classroom, I had the idea of creating a public-access computer center. There were three others in the world before that; one at The Boston Children's Museum, one at Lawrence Hall of Sciences in Berkeley, and actually one Dean used at the Lawrence Hall of Science. It was a mainframe computer that used Calnet, which was a phone line connection to the computer that you could use with a teletype. Also, there was a little public-access center that was just started called People's Computer Company. That was Bob Albrack. Dean introduced me to Bob, who is still doing this work. I said, "Hey, we need a computer access center here in Sonoma County." Also, I'd like to be proactive and take the computers into schools. So, Dean became one of the founding board members of the LO*OP Center, which I started a couple years later.

This whole computers in education movement started largely in museums. I was one of the people who had the vision to create a virtual museum, a number of us have sought each other out. In '75, after my second child was born, I rented a storefront and started LO*OP Center. We acquired a teletype to follow the Montessori school model of having a dedicated phone line to Lawrence Hall of Science. There was also access to computers at Call Computer in Palo Alto. I was in Sonoma County, ninety miles north of San Francisco. But, the phones reach everywhere. I had no training in computing, so I *knew* I didn't know anything. I needed to learn, and I gathered a bunch of teachers around myself.

So I started the Sonoma County Computer Club. I put a little ad in the paper inviting anyone interested in computing to come. And the computer club folks taught me to run my own computers. Through them, I found out about the Homebrew Computer Club based in Stanford. So, I went to check it out with some of my club members.

The club was run by Dennis Allison, who's one of the pioneers still at Stanford. Steve Wozniak was there, actually writing the *BASIC* language for the Apple during the time that he stepped out of the formal club presentation. There was, at every Homebrew meeting, a sharing session when everyone was invited to raise their hand, and give a little speech about what they were doing. And at the end of the meeting you could go talk to the people who'd talked about their projects. I raised my hand and said, "I have this little nonprofit company called LO*OP Center. LO*OP stands for Learning Options Open Portal, and is also my last name, and I'm taking computers into schools.

So, Woz sought me out and asked me what I was doing. I said, "Why don't you come up and be the guest at one of our computer club meetings?" which he did. Both Steves came up to the Sonoma County Computer Club and demonstrated the computer. He brought an Apple-1, which he gave to us. Years later, I found out that it was literally the first Apple. Someplace, among my papers, I have the sign-in sheet with Steve Wozniak and Steve Jobs' names there.

What he gave us was a motherboard; it wasn't a whole computer. I had no idea what to do with it. So, one of our club members who was working at HP—was an HP hardware engineer—took it and built a case and a power supply for it. It came with nothing, and no way to run it. And then somebody else told me where to go to buy a keyboard. Also someone gave me a monitor. And so it was like buying any kind of component system.

At that time we used the word "computer" for the Central Processing Unit, and for the unit attached to the motherboard. The early Apples all had sockets so these little chips—which were little black rectangles that are a half inch by an inch— and the integrated circuit looked like little bugs because they had little legs. The motherboard's green and it's about eighteen inches long and ten inches wide. One of the characteristics of the early Apples was that they get warm when they're running because of the electricity running through them. The physical effect of the heating and cooling is that those little chips work out of their sockets. So, when you were running an early Apple, after a few weeks, your Apple would only work intermittently, and what you had to do was take the cover off and take your finger and touch a piece of metal so you weren't carrying static electricity, and push those little chips back into their sockets. We really had to interact with the hardware in order to keep these machines running.

Bob - How did you find out years later that it was the actual first Apple-1?

Liza - Well, one of the founders (*sic*) of Apple was a gentleman named Jef Raskin (who has passed away). Jef was a pure genius, and wrote many of the early Apple manuals and worked with the two Steves to form the company. He was an early employee and a really important contributor. So, those early folks got Apple-1's. And at one point, probably about sixteen or seventeen years ago, Jef decided to sell his Apple-1. He put it on *eBay*, and he advertised it as "The first Apple-1." Woz was interviewed by *Wired Magazine*, and was asked about Jef's Apple-1. Woz said, "It wasn't the first, because I gave the first Apple to a crazy teacher by the name of Liza Loop." And that's how I found out. People who read that article began to call me and ask, "Are you that person he's talking about?" And I would say, "Yeah." That's how I found out that it was literally the first Apple.

Bob - Do you keep in touch with Woz?

Liza - Actually, you know, we don't talk very often. But you know, we give each other a big hug when we see each other at a conference. Because of the project I'm involved in right now, I'm about to get back in touch with him. Because I want him to be a member of our organization. But for me, it's the other end of the spectrum. I was computing before the Apple was adapted to educational purposes. It was an important technological milestone and stepping-stone toward where we are now.

When I got the Apple-1, there was almost no interface. I got a piece of hardware. I had to take it back to Woz and say, "Fix this thing!" Because it wouldn't stay running for the forty-five minutes of a class. I'd go into a classroom, and the first place I took it was Windsor Junior High School. I was invited by a math teacher there to demonstrate computer programming to his class. And at that time, there was no battery backup on the computers. So if you unplugged it, it lost its memory. The contents of the memory were stored on audio tape. So you had to take your little audio tape, put it in your cassette recorder, plug that in with an RCA plug, plug that into the receptacle on the board, and fiddle with the volume with a little screw you twisted. *And* fiddle with the volume on the tape recorder until you got it just right. So what sounded like a buzz on a speaker would re-load the *BASIC* language into the Apple-1. And that took twenty minutes.

And you never knew whether it was actually loading or not. You had to wait for twenty minutes and try it, and if it didn't work you had to take another twenty minutes and load the *BASIC* again, having fiddled a little bit with the volume. So, I'd go to the school early and load the *BASIC* in the classroom so I didn't have to unplug the machine. Then I could demonstrate to the kids how to program in *BASIC* on a keyboard, using a television monitor as the screen. As long as the Apple stayed running, we might be able to type in a little program and I could demonstrate something. But, the Apple itself often didn't run longer than twenty minutes. And when it crashed, its memory crashed as well. Well, it was a forty-five minute class. So, after two or three of these embarrassing situations where I'd start the demonstration and then the machine would crash and I'd have to do the rest of it on the blackboard, I took it back to Woz and said, "You know, we're really well-aligned on what we want to have happen here, but this is not an adequate tool for what we want to do." He worked on it to try to make it more reliable, and then said, "Well, don't worry I've got something else for you." And that was the Apple][, and I have Apple][number 10, which worked a lot better.

Bob - Do you still have both the Apple-1 and the Apple][?

Liza - Yes, I do. They belong to my company. They belong to the LO*OP center, so they're really owned... Something people often don't understand about nonprofit corporations is nonprofit corporations are owned by the citizens of the state. So, I don't own the computers. The citizens of California do. I'm just the custodian. And so I keep it safe for them.

Actually, I've tried to put the Apple-1 on exhibit in a couple of museums, and because it's a one-of-a-kind computer, it's priceless, and can't be insured. Museums won't take it unless I give it to them. And I won't do that. So it's not on display anywhere.

Bob - I guess you won't be able to sell it for two hundred thousand dollars, like they did at the Christie's auction a few months ago?

Liza - Well, I could, but I'm not going to.

Bob - I couldn't believe that computer sold for over two hundred thousand dollars.

Liza - Well, I couldn't believe it sold for so *little*. It's worth a lot more than that. I mean, they're priceless. The problem with priceless things is that you can't sell them for what they're worth. But this one will go to a museum, eventually. It won't get sold. I'll donate it. And, by the way, when Woz tells the story, he says that he talked with Steve Jobs about the fact that he wanted to give us the computer as a gift. Jobs wouldn't let him. He made Woz pay three hundred dollars for it.

You should verify that story with Woz. He's a very approachable, very sweet guy. He's one of the few people who had the smarts to do what he did. And he always wanted the Apple to be a gateway to learning.

Bob - Did you have a lot of interaction with Steve Jobs, or was it mostly Steve Wozniak that you dealt with?

Liza - Actually, I did have some interaction with Steve Jobs. I don't like him very much. The LO*OP Center was open for three years. Then one of my club members got a job at Atari and called me up and said, "We need somebody who knows about users, and we need someone to write the user's manual. Come down and interview at Atari." So I worked at Atari for nine months. And Steve Jobs was around, this was 1989. I'm trying to think of where else I've interacted with him. Not a lot. It's like, Woz is my kind of person, and Jobs was *so* focused. And it was Woz who got us the computer, and Woz who was interested in education. My sense is that the other Steve was interested in education as a market, as compared with interested in education as a mission.

If I had a choice of going to dinner with one or the other, I'd accept an invitation from either of them, but I'd probably have more fun with Woz. I mean, I'd love to sit and talk with Jobs. Because, he's an interesting person. He's intense. He's enthusiastic. But he's just not as nice. And he was more interested in forming a successful company, which is why he stayed with the company and Woz didn't. That doesn't reflect negatively on Steve Jobs at all. I mean, we wouldn't have the company we have if he hadn't been the person he was.

Early on, when the Apple-1 was new, we thought of computing as the new Latin. It used to be in prestigious schools, everybody was required to learn Latin. The slogan was, "Latin teaches you to think." So, what I was saying in those days was everybody should learn at least the rudiments of programming because it's the new Latin, it teaches you to think. I still think that.

But when the Apple-1 came out, we were teaching programming on it because that was all you could do with it. What you programmed on it was often a game. We were working with young people, and that's what was interesting to them. And little word games were the easiest thing to program. Something like, "Give me the name of a food, the name of your best friend, of a place, or the name of a piece of furniture." And then the computer would print out "Suzy and Jon were sitting on a couch eating asparagus and singing your favorite song." So, what you ended up with from the printout from your teletype was this personalized story you wrote on the computer.

Bob - Kind of like *Mad Libs*.

Liza - Exactly. We had *Mad Libs* then, too. So I didn't know people were still doing *Mad Libs*. Is it a computer program now?

Chapter 14

Burn In

I spoke with Bill Fernandez, the first Apple employee hired by Jobs, in August 2012 and told him the story about my Apple-1. I mentioned that I was from the Washington D.C. area and my machine had been owned by a colorful character who was in the tech business locally. He asked the name of the fellow and I told him it was Bruce Waldack. Fernandez said that he guessed I was going to say Bruce, because coincidentally... in the '90s, he'd been hired to come out to Washington D.C. and do contract work for Waldack's company.

Bill Fernandez - It's very strange that you're calling me about a computer that was originally owned by Bruce Waldack.

Bob - How long did your work for Bruce last?

Bill - Well, I just came out for one trip. Then, later on they said he'd left the company that he'd founded, and went on vacation or something, and then it died.

****

Bob - You originally introduced Steve Wozniak and Steve Jobs?

Bill - I grew up on a small street in Sunnyvale, and across the street and one house to the left was Mr. Taylor's house. Across the street and two houses to the left was the Wozniak's house. Mr. Wozniak and my dad

90

were friends, but Steve Wozniak was about four years ahead of me. It wasn't until junior high school that I got interested in electronics. And in the second year of junior high school, Steve Jobs transferred into our school. So, I met him and we became friends. Around the same time—because I was into electronics, and Woz was too—I started doing projects with Woz. Mr. Taylor had a garage full of electronics parts, so I used to do yard-work for him, and trade-in the hours that I collected for parts for my projects. That's kind of the setup.

So one day Jobs comes over to hang out. This was probably early in high school. And I say, "I want to get some parts from Mr. Taylor," so we walk across the street, and Woz is next door out in the street washing his car. So, I thought to myself, 'Here are two electronics buddies. They probably want to meet each other.' So I said "Steve, come over, I want to introduce you to this other guy, this other Steve." And so I introduced the two Steves together out in front of Woz's house. They eventually started doing... I continued doing electronics projects, and hanging out with both of them independently, but then, over the next several years, they started doing projects with each other. Ultimately, they started Apple Computer, and they hired me as their first employee.

Bob - Why do you think you and Jobs became friends?

Bill - Well, we were both loners socially. And both kind of intellectual, philosophical, introspective. Neither of us was interested in playing social games, and yet both of us wanted to be popular and have friends. We didn't necessarily want to be the center of a crowd, but we'd like to have some friends. Junior high school is very socially rough and nasty sometimes. Very cliquish, and so forth.

So, we were both kind of outsiders, loners, intellectual. I'd transferred into seventh grade at this junior high school (junior high school is seventh and eighth grade). I transferred in seventh grade, shortly after the beginning of the school year. I missed whatever the opening gambits are that all the kids play. I didn't really know what I was

91

getting into. Then Jobs transferred in somewhere in the middle of the eighth grade school year, and so he also was out of the social scene, and knowing what's going on, and whatnot. So, put all those things together. We met each other, we had some classes together, and we found that we shared style and interests, and we started hanging out together. I think it's likely that it was me that got Jobs interested in electronics. I got into the hobby first, and I exposed him to those sorts of things, and then he started doing electronics stuff.

Jobs never passed me in terms of electronics expertise. He was entrepreneurial, which I was not.

Bob - Tell me about the Apple-1 burn-in box.

Bill - When you're manufacturing electronic devices, a common technique to make sure the device is not going to fail prematurely out in the field, is to run it under power and at elevated temperature, hoping that any components that are likely to fail will fail during his period, so you can fix them before you actually ship the product to customers. This process of running machines under power at an elevated temperature is called 'burning them in.' I built a box out of plywood, and cut slots down either wall, so it was a bunch of slots on both sides so I could slide —this first one was for the Apple-1—you could slide Apple-1's into it. You could have them stacked up. And then the box closed, so it had a lid. I had to have a way of running power to all of them. I think we just relied upon the electrical components themselves heating up the air inside the box. Then we just let it run for a couple of days. Every electronic device loses some energy in heat. So I think we used that to heat up the interior of the box once we closed it.

Bob - That's an impressive quality control test.

Bill - We were all interested in doing a good, professional job, each in our own ways. And we all had experience working at Hewlett Packard, which at that point was one of the premier manufacturers of electronic engineering equipment. So we learned what you're supposed to do. 'Oh, you're supposed to burn these things in.' 'Well, how do you do that?' 'Let's build a burn-in box.'

Bob - Who worked at HP?

Bill - All of us. Woz designed the Apple-1 while he was working at Hewlett Packard, and while I was actually working there, too. Jobs had a summer job at Hewlett Packard during high school. And Hewlett Packard was all about quality. We all knew that. We all appreciated that. It was very important to us.

I asked if he recalled Charles Ricketts.

Bill - No, I don't recognize the name Charles Ricketts. I didn't realize really that we'd sold any computers directly from Apple. I know that we had two runs. The first was sold, I think, completely to the Byte Shop, and the second must have sold directly from Apple to the public, but we didn't sell all of them. I have no idea who would have bought them.

My understanding is that the first production run was sold to the Byte Shop. Then there was a second production run, and I know that maybe a dozen of them ended up on a box in a corner in the engineering area when we were working on the Apple][. When the Apple][came out, we kind of lost interest in the Apple-1.

I described my Apple-1's box.

Bill - Is it blue?

Bob - It's blue, yeah.

Bill - Is it like two-tone, like blue and medium gray light gray?

Bob - No, it's solid blue with a Plexiglas top.

Bill - Why don't you email me a picture of it?

Bob - Okay. What's the initial thought that made you ask if it was blue?

Bill - First, Apple never shipped a box. For the Apple-1, all we shipped was the board itself. But having a box was clearly the next stage in the evolution of the user-friendly experience of the personal computer. So we were interested in boxes. We knew that in the evolution of personal computers—and actually they weren't called personal computers then, but that's another story. Rather than just shipping the board and requiring that people add a keyboard hanging off it by a wire, and a transformer hanging off it by a wire, the next stage was to ship something in a box.

So we were interested in boxes. I think we had various prototypes built. Some were made of sheet metal, bent into shape. We also found that a lot of the early Apple-1 owners would make their own boxes, and then send us photos of them. I remember early on seeing that sometimes people would take a piece of plywood and mount the board and the transformer on it. Sometimes it was a fancy board, like a piece of lacquered maple. Sometimes they'd hand-build their own little box, often times with a sloping front with the keyboard in it. Like a very low slung, deep kind of thing. I remember that someone made some really nice boxes out of eighth-inch thick Philippine mahogany. It was made out of thin wood with a nice veneer on it, and they had it sort of naturally finished, maybe lacquered. We had some people who built them into briefcases. Open it up and the keyboard would be down, and the computer would be on the lid. So there was a lot of action in that area.

So it could be that the original owner of your machine built that case himself. Or it could be that some cottage industry had sprung up, and he bought something from someone. It could be that he had it custom-fabricated, or depending upon his interaction with Jobs, he may have bought one of the early prototypes. It's hard to tell. There's something that you're describing that kind of rings a bell.

Bob - What did you mean when you said sheet metal that was bent?

Bill - That's a very common fabrication technique for something in that era. When these electronic manufacturers made things, making them out of sheet metal, it would be something that you could prototype fairly easily, manufacture very easily. You take a piece of rectangular piece of

...usually it was aluminum. Cut it to size, put it in a 'break' and bend it. A 'break' is the technical term for sheet metal-bender. And you can bend it in angles and stuff, and fold it into a box with the little flaps, and drill holes where you needed them. Usually you mount some little aluminum standoffs, which are little aluminum dowels drilled and tacked to both ends and screwed in at each end. And you screw up from the bottom. Now you have four little sticks sticking into the box. You put the board on top of it and screw it down. Now there's a space between the board and the bottom. That's a very, very common way of a quickly fabricating something. And you'd paint it to make it look nice, usually with a texture. A hammer-tone texture, or a stipple texture were very common, because if you just paint it flat you tend to show scratches and oils and things, and it looks bad. And if you paint it, it tends to look better. That was the professional way to go at that point in the development of personal computers.

I asked him more relating to Ricketts, and about why Ricketts would have paid $600., not the $666. price that is always talked about, and controversial.

Bill - It might be that Ricketts asked, 'Do you know of a way to get a case?' or something, and maybe Jobs said, 'Yeah, I can give you this,' or 'if you give me fifty bucks, I'll sell you this.' Who knows? Anything's possible.

I think that where $666. pricing came from is that the manufacturing cost was a third of that. If you factor it out, how much it cost to buy the parts, then hired someone to sort the parts into little kits, and send it to over to this company that was going to solder the parts into the board, you add up all that cost, and you end up with a third, two twenty-two. His understanding was that, okay, from the retail cost— the manufacturer's suggested retail—the typical rule is that a third of that is manufacturing cost, and two thirds of that is wholesale cost. And so you would sell machines wholesale to the Byte Shop for $444., and the Byte Shop would sell them for $666.

So, if Steve had an Apple-1 hanging around that he hadn't committed to some other customer, I could well see him saying, 'Okay, six hundred dollars direct from me to you is between wholesale and retail, and that's fine with me.' It's all very possible.

Bob - The second check is for $193.00 and is labeled "Programmed by Steve Jobs."

Bill - Well, the thing that comes to mind is that maybe he bought a cassette IO board. Don't put too much stock in the word "programmed." Nowadays, we kind of know what that means. It means that someone wrote code in a programming language to create a program. But in those days, people didn't really know. So, you could have said 'configured,' or 'set up by' or, 'software preinstalled.' Or maybe he sold Ricketts a cassette IO board, and he copied a program into a cassette tape, and he gave him a cassette tape with the board. A person new to the industry could have called that 'programming.' Jobs never did any programming in terms of coding or writing in a computer language.

I do know that Jobs had an Apple-1 framed on his office wall in the Macintosh division for years, until someone stole it. It was in a metal frame with maybe a three-inch mat around it, a medium blue textured mat. It was actually double-matted, so the outside mat was a little bit bigger than the board, and the board was mounted on the bottom mat. You had a little bit of white for the bottom mat, and then the blue, and it was in a metal frame. It wasn't an expensive framing job. On the bottom was a little plaque that said, "Our Founder." That was on his office wall in the Mac division until it was stolen.

Bob - What was it like working in the garage for an eight-hour day?

Bill - I didn't have to clock in and out, we didn't use the clock. I think I had a salary. You know, I'd show up in the morning, do all the stuff that needed to be done, leave in the afternoon and go home.

Bob - Would visitors drop by the garage to purchase computers?

Bill - People came and went for various reasons. I don't explicitly remember a case where someone came in to make a transaction, or where someone came and said, 'Can I check it out?', 'Can I test drive it?' like an automobile showroom, and having a salesman pitch his product. I don't remember any instances like that. It wasn't like the garage was acting like a showroom. That isn't to say they didn't happen. There was certainly not a stream of people buying directly out of the garage.

Bob - That was probably because the first sale was a group of fifty machines.

Bill - Yeah, well, you know I was on the periphery of a lot of things. There was interest shown in personal computing. Everyone at the Homebrew Computer Club wanted their own computer; that's why they were there. When Jobs said to Woz, "Hey, we could build and sell these," he was probably thinking of just selling individually to hobbyists and aficionados, which is essentially what they did with the Blue Boxes.

Bob - What number employee were you?

Bill - Initially, working in the garage, there were no employee numbers. There were just people. And it wasn't until later, we hired Mike Scott to be the president of the company. Shortly after that, I left to go to another company. And then Mike Scott, as part of putting the company on a more professional footing, assigned us employee numbers.

Anyway, employee numbers were assigned after I'd left the company. And, of course, I heard the same story that everybody else did. It ended up that Woz, Jobs, and Markkula were one, two, and three, (which makes perfect sense to me,) and I was assigned number four. Which also makes sense to me, because I was the first person they hired after incorporating. Mike Markkula helped them get venture capital, and incorporate. And four is my favorite number, so I thought, 'This is very cool.'

I asked about the board serial numbers and board hand-numbering.

Bill - I do not have any recollection of that. I don't know one way or the other.

Bob - Were they Byte Shop numbers?

Bill - I don't know.

Bob - Regarding Steve Jobs' dad...was he was around much of the time?

Bill - He was kind of around all the time, when he wasn't at work. It was his house.

Bob - What he was like? Supportive?

Bill - Um, he was kind of a quiet, purposeful fellow. So, you say, 'Was he a supporter?' Some people might wonder if he was a like a cheerleader? Well, no. Not at all. But, on the other hand, he converted his garage, pretty much substantially, over to Steve's little business.

Bob - And part of the house, right?

Bill - Well, there wasn't much of the house to convert. Maybe there was a little room they used to warehouse things in. So that seems to me that shows a lot of support. He had a very strong work ethic; he was a blue collar guy, he was a machinist. So it was kind of like, 'Live and do things that are sensible, don't do things that are stupid. And just put your head down and do the work.'

Bob - Where was the burn-in box?

Bill - That was in the garage, in the middle of the floor. Stick them all in there; let them run for a couple of days. At least twenty four hours. And take them out, and hook them up, and see if they still worked.

Bob - Was there a steady flow of boards to burn-in?

Bill - Well, you know, these are twenty year old memories, so there're a lot of gaps. When I reflect, what I remember is that every day was something different. Okay, so, it's not like we were running a manufacturing facility. There was always something new that needed to be done.

Bob - Did working out of the house and garage end up as a 'bursting at the seams' situation?

Bill - Yeah, kind of. But in a way, in both cases, we were busting out. In the garage, there was only room for Jobs, me, and maybe one other person. But when we needed to hire a receptionist, an accountant, a marketing person, a president, a manufacturing person, and build an engineering department to do research and product development, you just can't do that in the garage. So, we had to burst out of the garage to go to the next stage. When it was clear that we needed to expand again, because Stevens Creek could no longer contain what we envisioned, for the next step then we needed to find another place before we burst out of Stevens Creek.

Bob - There was only room for three in the garage?

Bill - Basically. The thing about it was it was a two-car garage of a very small tract home. And we got two thirds of it, but *still*. Not a big space. And we had three or four work benches. And there's no office space there. To hire an accountant, where was the accountant going to sit? I think that what's really true is that, like any organism, you grow in growth spurts. And at each spurt, you develop a new capacity. You take up more room and you eat more food, or whatever. And, like some animals that have to bust out of their shell so they can grow a new bigger shell. That would be an analogy for the need to bust out of the garage, so we could move onto something bigger. Then bust out of Stevens Creek, so we could move into something bigger. Because we were growing and expanding; it was a natural progression.

Bob - Am I right to characterize you as an interface architect?

Bill - These days we call ourselves a 'user experience architect.' We keep changing our names because we think it's cooler.

Bob - Did you first apply that with the Apple][?

Bill - No, I didn't have any user experience role per se.

Bob - That was later that you first applied those skills?

Bill - Well, that particular specialty has gone through a lot of different stages in development. It wasn't even a specialty in the early days. Back then we were basically people who wanted to make great products. We wanted to make great user experiences, we wanted to make products that people loved and that served them. We didn't make a separation between designing the user interface, and so forth. It was all kind of, 'Well, we need a case, and the case needs to be great, and it needs to be approachable,' so we'd get various industrial designers to draw up sketches of cases they think we should get. 'This looks too old-fashioned. This one looks too technical, this one looks too dumb,' you know. So, we did everything by the seat of our pants; the engineering, the testing, the manufacturing, the marketing, the industrial design, the user-interface design. It wasn't until years later that user interface design emerged as a specialty that the people designing and building the product itself couldn't really do. Early in product development, we learned that industrial design is something you needed a specialist for.

We were, all of us—Woz, Jobs, and myself—interested in making beautiful, elegant products, and we expressed that in different ways. We were all interested in making products that are great. Part of that greatness is making the user experience wonderful, although we didn't have that term for it in those days. These days, our profession is changing to an awareness of the user experience and reflects on the maturation of the industry.

It used to be that everyone was interested in making great hardware, or efficient, or fast computers. And then, in making software that ran on it. Then, they started having problems with customers. And so the term computer/human interface became very popular. And there're three variations of that: human-computer, computer- human, and user interface. Yeah, human interface was the fourth, so there were four different variations on the same theme. But they're focused on the interface where man meets machine, but now that's expanded again, to

100

say it's not just 'where are the human touches to the machine?' It's the entire experience the human has buying, using, installing, and so forth. So, we need to expand our view to do the whole job. So, that's why we use 'user experience' now. Little by little, the industry has been learning that there's actually more and more to it. Woz, Jobs, and I were all implicitly interested in doing an excellent job in this area. Early on, we knew that having a printed circuit board was a more professional way to go than hand-wiring every board we sold. And burning it in was more professional than just shipping it out and hoping it didn't fail. And advertising with color ads was more professional than typewriting something and just putting it in the back of a magazine. 'How do you do a professional job?' was an early way of conceptualizing that.

Bob - Today products are so user friendly, you're not supposed to need instructions.

Bill - That doesn't always work, even with Apple products like the iPhone and the iPad. But we've come a long way.

My family or friends will have problems with things, and I'll explain it to them and they'll slap their foreheads and say, 'Oh, my God, how can I be so stupid?' Well, it's not that you're stupid, it's just that you had no way to know. And I can't imagine what it's like for families that don't have an expert in the family.

Chapter 15

Forty-one Chips

Steve Wozniak keeps a very busy schedule. He seems to constantly be traveling worldwide, so an appointment for an interview has to be set way in advance. But Steve also has a reputation for being a very nice guy. When we spoke in October of 2011, he was at home in California. At a later date, I got to show him my Apple-1 when he visited Washington, DC.

Bob - Before you created the Apple-1, you built The Cream Soda Computer?

Steve Wozniak - That's the computer I built five years before the Apple-1. I'd been designing computers back in high school, but could never afford the parts. I worked for a year to earn money for school, between my second and third year of college. I could never afford chips. One of these tech guys said he could get me some. So I designed a computer, entirely my own design. It was a very small computer, it had a little board with about 20 or 30 chips, and 256 bites of memory, of RAM. I got some chips from a company called Intersil, so it was pretty amazing.

It worked like all the computers of the old days. Computers start with a fundamental box and the box has things like memory, switches that you toggle into ones and zeros to get data into the computer. Very slow processing. If you wanted the number 15, you would toggle the switches to 00001111 and that equals 15. Press a button and the 15 goes into a memory spot. Then you can put another number in the next memory spot, and another number, and another number. All those numbers add up to a program. You pop the switches to the right address and it runs your program. So that's pretty much the heart of what's called a processor, which is the guts of a computer. And I had built that. It was an 8-bit computer, so that means it had eight switches for data, and numbers from zero to 255 could be represented in computer language.

It had 256 bites of memory, that's all, no more. By the time I designed the Apple-1, all these little kits had come out and that's all they provided for a low cost. To get enough memory to really run a computer was very expensive, so I hit on the formula. On The Cream Soda Computer, its only input was these eight little switches you'd toggle, and the output was the lights that represented ones and zeros. So it was very, very limited. It wasn't expandable enough that you could even have something like a keyboard, or a big teletype machine to type in and have a printout come back. It was a very small machine, but it was absolutely a full computer and it worked.

I built that in 1970, but even back in 1967 and '68, I'd designed all sorts of computers on paper in high school. I wasn't designing new computers, but more or less redesigning existing computers from companies like Hewlett Packard, Varian, and Digital Equipment. I got so good at it that I could generally design a computer in two minutes. That's about how long it would take me. I used very few parts, and I just got better and better at it. I just never got paid. I never got a grade. I was just doing it for the fun of it, you know, to see how far I could go and how well I could do it. I was trying to work with very few parts, so I learned a lot of techniques to minimize the number of parts. That's what I was known for.

After I did the design for The Cream Soda Computer, I got the chips from an executive in the company where I had programmed that year. I went down the block to a friend's house and the friend would then be the one to solder or wire. I can't remember how he did it, the method of getting the pins on the chips to make it actually turn into a computer that either works or doesn't. If it doesn't, I would test equipment and figure out how to fix it and make it work. I don't remember any problems with it, it worked pretty well. It's called The Cream Soda Computer because my friend Bill Fernandez and I would ride our bikes down to the local grocery store. We would buy cream soda because we both liked it. So we'd bring it back and drink it in his garage while we were assembling the machine. And right then Bill said, "You've got to meet this other guy Steve Jobs, because he knows digital chips and the like. Like *you* do." So that's about all I can say about The Cream Soda Computer. We did show it off for a local newspaper article. At the end of the interview, I showed them how to multiply some numbers, and I put in the switches. I stepped on a wire and that shorted out the chips and they smoked and the computer burned up. So it had a short life.

Bob - That was five years before the Apple-1?

Steve - Yes. At the time that I started designing the Apple-1, there were a bunch of companies putting out kits, and doing articles in magazines like *Popular Electronics*. It was like when I built my ham radio in sixth grade, fifteen years before that. When I built my ham radio, it came as a kit, meaning you'd have to put it together, using nut drivers, wrenches, and screwdrivers. You'd solder wires and transistors to all the parts you'd put in tubes. I'd built my own ham radios back then the same way: a kit of parts and a little booklet that tells you how to put them together. What was coming out had about the same capabilities as The Cream Soda Computer I'd built five years prior. I was advanced; way ahead in the game. You never go backwards.

I was ready for a real step forward, because I wanted a computer where you didn't have to use switches to input the little ones and zeros. I wanted a computer I could use to put in a program, and maybe figure out my checkbook, or play a game, or solve a puzzle in the newspaper, or a chess problem. My interests weren't really met by any of those kits. Those kits weren't really computers. They called themselves computers but they were really just a glorified microprocessor chip based around Intel's data sheets. The people who put out these kits just copied Intel's data sheets. They didn't design anything, they weren't engineers. They didn't use inexpensive parts because those, particularly memory, were very hard to design. You had to be an engineer. They took a very simple approach, and used the cruder, smaller, more expensive parts for memory called Static RAMs. What I used was Dynamic RAMs.

I had to design a lot of circuits, because a Dynamic RAM forgets all its data within two thousandths of a second. So every two thousandths of a second, you have to have some little circuits that punch their way into the memory, grab more of it, and write it back to keep it fresh. The kits all just missed the boat, totally, and I designed it right. They were putting out these early microprocessor computer kits that they said were cheap enough to afford in the home. Well, a technical person who knew computers could construct them. But to make them into a computer that could really run a game, you'd have to add the equivalent of thousands of dollars' worth of memory, and you had to add thousands more like the cost of a car—for a teletype machine you could punch buttons on.

They had big front panels, with all the switches, like my Cream Soda Computer. That was the old days; every computer had always been made that way. A bunch of switches on the front, toggle-in ones and zeroes, press buttons, and they'd go into memory. Every computer had a front panel, until my Apple-1. I totally had to get rid of the front panel. I figured, with the chips available and their prices, it would be a lot better approach to just type on a normal keyboard, and to see the input on a television set. Everybody owned a television set.

The best work I did was always because I had no money, and also because I was so brilliant at designing. I had no prior experience in any of the stuff I ever did for Apple. I had never done anything like it before. When you do it the first time, you have to sit down and say, 'How can I do this?' You have to write the book yourself. You have to develop the science rather than rely on something people have been doing for years or decades. If they have books on a subject and other people have been doing it, you just learn those methods and you've got it easy. I didn't have it easy. I had to sit down and say, 'How do you build a certain kind of device?' I always came up with how to build it with the absolute fewest parts and lowest cost. And that was what was needed.

I put my own little computer—a microprocessor and some memory on the board with my terminal—and now I could talk to my own computer, and my own computer could talk to my TV. That was the Apple-1.

Bob - Do you feel you got appropriate credit?

Steve - I do, I absolutely do. Having actually done the brainwork, the engineering, the design. All I wanted was to be known as a great computer engineer. A great computer designer. I was just an engineer. People will sometimes come up to me and say they studied the circuits or programs I've written, and they just couldn't believe how intricate and tricky they were. So short, direct, and economical. And that's just what I wanted in life. I didn't want to necessarily start a personal computer revolution. I did want to be a part of a revolution, because I'm kind of anti-authority anyway. I wanted things to be different, so I didn't have to compete in the same thing a hundred thousand other people are doing. I always wanted to think of something new, some other approach.

I didn't really want to be known for starting companies. Steve Jobs, though he was my best friend in this, wanted to be the most important person in the world, no question. He kept finding ways to sell things. The Apple][was the sixth time he found a way to sell something I'd designed. One after another, I'd design things, and he'd find a way to sell them. I didn't ever design anything to make money, never once. I only designed things for myself, and then Steve would say, '*Whoa*, this is good. I can sell it somewhere.'

Bob - Were you happy to sell products once Steve found a market?

Steve - Oh, I was happy for the money. We always split the money. It was really fun to have a friend to do stuff like that with. The first thing we ever did was an illegal device for making free phone calls. I didn't even use them to save money on phone calls, but having a device that could do it was so amazing. Who could believe it ever existed? So, I was proud of it, and not only that, I liked getting a little bit of money to buy myself Hewlett Packard calculators. So no, I never minded a little extra income. At HP, I did a lot of projects before building my own machines. When Steve found a way to sell something, it was nice to get a little bit of extra money. And then he made money by starting a company, and then marketing the Apple-1 and the Apple][. I'd have just dwindled and given away my designs, and told people what I had done. It probably would have never gone on to affect the world.

Bob - When building the Apple-1, did you ever envision Apple Computer and personal computers in general would go the direction they did?

Steve - I was at our club from the day it started, and Steve came back from Oregon. I'd already built the computer, and was giving the design away for free, at the club. He said, "Why don't we sell this?" I believed that everybody in life had a use for a computer, and it was my thing that I loved. I really believed that almost everyone in society would own a computer someday, but that they'd become technical, that they'd learn how to write programs and solve problems themselves. Since I found the time to be able to solve programs and create games, I felt everyone else would. And that was way off the mark. Not many people are going to become technical enough to write their own programs, even though they could enjoy it. Only a tiny percentage of society can do that.

I didn't see—even if you do have a product that you can start selling—what big business really means. How it totally brings life-changes for everyone. Steve and I never talked about a computer storing music. So we didn't foresee today's computer world. We foresaw computers everywhere, but doing different things, doing the limited things that they could do when we started.

The Apple-1 couldn't have gone very far, because the program was stored on a cassette tape. It would take a full minute to read. And then after a minute, you got a program that might run and play a game. It was very slow and awkward. It wasn't today's nice computer experience. But again, everything in computers increases. You just know you're going to have a better one the next year. You know you're going to have more memory. It's going to run a little bit faster and smoother. Quality is going to go up and speed will go up. That's just how it happens. That's happened all our lives with computers.

We were at a good starting point, and *boy*, we could sell as many machines as we could make. Especially when the first useful program came out, the first spreadsheet, *VisiCalc*. Instantly computers had so much value. By typing in numbers for income and month-by-month expenses, people could see the changes instantly. Something that would take them forever to do by pencil and paper. So, it was hugely successful right from the start. Almost nobody left Apple, because everyone who worked for the company thought we were the leaders of this revolution. Our product was so much better than the other attempts at early personal computers.

Bob - You gave Vince Briel and others permission to replicate the Apple-1, and even supplied designs. What are your thoughts on replicas?

Steve - I never had to give permission for him to use the Apple-1. It was already in the public domain. Back in the Homebrew Computer Club, when I designed it in 1975, I passed out my schematics. I said, "Here, you can have it. Build your own. It's yours." No copyright notices, no business, no charges, no money. So it already never belonged to Apple. I was very happy to see the replicas, because with technical, hobbyist stuff, there are people that like to go back to the early days, the foundations when you could actually build something. One person could build a machine themselves, and totally understand it and operate it. And, yeah, I've ran into a lot of people with their Apple-1 replicas. Recently, I ran into a little kid, the son of an Apple employee. I showed up by surprise at the building one day, and I talked to the kid and he showed me what he could do with his little Apple-1 replica, and it was pretty cool. He had to memorize a few special numbers and stuff, he had to be a real geek to use it, but he did.

Bob - Most Apple-1 boards were soldered by a company in Southern California, but were the first boards hand-soldered by you?

Steve - Basically, I only built one—hand-soldered the one for myself—the prototype. I might have built two Apple-1's. I went over to a high school friend's house and I actually hand-soldered one together for him. I did every single wire on it because not that many people soldered. Then, what happened was Steve and I started this company after Hewlett Packard turned it down. Because I wasn't going to cheat on HP. We paid a friend a couple hundred dollars to lay out a PC board for the Apple-1. He laid out little pieces of colored tape on a big drafting table, where all the little traces of lines on a PC board go. Then we could put chips in and make it easy. We sold it based on that PC board, with the chips in them and all the parts.

I remember one time I was driving in Orange County and I saw a computer store. At first, there were only a couple of computer stores anywhere. Then ten, then twenty, then thirty, and so on. But when I passed by this computer store, I went in to see what it was. I brought in my Apple-1 from the car. I hooked it up to a TV that I carried in the car, and I showed them how it worked. He decided he wanted to buy them for his store. But, by then we were selling Apple-1's in some local stores. Steve Jobs was handling all the sales, securing the parts, and getting the computers actually built. He was handling all that, the accounting and all, and we were then selling to stores all over the country. They would call up, and we'd say, 'Yeah, we'll ship you a couple. Here's the price.'

So, we started getting a little bit of a name in the hobby and electronics world. People knew of all these computers that came out, but Apple was the one that was different from all of the others. We had a complete computer, at a lower cost, that could do a real job. It was more 'bang for the buck.' A lot of the things about it made it a really incredible design. When we got up to the Apple][, all these hobby computer-makers dropped out. Like I said, they were using the wrong kind of memory, they didn't really have engineers designing them.

So, with the Apple II, we had competition from Commodore and Radio Shack. Commodore was funny, because we had shown them the Apple][, and tried to talk them into buying it from us, but they said 'nope.' They knew how to do it cheaper. They said, "Nobody needs color, nobody needs graphics, nobody needs game panels, nobody needs high-resolution." Nobody needs all these things we had; a lot of memory capability, a lot of expandability, and so on. And it really hurt them in the end. That's why they lost out.

So, early on, there were only three personal computers you could program, say, a game, and it would run. Or you could load it in from a cassette tape. Before that, there had been no such thing. But, if you bought the Apple][, right out of the box, turn it on, *beep*, it's already running *BASIC*. Then you can hook up a cassette tape recorder and have a program running. Maybe it's keeping track of your checkbook, or maybe it's teaching you math. Maybe it's playing a game where you shoot down some airplanes flying overhead.

I actually designed the Apple][from the ground up, and I started with an idea that I'd gotten when I was very sleepy. It popped into my head that there may be a way that one color chip could generate 16 bits of colors on a TV. Back then, color generators would cost a thousand bucks. They'd be full of complicated circuits involved in testing. I had a very clever idea. I designed the Apple][as a color generator at the core. Then, above that, I had the circuits you needed to make the computer memory operate. It started out as a color generator at the core, and it ended up using half as many chips as an Apple-1. It was an incredible design at the time. Half as many chips, ten times the computer; nothing else would be like it. Nobody ever expected color in a low-cost computer. That was why our first logo was the six-color logo. We brought color to the world.

And it had graphics for games, and it had high-resolution for things like photos. A lot of stuff in it was just totally... nobody would have ever dreamed of it before, so we knew it was a big winner. It took me three months to design the Apple][and have it working. I didn't even know if it would work when I started, but it worked, and it only took three months.

By then, we'd just barely started selling the Apple-1, and we had to keep the Apple][quiet until we found a way to finance it. Because that was going to be a big seller. We'd need money. Steve and I were in our early twenties, we had no business experience, we hadn't taken business classes in college, and we had no money of our own. There were no friends or relatives that could loan us money. We had to do everything, with no money. With the Apple-1, we got the parts that we couldn't afford on thirty days credit. Then we built the computers up real quick, and drove them down to the computer store and got paid in cash. So then we could pay off the loan on the parts, that's how we did it. The Apple][, though, we were going to sell a thousand of them and we had to raise money for that.

111

After I got the Apple-1 done, and we started selling them, it took just a couple months before I finished the programming language I was writing, called *BASIC*. Bill Gates had written a *BASIC* programming language for any computers built on the Intel chips, and he was kind of famous in our hobby circles. I thought, '*Wow*, I'd be famous if I wrote a *BASIC* for my microprocessor,' my device. I knew I just had to write it. I'd never programmed in *BASIC*, I'd never learned programming languages. It was basically one of those things where I sat down and worked out the scheme in my head. So we delivered our version a little bit later in the game. Somebody could load in this software off a tape player, and now they could write their own languages in *BASIC*, or they could run other people's programs written in *BASIC*. It wasn't like today's computers, though. It was only stuff where you could type words on a screen kind of slowly. That was the Apple-1. And, also another thing, after the buyer bought the computer, he could purchase what was called a 'cassette-tape interface,' a tiny board that plugged into the computer, that let you read-in programs from your cassette tape player. It was a second tiny board.

Bob - Liza Loop felt you were interested in education as a *mission*, whereas Steve Jobs was interested in it as a market.

Steve - When I was very young, my father explained to me the importance of education in our lives. I just sort of decided that teachers were the most important people in the world. And I told him—when I was very, very young—that I wanted to be an engineer like him, and that my second goal was to be a fifth grade teacher. I was probably in the fifth or sixth grade at the time. So, from then on I always cared about people in school, education, and teaching them things that would help develop their lives. And when I took classes in college, like psychology, I always paid special attention whenever we discussed the development of a child's mind.

I became aware that, *whoa*, there are stages of development. You learn one sort of thing before you learn another; cognitive developmental stages, if you will. And you can't reach one stage unless you master the one before it. So, the sequential step-by-step structure of programs and computers is a lot like a child's mind developing. This was always intriguing to me. I always had the goal in mind to teach fifth grade someday, if I could.

I never ever lost that goal. When we first came out with the computers, one of the things that inspired me to want to design one was that some of the people in our club were talking about how education was going to be revamped. There was going to be a revolution. Now students could get information from a book, type in some answers and get corrected instantly. 'You're right,' or 'you're wrong,' and then if they miss the question it would be re-taught a little bit differently. Basically, they'd wind up with a much greater education, and greater minds than we've ever had.

Well, that was very inspiring, because I wanted to be a part of a revolution. It was one of the things that caused me to take my talent to build a computer, and then give it to other people. 'Here, look how easy it is, how inexpensive it is. You can build one of your own.' I gave it away.

When we started Apple and I met Liza Loop, she was at our club (Homebrew) and talked about how she took computers and taught fourth through sixth graders. I talked with her and thought that was so admirable in an age when you never saw a computer in a classroom. I hadn't even had one in high school. During my first year of college—which was just a few years before then—Introduction to Computers was a graduate course. She somehow took a computer into the classroom and taught kids what programs were about, along with the fact that people develop the computers. The computers don't make mistakes on their own, it's the fact that someone who wrote the program made a mistake.

I was pretty intrigued by this, so I asked if I could come see her and I brought Steve Jobs along. We drove two hours up there and visited her at her center in Sonoma County. She told us all these stories. She told how she had this computer that was on a big rolly, like you roll a suitcase, and she'd roll it into a classroom and hook it up with a teletype machine. Then she'd let the kids play a computer game on it. I just thought that was so admirable.

When we started producing our computers, I'd go down to local schools and show them off. I'd usually bring one or two younger friends, like high school friends from Apple. We'd go into local schools in Cupertino or Sunnyvale, and we'd show them what it was all about. They weren't ready to be customers yet, but, you know, it was always close to my heart.

Bob - Dan Sokol helped you teach computer classes in the 1990s. Did you choose fifth grade because you always wanted to be a fifth grade teacher?

Steve - That came much later, after Apple had made a huge hit. We shipped our early Apple][s, the computer that was really going to turn over the world, the first computer to sell a million units, with just some tapes (and later, floppy disks) of a few programs we'd written ourselves. One helped people handle a checkbook. One was called Color Math, which used flashcards to teach arithmetic. Basically, we wanted to assert that computers could be used for academic purposes. So, I had kids of my own by that point, and I thought, 'I'm going to donate computer labs to the schools.' Computer labs were like the up and coming thing.

I figured I'll go to my hometown, Los Gatos, and I'll donate computer labs. I'd donate them to other cities, too, if I had a request. Pretty much any request, I fulfilled it. I started donating computer labs to local schools, and then I thought, 'You know, I had this dream to be a teacher.' Donating computers is fine if you have more money than you need. It's not that big a sacrifice. What you should really sacrifice, if it's meaningful to you, is your own time. And that's when I said, "Well, what I'll do is start a class, a voluntary class in how to use computers to

114

enhance and present all your school work." In other words, not to just teach somebody to be a computer geek, but how to use it as a tool for life.

I wasn't going to leave anybody out. I started teaching one kid, at first, as a try out. Then, my first class was six students. We had desktop computers. When Apple came out with laptops, we got laptops. Then some of the other kids at that school were kind of jealous, so by the summer I took twenty-two of the kids into my class. Every student in my class got a computer to keep. I could teach more and more effectively, and I really enjoyed it. I didn't know if I was going to be a good teacher. I always made the classes very fun, and I provided all the equipment out of my own pocketbook, so I couldn't really fail.

My first year, I just taught fifth graders. Then the second year I'd take fifth graders, and a class for advanced students. The advanced students' class, over time, usually became sixth-to-ninth grade. Then I started classes where I'd teach teachers in the school district, because that was very important. I wish I'd done more of it, because the students will always go down to a level that the teacher knows they can do. I want them to keep doing good work as far as using the right font colors, sizes, and spacing. Don't make things too childish in your homework. I did this for eight years, pretty much secretively, with no press. Apple wanted me to print out courses and books and CDs for a million people, but no, I wanted to do this like a normal teacher where you personally touch twenty students in your class.

Bob - You never ended up doing the books and programs?

Steve - No I didn't. You know, different things in life had meaning to me. I'd rather help one other person, even if it's just helping them tie a shoelace. It's more important to me than design a computer for a company. In the end, it's how you make people feel about other people around them, how much happiness you bring in their lives through personal contact, than it is through products you give them.

In my class, I hired young people that were interested in computers and technology, like eighteen or twenty years old, that didn't have a job, or had a job selling computer stuff. I brought three of those young people over time into my class, with full-time jobs as assistants. They wouldn't really do much of the teaching, but kids would have questions as I taught. The kids had a lot of questions while they're working on projects, so my assistants would roam around the room and help them get answered. And when I could, I'd stand up in the front with a projector. Rarely did I have anyone else actually do the teaching, because I had so many techie friends who'd want to favor the geek who wants to learn to do stuff you're not supposed to do. I wanted them to learn to be normal people with the computer, so my entire class got equal attention.

Bob - What's the significance of the Apple-1?

Steve - The Apple-1 was only about 41 chips, including memory. People would look over my shouldero at the club and see it. As soon as you saw it, you knew that it was a complete computer that could do useful things, and was totally affordable. Every computer before the Apple-1 followed the old formula, the old paradigm, where you had a front panel with those switches and lights. Every computer *after* the Apple-1 was going to have a keyboard and a video display. Basically, it pointed out the whole future of personal computers. This was the way to make them. The Apple][was really the big successful one that turned the world over, because basically you can add so many incredible features that nobody ever expected, and it was completely built out of the box. The Apple-1 was only partly built out of the box, but the Apple-1 gave the formula away.

Chapter 16

Footnote in History

All sorts of speculation having to do with the 'road not taken' get attached to Ronald Wayne, Apple's third partner as of its founding in 1976. He and Steve Jobs had met while working at Atari. Wayne had prior start-up experience. Wayne was intended to provide maturity and business experience for the fledgling Apple operation, and actually helped broker Wozniak's participation. But Wayne had come to equate risk with financial loss. Within twelve days, he sold his share of the company to assume a more peripheral role; writing the Apple-1 user's manual and illustrating its cover, among other contributions. That cover, Apple's first logo per se, was an ornate line-drawing of Isaac Newton in an apple orchard. The choice of subject matter was fitting, more or less, but its visual style was clearly already dated for such a forward-thinking company. As I've gotten to know Ron since first speaking in December 2010 and having spent time with him, I find he was probably a greater influence than most people think.

Bob - Did you leave before they started making the Apple-1?

Ron Wayne - I backed out of the situation twelve days after I drew up the contract. So I was never really involved in the workings of the whole Apple enterprise. I've been the 'unknown founder' for decades.

I've had many vocations in my life, failing at each. I'll put it to you this way. I've never been rich, but I've never been hungry either. And I've done a lot of fun stuff, and pursued many interesting things in my lifetime.

I'm absolutely convinced that I'll go down as a footnote in history, literally because I happened to have known someone. Steve Jobs' name will ring through the corridors of time. He's had a very phenomenal, very productive, and very dominant life of activity in the computer world.

Bob - We read so much about Steve Jobs' personality, what was he like back then? Does it reflect what you hear about him today?

Ron - Well, I think today's general understanding of him was pretty accurate. He was very dynamic, very focused, and very aggressive. When he had an idea, he did everything he possibly could to realize his ambition.

That's the kind of dynamic personality that it takes to do the kind of things that Steve Jobs has done over the years. Sometimes people regard that kind of personality as not very nice. But it's what it takes to get things done, to accomplish things in the face of all sorts of obstacles.

He and I worked together at Atari. He was a consulting agent for them. He was responsible for games like *Breakout*, and I was the chief draftsman and development engineer there.

Bob - After you quit the initial Apple partnership, you worked on box designs for the Apple-1 or Apple][?

Ron - I was asked by Steve Jobs to do an enclosure design. I think it was for the Apple][, because the dating I have on the thing is January of '77. So anyway, I did a design. I did a design based upon the assumption that these kids had nothing, and therefore you wanted a design that wasn't going to cost a lot of money for tooling, something that could be fabricated at reasonable cost. So I did this rather innovative design for the thing.

118

And I did the documentation, I think Jobs paid me fifteen hundred dollars for the effort. But the cabinet was never built. And then later on, out comes the first Mac. I think it was the first Mac, or one of the later Apple versions, in this foam-molded cabinet from a tool that must have cost fifty grand. I didn't know at the time that Steve had asked me to do this design, that apparently he had gotten together with Mr. Arthur Rock, who was a venture capitalist. Rock actually raised twenty-five million dollars for the formation of the Apple Corporation. So anyway, my design never got built.

But at the same time, there's an interesting twist. Modern computers are composed of a tower, and separate to that is a keyboard, and separate to that is a monitor, and they're all linked together with wires. But all of the Apple designs use an integrated design, wherein the enclosure for the circuit board is mounted not vertically, but horizontally. It has an integral keyboard, and is designed to have the monitor right on top of the enclosure. That's exactly the approach that I had taken in my design. And so I amuse myself, or possibly even deceive myself, into thinking that that fundamental approach was what Apple had used in the building of their first well-financed product.

Bob - Maybe they were going back and using the design you originated.

Ron - Precisely. Because they followed that integrated approach throughout all the products that they made. And, of course, that integrated concept was not used by anybody else.

Bob - Everybody else went the other route.

Ron - That's correct. The only thing that went into my design that has never been used... Are you familiar with something called a tambour door? Are you familiar with a roll-top desk? Okay, well that roll-top is called a tambour door. And I had designed into the thing a tambour door that would slide up over the keyboard. You close the thing and the computer is off, and you open it and it turns the computer on. It keeps the dust and crap out of the keyboard.

119

No one has ever used my tambour door approach. Of course, good ideas take a while; thirty-five years isn't enough time. It'll come to pass.

Bob - So you have the original drawings?

Ron - Not exactly. The original drawings, the vellums, went to Steve. That's what I was paid for. But I do have blue-line prints that were taken at that time. They've aged, shall we say. They're browning at the edges.

Bob - And certainly those are the only copies that would exist today.

Ron - As far as I know that is the case. So, I have the set of prints and the Xeroxes, and I also have the galley proofs, which are actually Xeroxes of the Apple-1 manual. I'm putting that together in a package and I'm going to offer the whole thing at auction.

It seems that I made a very foolish mistake many years ago, roughly twenty years ago. I ran across an ad that somebody was running, a guy who deals in famous autographs. And I'm thinking to myself, look... I've got this old contract sitting in a filing cabinet collecting dust. Maybe I can turn this into some money, which at the time I could use. So I got in touch with the guy, and we negotiated, and that contract was sold to him for five hundred dollars. And you know what happened to that contract?

Bob - It sold at auction for one $1,500,000.

Ron - *Now* you got it. I've always been a day late and a dollar short.

About two months after Steve Jobs passed away, the documents went on the auction block. Sotheby's expected the final price to range from one hundred thousand dollars to one hundred fifty thousand dollars. "The 1976 document, which once belonged to Ronald G. Wayne, one of Apple's founders along with Steven P. Jobs and Stephen G. Wozniak, is the first chapter in the story of one of America's most important companies," Sotheby's said in a press release. The auction lot included one of the three original partnership agreement copies, signed by Jobs, Wozniak and Ron Wayne on April 1st, 1976. Also included was a

*dissolution of contract, in which Wayne resigned from the partnership
in exchange for eight hundred dollars.*

*The final selling price at auction was considerably higher than the
estimate, at a final price of $1.59 million. The purchaser was said to be
Eduardo Cisneros, CEO of Cisneros Corporation. Cisneros tweeted after
the auction, "Very happy to own a piece of American (World) history."*

Ron - Well, out of all this came one thought. When Jobs and Woz and I
got together, after our evening's conversation where I resolved the
modest dispute that existed between them, Steve said, "Lets form a
company." So, I sat down at the typewriter, and I typed out the three
contracts. So, with my own hands, I made something that was actually
worth a million dollars.

To quote the Bard, "Who can look at the seeds of time and tell
you which will grow and which will not?"

But then my actual involvement drifted away fairly rapidly. I
took my name off the contract twelve days after I signed it. I did some
work for Steve and the Steves, and I did the logo and so on, and then
essentially they went off and did their thing, and I went off and did mine.

Bob - So, were you a man of many talents? I mean that Apple-1 manual
cover artwork is fantastic.

Ron - Well, I am an illustrator. I'm a draftsman who could probably lay
lead three times faster than anybody else, which is why I didn't even get
into *AutoCAD* until 2002. I'm a machinist, a circuit designer, I taught
myself electronics. I taught myself engineering and finished up my career
as chief engineer at an electronics company for sixteen years, in Salinas,
California. So I could legitimately call myself a Renaissance Man.

Bob - The vast majority of people who call themselves qualified
draftsmen-engineers could never draw something like that.

Ron - Well, I've tampered in many fields.

Bob - It was quite a piece of art.

Ron - It was fun. It was a fun thing to do. To be absolutely candid, I knew at the time I was doing it that this was not a practical logo for the twentieth century, it's a nineteenth century logo.

Bob - So you knew it would be temporary?

Ron - Oh, of course, it had to be. There are no logos like that in today's world. But, I'll tell you this. Steve was sufficiently impressed with my design that he had a huge print-out made of the thing which was suspended as a banner over one of his computer convention booths. And of course, it was used on the cover of the Apple-1 manual.

Bob - Steve Wozniak seems like such a nice guy.

Ron - Oh, he is the most gracious man I've ever met in my life. Absolutely wonderful. He wrote the forward, to my book, *The Adventures of an Apple Founder.*

Bob - People we've interviewed have told me things like that he was the fastest typist that they'd ever seen, that he would write programming language out of his head, and even that he was a terrific athlete. Talk about a Renaissance Man, I think people think of him as having kind of a singular success. Did he seem that way to you at that time, that he was kind of multi-talented?

Ron - Uh, to be candid, no. I actually had very little time spent with Steve Wozniak. I've met him, of course, several times since over the years. One thing that occurred for instance, I told you about this experience at the Macworld convention. And while I'm at the convention, in this crowd of people—here comes a guy charging through the crowd at me—and he's greeting me like a lost brother. And it was Steve Wozniak. We spent the next two hours in fascinating, trivial conversation. It was wonderful. And to have taken that approach, I thought, was extremely gracious of him. Very easygoing, very pleasant guy. I had no idea of his talents, other than the fact that he was a magnificent circuit designer. Of course, he was extremely whimsical, which added to the aura of his character. And I saw a good deal of that in the limited time I spent with him.

Boy, did he have a sense of humor, and was he ever a prankster. I got it from somebody who was there at the time he was in Vegas with his family, and going up to the room, the bellboy is taking up his luggage. When he's all done, he reaches into his pocket and he pulls out a strip of uncut two dollar bills, you know? Tears one off and gives it to the bellboy. And then, of course, about an hour later, so I heard the story, there's a knock on his door and these straw hat types, you know, from the Treasury Department, wanting to know about the two dollar bills. That's the sort of character he was.

I had much more involvement with Jobs, and I was one of the few people that ever said no to him.

Bob - It sounds like he really respected you, partially because you're older than him and your experience in business. You were probably a role model to him.

Ron - Well, I was in my forties, and these kids were in their twenties. And one of the main reasons I think I backed away in the beginning— these kids were whirlwinds. It was like having a tiger by the tail. I figured, if I stayed with Apple, I was going to wind up the richest man in the cemetery. So I figured, I've got my own spark of divine genius and I'll go off and do my own thing. My passion. I recognized the significance of the product they were putting together; it was the right product at the right time. But my passion was slot machines, believe it or not. In the early '70s, I got a dozen or so patents under my belt, and I had some pretty spectacular ideas, none of which ever came to fruition.

Bob - What was it that made that your passion?

Ron - Okay, I give up. What motivates us? What drives us?

Bob - I guess the underlying question is whether you were a gambler? Were you a fan of gambling? Or was it the mechanical engineering aspect of it that interested you, and you might not have had an interest in the gambling part of it?

Ron - There were various aspects of it. When I became interested, the machines were all mechanical. And I had taught myself electronics. I wanted to get on the other side of the table, I saw this as a potential for making a great deal of money. I wanted to become a part of the historical aspects. I wanted to be a participant in this fascinating industry.

Bob - An inventor.

Ron - Right. And I knew the history of the slot machine, going back to 1895 and Charlie Fey. And I've even actually seen one of the Liberty Bell Slot Machines, one of the first machines he ever built. So there was the historical aspect of it, the psychological aspect of it. In fact, what I have done over the last half dozen years, is I designed a modern machine, which is built to look, and feel and behave like the old mechanical machines. Coins in, coins out, okay? Because the whole industry's been taken over by paper in and paper out. And that has really tarnished the aura entirely.

People like myself remember the character of the old casinos with the old mechanical slot machines. And there is no feeling in the world equal to when you hit that jackpot, and you get this *crash!* of coin that drops into this pot. Alright? That's something that's totally missing in today's world.

Now, there was a legitimate reason for getting away from that world. For instance, when a machine dropped a jackpot, all you could do was stand there and wait until they came out and refilled the jackpot box. Well, that was bad both for the player and for the house, because the machine's not getting played. Okay? So they had a legitimate reason for it.

Well, my machine—if I could ever find the financing to build and market it, I've got a marketing outlet for it. If I could find the financing to build it—has a quick-drop jackpot. It pays out coin at the feed rate of a

124

light machine gun, but without the force. And the jackpot box, once it drops, there's a hopper inside that automatically refills the jackpot box. And as far as the player is concerned, the machine might just as well be an old mechanical machine. Because all the innards, the logic of the machine, is electronic.

But the reels, the percentaging is still done on the reels, and the reels spin and stop at random, and the game is played that way. Now, this is not a design for a machine that would fill a casino. In a major casino, they would slice off a corner of the casino and style it in the 1920s or '30s, and put in a bank of forty or fifty of these things with a little coin cage. And people like myself, who look back with nostalgia at that era, will have an opportunity to live that environment again. Or even younger people, who've seen that kind of casino in the old movies, would like to play in an environment like that, which simply doesn't exist now. Anyway, that's one of the things I'm hoping that I will have an opportunity to do before, you know, the last bell sounds.

Bob - You were telling me your interest was always in slot machines, and you said when I asked about Woz and Jobs, your heart wasn't in it. At the same time, when you talk about them being a whirlwind, and when you're around a whirlwind, success can come, but trouble can come along just as easily.

Ron - Well, there was that risk. And I had had my own unfortunate experience years before. I'd formed my own corporation, and gone into business for myself before I realized that I had no business being in business, because I was a much better engineer than I was a business man. There was also the reality, the distinction of the fact that both Steve and Woz were in their twenties, and I was forty; an old man. I really did know, at the time, I was standing in the shadow of giants. Um, but that had an adverse effect, because I knew that I was never going to have a chance—I was a product development guy myself—and I knew that I would never have a chance to have a project of my own. And these guys were certainly not going to get into the slot machine business.

He offered me jobs at Apple at least two or three times, and I declined each time. I was a little more diverse than that; I wanted my fingers in everything.

I knew Apple was going to be a very successful enterprise. But I also felt that it was going to be one hell of a roller coaster. And I felt I was getting too old for that kind of thing.

Bob - So, there was not only potential reward, but risk, too.

Ron - Oh, there was enormous risk. As a matter of fact, I'd just climbed out of a business disaster of my own, only a year or so before, and I wasn't anxious to pursue that kind of adventure.

Bob - Going back to when you first met Steve, I guess you first met him at Atari.

Ron - Oh, yeah. We chummed around quite a lot. We went to lunch and dinner and talked about literally everything. There were no subjects that were off the table.

Bob - Was he kind of special from the beginning when you met him?

Ron - Very unusual individual, very focused, very intense. And he was looking around early on at a direction. He wanted to do something. He knew early on that I'd been in the slot machine business. And, of course, he knew my own personal failure, which had occurred a few years before. And he walks into my office one day and says, "Hey, I can get my paws on fifty grand. Suppose we go into the slot machine business." And my response to him was, "That would probably be the quickest way I could think of to lose fifty thousand dollars. You don't want to do that."

Bob - I know what you mean, though. You knew that he was looking for his best opportunity. He was going to be doing something. He wasn't going to be there two years from now doing the same thing.

Ron - And he was an absolutely perfect foil for Steve Wozniak. Wozniak did things just for the fun of doing it. He'd built that computer, "Just look

126

what I did, this was just great! Boy, this was fun! I've got to do some more of this!" Jobs, of course saw it as a product, and a potential for making huge amounts of money. And the two together, they were a perfect match. The third element in the equation, the thing that I regard as key to the success of Apple was when Jobs got tied up with Arthur Rock. I don't know how that occurred, but Arthur Rock was a very, very unusual venture capitalist. In that he recognized the importance of having the creators of the product in control of the product. And he made sure that Jobs and Wozniak had fifty-one percent of any agreement that came out. And that was very, very rare. Every involvement that I'd had in years before with somebody coming up with the money to do something, they wanted absolute control. That was critical, I believe, to the success. It showed up later on, when Jobs got overridden by a board of directors, and he left. Of course, once he left, the company went into the hole and it didn't revive again until he came back.

In May 2013, I traveled to Pahrump, Nevada to meet with Ron. He suggested that we meet in the coffee shop of what must be the little town's biggest casino, The Nugget. In the coffee shop, which is basically your traditional coffee shop...like in Seinfeld. *Ahead of time, I told Ron what I would be wearing, so he might pick me out from a crowd. And then he told me he would be in his standard 'uniform', a black suit. It was a Saturday morning meet-up in a coffee shop, and sure enough...black suit, white shirt, and a conservative tie. Ron is a sweetheart of a guy, seventy-nine years old, and I suspect that he would not be comfortable in anything other than that suit.*

By the way, Ron has been involved in so many pursuits in his life. Apple, slot machines, electronics, currency, rare coins and stamps, graphics and drafting, I think the list goes on and on. But he has an interesting

127

twist on the old hobby of stamp collecting. Seems that stamps that are not old enough or interesting enough to be collectible, often trade for less then their face value. Presumably some collectors die off and their widows end up with lots of stamps that are not in demand by collectors. So Ron amasses them and sells them in bulk to small businesses, to use on their outgoing mail! He makes a margin, and they are still getting their stamps for a good discount off the face value. So that explains why you might once and awhile get some mail that has stamps on it from the 1970s.

Bob - You were saying Jobs was an interesting character.

Ron – He was very single-minded. Which meant that if there was something that he was after in particular, you never wanted to get between him and it. You'd wind up with a cat's paw in your forehead.

Bob - You first worked with him at Atari?

Ron - Yes. Two years. And we were pretty chummy for that two years.

Bob - Did you consider it as a friendship, and also did he look to you as a mentor?

Ron - To some degree, because I was in my forties, and those kids were in their twenties.

Bob - When you did the artwork for the logo, do you recall asking, 'Why is it *Apple*?'

Ron - I never did, and it amazes me that I didn't. And I still to this day don't know where 'Apple' came from. But you can tell from the line in the margin here, what the first thing was that popped into my head, why I went to the Newton and the apple thing, the line that you see here, "A mind forever voyaging through strange seas of thought alone," okay?, is the last line of a fairly well-known sonnet by Wordsworth. And that line popped into my head, and I figured I ought to have that in there.

Bob - And that was your idea to put that in?

Ron - Oh, yes, the whole thing was my idea. And the artwork itself. And I was, I think I caught some of Steve Wozniak's whimsy. It was fun. I enjoyed it. Just as everything that they did was fun. At least Wozniak, whatever he did, he did for the pleasure of doing. He did the prototype, design and model for the Apple computer to say, "Look at this! Isn't this great?" Okay? And goes on to something else. It was Jobs who was the dynamic businessman who saw this as the basis of an enterprise. Of course, it was Jobs who drove everything that Apple Computer really did and became. And it was fairly obvious, Apple grew and matured and became what it was until he got into an altercation with the board of directors. He left and the company went into the toilet. Until he came back, and it grew again. So that tells you something.

Bob - Back to that artwork, did you use an existing image of Newton? You did it from scratch?

Ron - Yeah. Just imagination.

Bob - Do you consider it the Apple logo, or the cover, or both for that period?

Ron - Alright, at the time, it was the logo, alright? And of course it was cover art. And Jobs apparently thought enough of it to have a large photocopy made of it as a banner which was hung over their booth at a convention. I'll tell you something else. On the lower left hand corner, I had inked in "R.G. Wayne." Alright? Jobs saw it, and had me take it out.

Bob - The evening that you three executed the partnership, you said that you first resolved a modest dispute between the two Steves.

Ron - That's correct.

Bob - Can you elaborate on what that dispute was?

Ron - The dispute was simple. Wozniak as I said was a very whimsical character, and he was also very proprietary, parental I should say, about his circuit designs. And he wanted to reserve the right to use those circuits elsewhere. And Jobs was telling him, you can't do this. Well, apparently Jobs was not articulate enough to get Woz to understand. And seeing me as something of a mentor, he asked me if I would help him get the idea and the understanding across to Wozniak. Which I did. Woz was a reasonable fellow, it was a matter of how it was presented, that's all. In that evening's conversation within an hour he concurred that it was proprietary and that it was the core of the corporate assets, or the company assets.

Bob - And you sat down and typed up three copies.

Ron - At that moment in time, I sat down and copied...wrote up three contracts.

Bob - *Typed* up, right?

Ron - Typed up three contracts.

Bob - And then everybody signed the three?

Ron - And all of us signed each of the three. Woz was apparently quite impressed that I could write up a contract in legalese.

Bob - I'm assuming that there was no significance to the fact that it was April Fool's Day?

Ron - No significance. None whatsoever. You have to understand that while this was a turning point in history, a real turning point in history, at the time you don't realize that.

Bob - Of course.

Ron - Alright. It's just another day, another series of events, and we were having fun is what it amounted to. Even at forty I was able to have fun.

Bob - By any chance, do you still have that typewriter?

Ron - Oh, no.

Bob - And then, for Atari, you were Senior Engineer?

Ron - I was the Chief Draftsman & Product Development Engineer. I was the guy who designed the cabinets for the games. And they also engaged me as International Field Service Engineer. And I spent about three months in Europe, qualifying potential distributors of Atari products. At least that's what I thought I was doing. I didn't realize until partway through the game that it was a perk.

130

Bob - A what?

Ron - A perk. A thank you from Nolan Bushnell. Oh, yeah. What I was doing could have been done by a trained monkey.

Bob - It was like an ambassadorship or something?

Ron - Well, it was more than that. It was a thank you to me, personally. He just gave me three months in Europe on the company dime. That's what it amounted to. They really didn't need me to do that. And it was fun, it was enjoyable.

Bob - Do you remember meeting Jobs at Atari?

Ron - Oh, of course. I spent a lot of time with him there.

Bob - Do you have a recollection of your first impression?

Ron - Not my first impression. Because first of all, he was not a direct employee, he was a consultant. And they brought him in to do various things like for instance that situation in Europe where they had bought a huge warehouse full of circuit boards. And a lot of them didn't work. It was quite a problem. Bushnell had sent a technician out to service these boards. The technician, not to put too fine a point on it, was something of a klutz. But he (Bushnell) had to solve the problem. So he engaged Jobs, and said, "Go over there and service these boards. It's desperate. We've got to get these boards serviced. First Class airfare, I'll set you up in hotel, and have a grand time for yourself, and a good rate of pay." And Jobs said, "On one condition. That you give me a one way ticket, and I'll take the difference in cash," because it was after that that he made his excursion to India. And being international field service engineer, I was getting these rather nasty phone calls, which as soon as Jobs got there, the tone of the calls changed dramatically. In record time. He was just spitting those things out like popcorn.

Bob - Fixing them.

Ron - Getting them all serviced and working.

Bob - He figured out how to do it?

Ron - Oh, he was a highly skilled technician.

131

Bob - Wow. Incredible.

Ron - He did the job.

Bob - That's an interesting story. So the fact that he didn't report to you, for instance, how did it come to be that you all became friends?

Ron - Well, as Product Development Engineer, I was involved in virtually every project that the company went into, so any product that he was involved in developing, I was there. Cabinet design, or whatever. I did a little write up in my book about the fact...of course, I'm an electrical engineer in my own right. Circuit design and so on. It was quite amusing, when they did the *Gran Trak*. Did you read about that, the *Gran Trak*?

Bob - No.

Ron - *Gran Trak* was the Atari racing game. Driver game. The guy had a steering wheel and gas and brake and so on. And he would drive his car around a track trying to beat the clock against various obstacles. And it was so much fun that they decided to make it competitive.

Bob - More than one player?

Ron - Two players, so I had designed a cabinet for two players. And they took the same power supply essentially, which was fairly beefy, and they put it in there, and it powered both circuit boards. No problem. And then they went to *Gran Trak 4*—four players—so they had a box with the TV set facing up, and in the four sides, you had steering wheels, and guys raced their different colored cars around the track. They took the same circuit board and they beefed up the components, to handle more current. Okay? That was fine. And it worked. And then they decided to go to *Gran Trak 8*. And they had eight drivers around this thing. Well, the first machine they put together, one of the engineers came in to my office and he's got this power supply. Circuit board, with all the bits and pieces on it, transformer and so on, and he's holding this thing up by the leads like a dead rat. 'Wha' hoppen?' The traces had blown off the board. And I was absolutely amazed. I mean here are the guys who could take these little integrated circuits, plastic centipedes, and sew them together to do

132

all sorts of wonderful stuff, and they didn't understand a simple power equation. The traces on that circuit board was fine for one circuit, or two circuits, or four circuits. By the time they got to eight circuits, they were running so much current, that these traces just literally blew off the board. These guys didn't recognize what was going on.

Bob - They thought they could just keep adding players.

Ron - Right. Well, I sat down designed a new circuit board, and within a week they had new circuit boards and the problem was solved. But I was so amazed that these guys who could do all these wonderful things with integrated circuits couldn't understand a basic power equation.

But I will let you in on a little anecdote, in terms of Steve Jobs' personality. He was an interesting guy to know, a fun guy to know, but he had two interesting aspects. One, he was absolutely well-informed on the subjects in which he was interested. The subjects he was not interested in, he had absolutely no interest and no knowledge. I almost lost my upper set one day when in the course of conversation I discovered he didn't know that aluminum was a conductor. Not his realm of interest! The other aspect of it was, that being as dynamic as he was, if you had to choose between Steve Jobs and an ice cube you would nuzzle up to the ice cube for warmth. Okay? Now I do not say that in a derogatory sense. I'm simply describing it as his nature. And essentially that's what it took to do what he did.

Bob - Can you just talk about the original partnership agreement, how you hung onto it for a long time? I guess you probably didn't think anything about it. It was in a file, right?

Ron - It was in a file for years and years and years. I came across an ad from somebody who dealt in autographs. And by that time Apple had risen to some prominence. And I'm just a humble employee; I was Chief Engineer at a company in California called Thor Electronics, a position I held for sixteen years until I retired. Modest income, but you know, you can always use a few more shekels. And here's this ad for somebody who buys autographs, okay? Well, I got this thing sitting in a file, it's collecting dust, why not? So, I got in touch with the guy and he was interested, and we settled on five hundred dollars. And I sold my copy of the Apple Computer contract to this guy for five hundred dollars. That was the same contract which about a year ago sold at auction for one point three million. Story of my life.

Bob - And that was the contract from April 1st.

Ron - 1976.

Bob - But you did tell me that there was one aspect of it. About how at least you have the feeling now that you...

Ron - Yes, that is true. At least I can say that I created something in my lifetime that sold for a million dollars.

Bob - I think there were two or three documents that were part of that, is that right?

Ron - There were three pages to the contract, yeah.

Bob - Because I thought that I read about the auction that it included the paper where they bought back your interest. Something like that, that that was part of it.

Ron - Bought back my interest? Okay, that's...I find very strange, because either my memory is faulty, or, they never really actually—I say *they*, Steve Jobs and Steve Wozniak—never actually bought back my interest.

Bob - Oh, they didn't?

Ron - Not really, not in that sense.

Bob - What was it like when you all did the original partnership agreement, how was it determined that you would get ten percent?

Ron - Well, that was Steve Jobs' totally spur-of-the-moment idea. He was so impressed with my skills at diplomacy working with Steve Wozniak, he instantly said, "Okay, we're going to form a company," and Jobs and Wozniak would each have forty-five percent, and I would get ten percent as the tie-breaker. Because Jobs felt that any serious dispute came along, he could rely on me to come down on the side of reason. Diplomacy. You know what a diplomat is, don't you?

Bob - No.

Ron - A diplomat is somebody who can tell you to go to hell in a way that makes you look forward to the trip. Yeah. It was a fun relationship.

He held up my Apple-1 manual, as I video-taped our meeting.

Ron - I drew and typed this manual.

Bob - You're kidding. I forgot about that part. Can you show me the cover of it? Okay. So, you didn't just do the cover of it.

Ron - I did the whole thing.

Bob - You did the whole thing. Now did you do it with Jobs?

Ron - Yes. This all happened after I had separated myself from the company. I didn't stop assisting them in other words. I was still working with them afterwards. That's what I was going to tell you before I forgot. I drifted off into something else. You were talking about having my share bought out. My share was not bought out. I simply went down to the registrar's office and had my name taken off the contract. Essentially that's what it was. And then after he, they had gotten together with Arthur Rock and had founded a new situation and had their money, I knew nothing about any of that. I get a letter in the mail, because they're going to found a new corporation, and the letter says, if you will accept, if you will sign this letter of separation, then please take the check and sign. I think the check was for fifteen hundred dollars. And I had already separated myself from the company. So, fifteen hundred dollars as far as I was concerned was found money. So, sure, fine, I did that. But that was after the corporation was founded, and they're just crossing T's and dotting I's. That's all they're doing. So that was the extent of it. The only other thing I ever realized out of them was Jobs asked me to do a cabinet design.

135

Bob - Can I ask you again about the manual? So you all did that after you had separated yourself in terms of the partnership.

Ron - That is correct.

Bob - And so that was contract work you did?

Ron - Well, assistance I should say, because I was never paid for it, or asked for anything for it. It was fun to do. Like the artwork itself was fun to do.

Bob - So did you and Jobs sit down and go through to do this?

Ron - He gave me the technical information, I drew the schematic.

Bob - You drew that schematic?

Ron - Yes, of course.

Bob - Wow.

Ron - And I was used to justified typing, and I did the justified typing of this, alright?

Bob - You did the whole thing?

Ron - I did the whole thing.

Bob - So he gave you the schematic and the basics and you basically...

Ron - I was documentation. I'd set up the documentation system at Atari and several other companies. So that was essentially what I was doing.

Bob - That's incredible. It's not just the cover, then.

Ron - No.

The following month, Ron and I caught up by phone. We discussed how he'd really missed out when he sold his original copy of the Apple Computer partnership so cheaply. The only items that he still retained from his Apple days were his copies of the design renderings he'd done for Jobs in 1977, and his copies of the proof sheets for the Apple-1 manual. He was interested in selling those items, but wanted to make sure that he did not 'give them away' as well. He said he'd like to have the proceeds soon enough so that it wouldn't just be used for his gravestone. In other words, he'd like to turn those documents into a little spending money. I quizzed him as to whether he might have anything else related to Apple or Jobs from those days. How about any photos he might have taken? Nope. This was the last of what he'd retained.

Bob - Let's see. I was just looking at a couple of dates. So what I wanted to have you do is go back the time prior to when these drawings were done and...

Ron - Okay, I have been reflecting on that, as best I can. And Jobs came to me essentially and said, 'Hey, we're going to build a new version of this and we need an enclosure.' The enclosure situation was rather important to him because of his first experience where he had sold a bunch of computers to the Byte Shop and the Byte Shop almost lost their upper set when he walked in with all these circuit boards. They weren't in cabinets. And I don't know how he ever got himself out of that situation.

Bob - Yes, Paul Terrell explained to me that he was disappointed because he wanted something more integrated...

Ron - He was expecting a product. It was a miscommunication of course. But a rather embarrassing one. And, of course, it led inevitably to the situation between Jobs and myself where he comes to me and he says, "We're going to build another version of this. We need an enclosure. Can you design one for me?" And, of course, why not? I was the package designer for all the video games for Atari. But anyway, I had been their chief draftsman and product development engineer, their package designer for the enclosures. So, naturally, he comes to me and says, "Can you do a cabinet for us?" I said, "Certainly I can." And I think he put the number of fifteen hundred dollars on the thing. And said, you know, have at it. I think we had a brief discussion on it; I did a couple of these drawings that I now have which were concept sketches, and then approached him with these drawings and he looked at them and he said, "Yeah, that's alright, that's alright, maybe not like *that*," etcetera,

137

etcetera. We hashed it back and forth. And eventually, I believe between the two of us we wound up with the aircraft profile that you see in the drawings now is the finished design. And that finished design was, of course, side-panels in solid wood with brushed aluminum plated, brushed aluminum rim that you see to run around these outside panels.

Bob - Wow.

Ron - And then, by having a cover back and base essentially wrap around sheet metal, it made for a full box and it allowed me to incorporate the tamour door thing. And at any rate, after we had pretty well settled on it, I then went to work literally and started churning out these drawings. A week or two later, perhaps probably two weeks later, I got ahold of him and I said, "Okay, I've got your design for you." And it was the full package design; assembly drawings, sub-assembly drawings, detail components, the extrusion drawing for the tambour door and so on. And that's basically how it was, and I turned the whole document package over to him. Somehow or other the extrusion drawing either was a drawing I decided either to redo or something. Why I still have that extrusion drawing for the tambour door I'm not entirely sure. But nonetheless, that is essentially how this all came about. And then of course, essentially I found out later on, when their later computers came out with these molded cabinets. Fifty thousand of the seed money went into their first cabinet design. But my design would have been entirely different had I realized that they had money available to them. I mean perhaps the concept would have been the same, but the actual technical approach to achieving that profile and contour would have been different.

Bob - And that's because you were building...you were designing something that could be built without expensive tooling?

Ron - With virtually no tooling needed, woodworking people would have a fixture they could then profile out all the side panels they wanted, and the fabricators doing the fabricated aluminum strips and so on, that's fairly straightforward stuff, it doesn't call for tooling. And of course the rest of it was either sheet metal, or machining. Machining could be done on CNC (Computer Numerical Control). CNCs were out by that time.

Bob - What part is it, which on one of the drawings says quarter inch thick black Plexiglas?

Ron - That was to be the top cover.

Bob - And then the tambour door kind of went in front of that?

Ron - The tambour door went over the keyboard.

Bob - Right.

Ron - Alright. And it slid in grooves on the side, there were grooves milled into the side panels into which the tambour doors would slide. And being a tambour door it's articulated so as soon as you pull down, it automatically slides in underneath.

Bob - Right.

Ron - And that's where it actuates the selector switch, the cricket switch rather, and it turns the equipment on or off.

Bob - What was the finish or the material of the tambour door to be?

Ron - I believe I was going to go for an aluminum extrusion for that.

Bob - Boy, that would have been beautiful.

Ron - Yes, I agree. It's rather bothered me all these years that nobody's ever picked up on that concept of covering up a keyboard when it's not being used.

Bob - So do you recall if there was ever any follow-up dialogue after you delivered the drawings to him and he paid you?

Ron - No. There was no follow up at all, which was also something that surprised me. But somewhere in the archives, the hidden vaults of Apple, I'm sure that those original drawings still reside. They would have to; it would have been part of their records.

Bob - Yup. I was looking at some dates. April 1st, 1976, that's when you all did the first partnership agreement.

Ron - Correct, and then the drawing I have of the tambour door is dated January 8th of 1977.

Bob - It's interesting, because when I look at the Apple history data, Apple was incorporated... It was a partnership when you all drew up that agreement, April 1st 1976. And then January 3rd, 1977 is when it was actually incorporated. The date on your drawing is coincidentally five days after the actual incorporation.

Ron - That's correct, although I knew nothing about that. Of course, they wouldn't have gotten the twenty-five million until they had a corporation to put it into.

And that would have happened probably shortly after I delivered the drawings.

Bob - The other date that I wanted to include in that was then when the Apple][was introduced, because your drawing was clearly intended to be the housing for the Apple][, when he first contracted with you to do that.

Ron - Yes.

Bob - And so that was April 16th 1977. So your date of January 7th is a little more than three months before the Apple][came out.

Ron - Yeah, the proper gestation period.

Bob - We know things were happening pretty fast at that time. You said that the one copy you re-did, changed it, and that you ended up retaining that one because it was replaced.

Ron - You're talking about the original drawing. Of the extrusion.

Bob - Right. The various concept sketches that you've described in your list as pencil on vellum, would those have been working concept sketches?

Ron - They would have been the preliminary concept sketches that I discussed with Jobs before we settled on the aircraft profile.

Bob - Would you have ultimately delivered him something like blue-line prints?

Ron - No. Well, I may have delivered him blue-line prints. That's possible. But at the same time I would have delivered him the original vellum.

Bob - The ones you retained were your original working sketches? And then the vellum he would have gotten on delivery would have been the finished vellum sketches?

Ron - Correct. A point of information as I recall now, I owned a Bruning machine at that time. Yeah, and I think I made these prints myself.

Reference to Ron's list of engineering drawings, a total of eight pencil on vellum. Seven Bruning blueline prints and then ten Xeroxes.

Bob - Going back to when you did the Apple-1 manual, I guess you would have done the manual after the partnership was created?

Ron - Oh, yes. Immediately.

Bob - So the timeline would be, the partnership was created. Then twelve days later, you then withdrew from the partnership.

Ron - That's correct.

Bob - So that would have been April 13th, let's say. And then, so now you're in a position where you're not part of the partnership but obviously you've continued working for them or with them?

Ron - Absolutely.

Bob - Was it shortly after that when they asked you to do the manual?

Ron - Are you talking about the manual for the Apple-1?

Bob - Yes.

Ron - No, it was during the twelve days.

Bob - That was during the twelve days?

Ron - Yes.

Bob - I didn't know that.

Ron - Yes. In fact, I had a slight disagreement with Jobs. Because it had been my practice over the years, to...when you draw a schematic diagram to identify each component...resisters were R numbers, and integrated

141

circuits were CR numbers, or diodes were CR numbers, and so on. Coils were L designated. Capacitors were C designated, and so on. And so what I wound up with when I finished the schematic was all of the numbers which then went together make up a tabulated parts list. And you could trace each component from parts list to schematic to finished assembly, and so on. And Jobs wanted to know why I was doing these C numbers and R numbers, and so on, on the drawings. I said because that's the way you do it. I've been doing that for fifty years. Okay? You're supposed to do it that way. He says, "No you don't." So he's telling me how to do the documentation. And, this was one of the things...it grated on me a bit. And it's one of the things that added up to...a number of other things that all added up to my separation from the company. We didn't have any flaming disagreements, don't misunderstand me. But there was an aura there, a character of what was to come that ran against the grain. And that coupled with the fact that I was in my forties, and the only guy that was reachable through this company in case everything blew up, you know, I was the only guy that was going to end up getting nailed, and I didn't know where I'd get the money to recover fifteen thousand dollars. There were all sorts of reasons.

Bob - Well, it's interesting because you went from being a friend and mentor to Jobs, to the point that you all signed that partnership, now you're partners in business. And things tend to change, when that happens.

Ron - Especially when you're in partnership, you've got a house and a car and a checking account, and savings, and your partners haven't got two nickels to rub together. Okay?

Bob - I see.

Ron - So there was that element in there.

Bob - You were the guy with the exposure, basically.

Ron - The exposure, yes. Again, I repeat. That was not the reason for the separation. It was just one of many reasons. It included things like, I was a product development guy myself. Now, I had a talent for putting documentation systems together. And Jobs was extremely impressed with the documentation system that I had put together for Atari. And, you know, it filled a volume. The whole thing, it took me months to put this thing together. But it solved the problem that they had.

Bob - That was related to parts.

Ron - That was related to the purchased parts. They'd already done the documentation system for... And I was absolutely sure at the time the partnership was formed, that Jobs was going to want me to run the documentation group. Why not? I had that skill demonstrated, right?

Bob - And because you'd already worked together at Atari, he was familiar with it.

Ron - Precisely, but for myself, my passion was not computers. My passion was slot machines. And I just was looking ahead in time and I really couldn't see myself in a big office in the back of a building pushing papers around for the next twenty years. Then too, I also realized, that I was standing in the shadows of giants. Was I ever going to get a product development project of my own? Probably not. Especially the way I usually do things, which is I like to take things from beginning to end. I'll design the labels that go on the box. I want to do the whole thing from beginning to end. Modern business doesn't work that way. You know, you've got graphic artists, you've got package designers, you've got circuit designers, you have all these different people under a manager, who plays these people like pieces on a chessboard. That's the twentieth century engineering style of doing things. I'm more of a nineteenth century guy. And all of these things that I'm describing to you rolled together to say, hey, wait a minute, I really had better back out of this thing.

Bob - You've described your execution of the design and layout of the manual, all of that happened in a twelve-day period. So was it after you executed the partnership, would it have been something where they said, 'Okay, Ron, the first thing we'd like you to do is do this manual?'

Ron - Yes, oh, absolutely. They knew that they had to have a manual to go with the product. And I was the graphics guy, so I did the manual.

Bob - Was the job of doing the manual completed before you backed out of the partnership?

Ron - Probably, yes.

Bob - Because it wasn't something that took you that long to do.

Ron - Oh, no, no, no. First of all, I had an IBM typewriter at that time. The original manual is in two justified columns of typing, okay. I could do that trick on an IBM Executive. And so I owned my own IBM Executive and so I could type up these two-column pages that were justified.

Bob - My reason for asking is that you have your copies of the manual, you had taken a close look at them to determine that they were printed in lithographs, yeah. So, I guess when you finished the manual you were still involved in some aspect of it, like having the copies printed up...

Ron - As a matter of fact, I think Jobs himself, or possibly Wozniak, took on the mechanics of going to a printer and getting it printed. But I had all the sheets prepared, all of the artwork prepared. So they could do the photo-plates.

Bob - I'm just guessing that the reason you ended up with some of the sheets, it's effectively a proof set for you.

Ron - Yes, I think it was.

Bob - And one part that you didn't retain is the schematics, that sometime over the years that was separated from what you...

Ron - I'm afraid so. It's really kind of too bad. Because, it was quite a nice schematic, too.

Bob - When the manual was printed, would those have been printed like a two-sheet, would they have been printed both sides?

Ron - They're probably galley proofs, is what they are. Because they're only printed on one side.

144

Bob - Because if they were actually pieces of a manual then they would have been printed on two sides.

Ron - I would think so, yes. I say I would think so because I'm thinking back thirty-odd years to what the manual looked like. I haven't seen the manual since then.

Bob - Except for the day you saw mine. With mine, all we were doing was focusing with the logo on the cover. If those are galley proofs, is it two pages, or one page per sheet?

Ron - One page per sheet. Now, an 8 ½ by 11, hand-printed on one side. Definitely lithographies, okay, they're not Xeroxes.

Bob - The other documents that we're talking about have that kind of aging look to them. Do these pages have that?

Ron - No. You would expect the blue-lines to have an aging look because they were printed on a fairly coarse paper that is probably an acid-based paper. And the edges, wherever the air got at it, *toned*. So, wherever the air got at it at the edges, the pages were toned.

Bob - It was never intended to last for forty years.

Ron - No.

Bob - One other question came to mind, going back to that time when you did the partnership, do you recall hearing about the order from the Byte Shop, was that talked about?

Ron - Yes, toward the end of that twelve-day period, I remember that. And one of the things that bothered me and added to my determination to leave was hearing that the Byte Shop had a terrible reputation for not paying their bills. You can see what effect that would have, especially after Jobs had gone out and done what Jobs was supposed to do. He got his paws on fifteen thousand dollars for materials to fill the order.

Bob - So you saw threats from every angle.

Ron - I saw things that weren't comfortable from several angles. Okay? And this is one of the interesting things; every single interview, everyone

I talk to, "You must regret terribly having made that decision." Sir, I did not regret it. Not then, not ever. Not now, okay?

Bob - Certainly from what we've talked about from the time you were making the rational decision. And that was the best thing for you...because of a lot of factors including piece of mind.

Ron - I really had this feeling that the product was going to be immensely successful though nobody could have anticipated what it became.

Bob – Going back to these drawings, I was looking at photos of an Apple][, and that case, it certainly is similar to your design.

Ron - Okay, was it a fabricated case? The Apple][. I've never seen an Apple][. What sort of a case is it in?

Bob - Well, there's an Apple][that someone's selling on *eBay*, and by serial number, it's one of the first one hundred Apple]['s. I can send you the link to it.

Ron - Please do, because I've never seen it and I'm curious to know what sort of cabinet he did put on that.

Bob - You talked about how on the top of your design you had had a flat surface for the monitor, a recessed area for the monitor.

Ron - Right, just a flat surface essentially, and the top was supposed to open up like a door so you could get to the circuit board.

I then promised to email Ron a link to pictures of this early-model Apple][. And we ended the call, but got back on the phone a day later.

Bob - You were telling me that you did these drawings in a different style, not really the style of the time?

Ron - The style that I used, the style I've used all my life is called armory drafting. Which in modern terms, about the only place you'll see it nowadays is in patent drawings. Certain kinds of patent drawings now use armory drafting. And it's weighted, you'll see the surfaces are shaded. So you can see if they're sloped or curved, or tilted. And that kind of drafting is a period drafting. That's the kind of drafting I preferred. First of all, I think where the style of drafting really helped is in machine drawing, and one of the reasons I used it is because when you do a complex machine part, when a machinist picks up a drawing, the first impression is the one that he's going to act upon for the rest of his interpretation of that drawing. And if you have no weighting of the lines, no shading at all, then is a circle you're looking at a hole, or is it a post standing up? He has to look at other views of the drawing to see this. But with my kind of drawing, you look at it and the drawing...the contours of what you've drawn jump out at you, and it minimizes the chances of his making an erroneous interpretation. And get halfway through a part and said, 'Oh, my goodness, that's not what they meant.' And, you know, you've thrown a couple of hours work away.

Bob - Okay. And since I'm looking at this one. The tambour door, when it was fully recessed, was the design that it would roll up?

Ron - Well, the whole thing. If you look at the tambour design, segments would slide in to one another. So that each segment articulates in relationship to the next one. It works like a roll top desk. Roll top desks are built like that. And there's a micro-switch there, which the door hits as it goes past.

Chapter 17

All One Farm

Dan Kottke is well known to have been the former college classmate of Jobs, who traveled with him to India. We first spoke with Dan in March, 2011.

Dan Kottke - Steve Jobs and I became friends at Reed College when we were freshman. We both got *Be Here Now*, a spiritual book written by Ram Dass. It was quite a landmark book, and I had never seen anything like it before. Our initial mutual interest was Eastern literature. It started with *Be Here Now*, and then we got *Autobiography of the Yogi*, and *Cosmic Consciousness*, written around the turn of the century. Also *Ramakrishna and His Disciples*, and *Zen Minds*. That was one of Steve's favorite books.

Zen is all about emptying your mind. I never was that attracted to Zen myself. At the time that Steve was starting Apple, there was a part of him that was so attracted to Zen and emptying his mind, and yet he was furiously thinking all the time about how he was going to become rich and famous. A little bit of a dichotomy there.

I was very much into Buddhism. I wasn't into Zen. Comparative religion was my interest; the survey view of all the different approaches. You know, if I had found a comparative religion program like at Reed or at Columbia, I could have ended up majoring in comparative religion.

Philosophy didn't appeal to me, because it was just too many words and too many papers I would have to write.

We stayed in touch, and in 1974 Steve and I went to India together to the Kumbh Mela, the biggest religious gathering on Earth. We didn't have any money. It was summertime and it was one hundred degrees, one hundred ten degrees sometimes. It was really hot, we just wore thong sandals, flip flops. I think I had bamboo sandals. We visited a bunch of ashrams. The main goal was to get to Neem Karoli Baba's Ashram. He's in the book *Be Here Now*. He's also known as Maharajji, but that's just a title. It was in Kenchi, which was a tiny little village.

We also went to the Ashram of Hariakhan Baba. That was our pilgrimage experience, hiking all day up a dry river bed. It was a five mile hike into the wilderness. We didn't know where we were going. It was an adventure. Hariakhan Baba is kind of like a Paul Bunyon figure, a mythical figure. We got to this ashram and he wasn't some old guy with a beard. He was a young guy. He was a little bit gay, wearing pastel covered saris and changing his clothes three times a day. The men would stand around and argue philosophy, and the women were doing all the work – cooking, fetching the water—typical Indian scenario. The whole thing was kind of goofy. So we only stayed there one day.

We visited other ashrams too, but those were the main two that we actually had as a goal to visit, as opposed to just kind of bumbling across India. We had a really dramatic moment where we were caught out in the open in a very dramatic thunderstorm and we had no rain gear. I think we had shoulder bags; we left our sleeping bags behind. It was so warm out you just didn't need it. I remember the night before that, we spent the night sleeping on this concrete bench in the steaming heat. The mosquitoes were bad and you're sleeping directly on the concrete with your little sheet, my little dhoti, I think they called it, to keep the mosquitoes off me. Very uncomfortable. Then this rainstorm happened and we were just huddling in the dirt being pelted with big drops of rain and there was lightning and thunder and it was quite terrifying. We had no protection at all, we were just out in the middle of it. We didn't know where to hide. So we're just like huddling under our sheets from the rain.

Then when we left the next day we had this really long hike to get back and the ground was one hundred degrees. You could not walk barefoot. We were crossing a stream and Steve lost his sandal. And I see his sandal sailing off down the creek. And I thought, "He's going to be in deep shit." I took off running and I found his sandal for him. So he owes me. Anyway, so he was grateful.

In the spring or summer of '75, I didn't know what I was going to do. I came to visit Steve in California. That's when we went up to the All One Farm in Oregon. Later Steve had a job at Atari, and I applied for a job with him, but I didn't get it. I had no experience. Then I went back to New York. I was accepted at Hampshire College, but they wouldn't take me in the fall, and I was too impatient. My parents just wanted me out of the house and I didn't have any money. I was basically looking to go back to school, so I enrolled at the Colombia School of General Studies—which is like adult education—just to get my foot in the door. I had a friend that was there, so I bunked with him at his fraternity house. That was in '75, and then the summer of '76 was the end of my junior year at Colombia.

In 1976, Steve was starting the Apple-1. That's when I came out and spent the summer working for him as an employee, as the assistant building the Apple-1's. Probably for three fifty an hour. It was all very low key. And I was just like, "Yeah, fine, I'll help." Actually, when I arrived, his sister Patty was plugging chips into the Apple-1 on the coffee table in the living room while she watched TV. So I saw a market opportunity! I said, "I can do a better job than that," so Patty lost her job plugging the chips into the Apple-1. I've never apologized to her for it! Maybe she can claim to be the first Apple employee. But usually I claim to be the first employee.

150

I was the first paid employee, although Patty probably got paid too, so maybe she was the first employee. However, she already had a job. She worked at Taco Bell, and she was family. I was the first non-family member to get paid to work for Apple. That was Apple the partnership, and there were no employee numbers. When Apple incorporated in early '77, Bill Fernandez was the first full-time employee with an employee number. So he was probably number three, after Woz and Jobs. Then Mike Markkula was the third founder of the company. He put all the money up, wrote the business plan, got the board of directors and hired the president, and so on. He had an Apple-1. He had a passion for it. He's a billionaire.

I mostly hung out with Steve and answered the phone when he was gone. I kept him company making deliveries. The Apple-1 was a board with sockets on it. My first job was plugging the chips. There were probably twenty-five chips; I didn't know anything about chips, but I could read the numbers. The main reason a board would fail was bent pins when you plug the chips in, and I was good at that. I could plug them in, you know, *not backwards*. I just assembled the Apple-1's—of which there were dozens—I don't even know how many there were, but my main job was assembling and testing them. Each one might take fifteen minutes. You would assemble them all at the same time and then test them. Assembly might take fifteen or twenty minutes, and testing took fifteen or twenty minutes.

You'd plug everything in, inspect it all carefully, make sure nothing was backward, and turn on the power. Sometimes something bad would happen, and there'd be a puff of smoke and it would be dead. But usually not. If everything was right, you would look for video on the screen. I would test all the keys on the keyboard.

Do you know what the monitor ROM is? The monitor ROM is the memory program that's built into chips on the board. When you turn the board on, that's what's running the monitor program. It's scanning the keyboard all the time. Every time it sees a key press it starts to interpret it. Steve (Wozniak) had written little monitor commands for filling and comparing memory. There was a little one-line program I could type and fill all the memory with one thing, like zeros. We would fill the memory with zeros, and then fill the memory with ones, and then loop. If it worked properly, the screen would get white, black, white, black. That's the very simplest thing you could do. That would tell you that the video portions were working properly.

Anyway, back to the processor. The key is based on the reset, it's based on the clock. It's based on the assumption that the very first value it gets is going to be an instruction, and every single value after that is going to be an instruction, too. If the memory somehow gets corrupted, the instructions won't make sense. And then the processor is lost. You would call that crashing. It crashed.

Bob - Was there a way at the time to fix it, if it crashed?

Dan - Well, there was a reset button on the keyboard. The program its running is in the ROM. So if the computer works as it's designed to, it should never crash. It's just running all the time, waiting for more instructions. That's what computers do. They're running in a loop endlessly waiting for more instructions. And the loop is looking for keys on the keyboard and that's it.

As computers got more complicated, there're a million things the computer is doing while it's waiting for more keyboard instructions. Nowadays you have the interrupts and all kinds of things. But back then it was very simple. Anyway, that's what the processor does. It just goes from one little cubby, instruction, to the next. It increments forever. The program counter is the place where the processor is going to go to get its next instruction. It just increments automatically. That's another thing it never said that in the manual. But the program counter starts at all 1's, and then it loops back around to zero. The very next clock cycle it rolls over to zero. Zero is called the *reset vector*. When you press the reset button on the keyboard, it puts the processor in a known state and it starts at zero, fetching instructions. And that's it. Isn't that simple?

A five-year-old can understand the idea of having a row of mailboxes. You go to the first one and it gives you an instruction about something to do. It's kind of like playing hide-and-go-seek. You go someplace and you find an instruction about what you're going to do next. But Steve Jobs couldn't explain it to me.

Bob - Do you think it was because you weren't asking the right question? Or because he himself didn't understand the programming side of it?

Dan - I think it was a mixture of various things. He thought it was too obvious. And I wasn't asking the right particular questions. If I had asked him, 'What does the reset line do?' that would have been the jackpot. But I never thought to ask that, and it never said anywhere. I didn't know. I thought, 'Reset? You would only reset if something breaks.' But 'reset' is actually like the ignition key in the car. Nothing is going to happen without it.

I was working for three twenty-five an hour. You'd think he would have wanted to educate me; there were a lot of tasks to be done. But he kept me in the dark.

That's kind of nerdy, but that's what we did. What I had to do for every board (now it gets tedious), because we were selling the cassette interface. The cassette interface was the only way to store a program once it had been typed in. The cassette interface was just a little port, it worked with a cheap home cassette recorder. It was very tiny and plugged into the audio. An audio cable went into a cassette, and we would load *BASIC*. You would type in the load instruction, and then you would start the cassette player playing. It would make a lot of noise, you would hear a beep, and then when you heard the beep (as if you were sending a fax) and you'd hit the character return. It took thirty seconds or a minute to load the *BASIC* that Steve had written. Then, I would actually write a simple one-line *BASIC* program. That had to be done for every board.

153

Even though the cassette port was a separate purchase, everyone would want it.

Anyway, if it passed all those tests, I put it in a box. I was the person who would address them and mail them out. There weren't many to mail, most were just delivered locally to the Byte Shops.

Steve and I wrote the first flier that summer, the flier for the Apple I that we handed out at the Personal Computer Festival, in August of '76, in Atlantic City, NJ. Stan Veit is the guy who organized it. He was a character, an East Coast guy. For that Personal Computer Festival in August, it was Steve Wozniak, Steve Jobs, and me manning a folding card table. That was the Apple-1 booth. That's where we gave out the flier. You know, that flier was such a classic, vintage thing. Steve and I spent hours at the kitchen table writing that flier about the Apple-1 and how great it was. 'No more switches, no more lights.' I remember that line. 'No more 2102's.' The 2102 was the 1k static RAM that everybody else used on the Altair and the IMSAI. The Apple-1 used 4k dynamic RAMs, which was 4k dense. It was much tinier. The 2102's were big chips, they were double-wide chips and each one was 1k bits, and they were static, which was nice. But Woz is the genius. And he figured out how to refresh the dynamic RAMs. You know, a dynamic RAM is like a leaky cup. To have any water in the cup, you have to keep filling it. That's the way a memory bit works on a dynamic RAM. So 'refresh' means you're filling the cups that are supposed to have something in them every four milliseconds.

That was my contribution; I built the boards, tested the boards, kept Steve company, we made deliveries, I answered the phone a lot. There were lots of people who called, so I was the office secretary. However, my main job in my mind was to read the 6502 hardware processor manual and understand how it worked. And I have to say, I failed. I'm a bright lad but I could not figure it out. It was a very frustrating summer for me. I was working on the Apple-1, and I really didn't understand how it worked. I was too intimidated. Although Steve

154

and I were good friends, I could not ask him how the processor worked. When I asked him, he couldn't explain it. I puzzle about that now because I could explain a processor to a two-year-old. I just kept thinking, 'I haven't read enough yet. I just have to read more.' I didn't have enough electronic knowledge yet. Steve was already operating at another level; he wasn't interested in the hardware at all. He was interested in making his first million, I think.

I was a self-taught engineer. It took me years to figure out how chips work, much less to design a computer. I was actually doing engineering work by 1980, and by the time of the Macintosh, which was 1981, I was made an engineer. For people who are beginners, interested in the core concept, the other important part of the Apple-1 story is it started out as a TV Typewriter.

Bill Fernandez and Steve Wozniak built a computer when they were in high school. It was called The Cream Soda Computer, because they were drinking cream soda at the time. It probably didn't do much of anything. The processor was probably discrete; it wasn't a microprocessor. That's what got the Apple-1 going. The 8080 was really the first processor. Well, the 4004 was really the first. That was only a 4 bit processor. Then they came out with the 8008, and then they came back with the 8080 but the 8080 was expensive, hundreds of dollars. The 6800 from Motorola was cheaper, but still hundreds of dollars. When Woz designed the Apple-1, if you look closely at the Apple I board, there's some little legend portion where it says the 6502 was compatible with the 6800. There was just a small difference in the clock signal. Woz designed the Apple-1 so you could run it on a 6800.

What galvanized the whole thing was when the 6502 came out they were selling them for twenty-five dollars. *Oh, my God!* Woz has told that story that he was at a trade show and couldn't believe he got a processor for twenty-five dollars. So, The Cream Soda Computer probably didn't have a microprocessor. It was probably a very simple logic thing. It didn't have an instruction set. My guess is it just let you add two numbers. It was like a glorified calculator with logic gates.

I never understood the Apple-1 schematic. I couldn't make sense of it. It just didn't make sense. It *doesn't* make sense. Years later, thanks to the Computer History Museum, I was standing next to someone who was from the Homebrew Computer Club, and he explained to me that Woz had built the TV Typewriter the summer before. The TV Typewriter came out in 1975, and it was the cover of a hobby electronics magazine. The design was given away free by Don Lancaster. The TV Typewriter was a complicated design because it was a frame buffer. It was a text frame buffer that put out a video signal that would connect to a video monitor of television set. It was the circuit for the keyboard, and how to interface the keyboard, and how to type on the keyboard and have letters show up on the screen. I thought Woz had invented all of that. What Woz really did is take the TV Typewriter, and the 6502 processor, and he stuck them together. Then he stuck the dynamic memory on so that the processor would have some memory to read a program and execute it. And that's what the Apple-1 was. It was a hybrid design. I never would have known that if I hadn't been standing in front of the TV Typewriter at the Computer History Museum.

I went to a couple Homebrew club meetings with Steve Jobs, but I didn't know enough about electronics to benefit from it.

Question about the metal box, painted blue, with the Plexiglas top...
Dan - We didn't make any metal boxes. Steve Jobs would not have done that. He didn't like metal. We spent a fair amount of time talking to some guy who was going to make boxes out of Koa wood, semi-exotic wood. I assume that a few were made, not like a production run, but I never had one. I just remember talking about them.
Bob - *Ricketts question.* Does that name ring a bell to you at all?
Dan - No. Did he buy it from the Byte Shop or directly from Apple?

Bob - The check is made out to Apple Computer.

Dan - They must have just given him a discount. Mostly it was the Byte Shops that sold them for $666. But who knows?

Bob - The check from July 27, 1976, is in the amount of $600. Then there's a second check from August 5, 1976, with a note attached that says "software NA programmed by Steve Jobs 1976" and that check was for $193.00.

Dan - I don't remember that. We didn't sell any software, to my recollection. I wonder if he didn't buy a cassette interface. The cassette wasn't included in the *BASIC* cost, it was a separate item. I don't remember what we charged for it. I would have thought that almost anyone who wanted an Apple-1 would want that. The Apple-1 would come on a cassette tape. Well, maybe it wasn't finished yet that summer. Maybe we were testing it. I don't remember shipping the Apple-1 *BASIC*. So the question is whether Ricketts had the Apple-1 *BASIC* on a tape. I was one of the people who did the tape duplication the next summer when we were doing the Apple][. We had a whole bunch of tape recorders all plugged in together. You duplicated like eight at once.

Bob - Dan Sokol said he was the first software pirate for copying the *BASIC*.

Dan - Well, that's something else. There was a famous incident at the Homebrew Computer Club where Bill Gates showed up. They were based in Albuquerque, New Mexico. Bill Gates showed up and was holding up a paper tape copy of his *BASIC*, which competed with the Apple-1 *BASIC*. He and Paul Allen, that was their first product. Somebody had stolen the paper tapes! Famous story. Not only stolen it, but duplicated it and started giving it out for free. Gates got really bent out of shape. There's a famous letter that he wrote about how 'this is theft, this is our hard work, and you're just ripping us off.' Dan Sokol was blamed as the culprit. But years later it turned out it was Steve Dompier.

157

Ed Roberts had offered to hire Bill Gates because he had *BASIC*. Bill said, "Uh, thank you very much. We're starting our own company." Bill might actually have worked for him briefly, but he was a Harvard student and dropped out to start his own company. The Altair and IMSAI were quote similar. They were both big metal boxes with switches and lights. And the famous s100 bus. So, meanwhile the Apple-1 had no bus. It had a little breadboard area where you could theoretically put a chip that did something. I don't think many people knew that. But, a couple years later, in 1978, during the Apple][era, one day Wendell Sander handed me a schematic and gave me his Apple I and asked if I would wire up... What he did was to take the Apple-1 *BASIC* and burn it into a prom that was now a bigger prom. It was now 2k bytes instead of 256 bites; a big expensive prom. I wired it onto the bus of the Apple-1 in the breadboard area. What that meant was he now had an Apple-1 that would come up in *BASIC*. You didn't have to load it. That's what the Apple][did. That was the big appeal; you turned it on and you were immediately running *BASIC*, and you could run a *BASIC* program. That was a pretty obvious thing to do with the Apple-1. In fact Steve Jobs had me do it for him, also. And I don't remember him ever thanking me!

On another side note, the most promising customer for the Apple-1... out of all the people that came by the garage to look at it...was some guy who had a big car dealership where they did repairs. What he wanted to do was put a monitor in a waiting room, and instead of announcing it over the PA when your car was ready, someone would just type on the screen, 'Car number 57, your car is ready for pickup.' At that time, there was no way to put text on a screen. Or, that's to say, the Apple-1 was the cheapest way to put text on a screen. (But you could almost do that with the TV Typewriter. The TV Typewriter let you type and put text on a screen. Maybe the guy didn't know that.)

Bob - Would this guy have been interested in technology as a whole? Was it kind of like he wanted to be a forefront of technology?

Dan - Yeah. I mean it was a progressive angle. You'd think it would be easy enough to have someone accomplish the same thing with a PA system, but who knows? I'm not sure what the dealership was or what the guy's name was. I didn't even have a notebook.

Which sounds... Well, every engineer has a notebook where you write down all the stuff you're dealing with. There was a list of things that I did to test the Apple-1 but I don't ever remember that it was written down. I definitely do remember having a copy of the 6502 hardware manual, and underlining the parts and trying to figure out how the processor worked. I should try and find that manual. I must have it here in my house somewhere.

Bob - Randy Wigginton said that his brother built some of the original cases, so would that have been the wooden ones?

Dan - Well, I don't know, because I don't know his brother. That's rather interesting. I've known Randy all these years and I never knew he had a brother. He and Chris Espinosa, in 1977, were still in high school and they would come to Apple after school to help out. Chris used to give the little demos in the waiting room and Randy was Woz's helper. They got along very well.

Bob - What was the point that made you all realize you had to expand beyond the Jobs house and garage to start producing more computers?

Dan - That was up to Mike Markkula. Markkula showed up in the fall of '76, after I'd gone back to Colombia to finish my degree. He incorporated Apple. I think he put up ninety-thousand dollars for some percentage of ownership. I don't know if he was an equal third with Woz and Jobs. I think once I heard it was only ten percent. But anyway, he's the one who incorporated it, he got the line of credit with the bank, and hired Mike Scott as president. He rounded up the board of directors, he got the venture capital investors. Markkula's the one who found the office on Stevens Creek Boulevard. Mike Markkula was pretty much responsible for that whole phase.

Bob - When you all went to the computer festival in Atlantic City in 1976, did you all think you had a big success on your hands?

Dan - Well, the festival was very homegrown. I didn't know enough about computers to really appreciate it. What sticks out in my mind the most is a guy with an electronic music synthesizer, and he'd built his own sequencer. It was playing weird electronic *beep boop* music. And I thought that was really cool because I'd majored in music at Colombia. That's what captured my imagination the most. I didn't know enough about computers to really be excited. I had no idea. We just had a bare circuit board. All these other companies had stuff in boxes. We were amateurs. I certainly didn't have any feeling about how hugely successful we were going to be.

Bob - Do you think Jobs and Wozniak had that feeling at the time?

Dan - I don't know. It was a big expense for them both to fly across country. I never really talked to either of them about it. I was the hourly technician; I wasn't like a partner.

Bob - What was the convention like? Was it casual or a big party?

Dan - No, no. It was definitely not a party. Because it was only a three-hour drive from my parent's house, I may not have even stayed overnight. I bet I borrowed my parent's car. I do remember I brought Steve Jobs to meet my uncle. My uncle Guy was head of the pension fund for General Motors. He was a finance guy, and he had this huge pension fund worth a billion dollars. I took Steve Jobs to visit him to see whether he thought there was anyone who would want to invest in this start-up company. We must have had the flier, but that was all we had. There were no pictures, and no demo. Uncle Guy recently passed away and I *just* heard the story that he'd told my mother, '*Jeez*, Danny was there with his partner about this computer company. It looks really interesting, but I can't give him any money because then he'll drop out of college, and his mother will never forgive me.' I'm surprised I'd never heard that before. It takes a funeral before you hear these stories.

Bob - Did he or Woz seem like they had any idea of how personal computers in general would go? Did they think they were a part of something big that early on?

Dan - Well, Woz, in the summer of '76, was already deep into the Apple][. He wasn't really interested in the Apple-1 anymore. Immediately after doing the Apple-1, he did the thing that you would think, which was he redesigned it so that the video memory and the processor memory were one and the same, and that was the Apple][. He actually got some kind of patent on that. But the Apple][uses dynamic RAM and a bitmapped screen. So the screen memory is the same as the processor memory. Which is what makes sense. He came over and gave us a demo of his Apple][, which was a much bigger project. He was very excited about that, and so were we, because it was in color. We had these little RF modulators so we would connect it to the home television in the living room, and play color games. That was clearly exciting. That was going to compete with Atari. We were going to have video game on the television in color. So Woz added game paddles to the Apple][, and he had a speaker so it made noise. That was exciting.

Bob - So, the Apple][was a more exciting project for everyone than the Apple-1?

Dan - Yes. So I remember seeing that Apple][prototype in a shoebox. And I asked Woz where it was nowadays and he said he didn't know! "Maybe in the attic." That surprised me. It should be in the Smithsonian.

Bob - What was your first impression of Steve Wozniak?

Dan - Oh, Woz was a whirlwind. The only time I ever saw him, he'd show up at Steve Jobs' house, very, very focused. He wanted to show Steve the new routines he wrote. Or show off something. I couldn't follow what they were saying. I was just in awe of the guy. I do remember going over to his house that summer, and his kitchen table was just piled a foot deep with electronics parts, soldering irons, and pieces of equipment that were torn apart. It was just chaos. Well, my dining room table looks like that now, because I'm an inventor. But I'd never seen anything like that.

Bob - Would you say they were equally intense back in the day?

Dan - Oh, Woz was way more intense.

Bob - Really? That's not what you usually hear.

Dan - Well, I mean, they were both intense, but Woz was a very technical guy. I never went to the Homebrew with Woz, I would go with Steve, but Woz was always there. I think I remember him standing up in front and holding up his Apple-1 and saying, 'Hey, we've got Apple-1's for sale, it's really cool, come and buy one.' I remember Adam Osborne being there. He was the one that started the Osborne computer.

Bob - Did you end up keeping in touch with Woz?

Dan - Oh yeah, I see Woz at the Computer History Museum. And when I saw him on Kathy Griffin, I probably sent him emails. I've sent him emails from time to time. And occasionally he actually replies. Occasionally Steve Jobs replies, but not very often.

Bob - Did you know what you wanted to do with a music degree, or was that just your interest at the time?

Dan - No, no idea. I was actually interested in literature and philosophy, but I thought if I majored in music I wouldn't have to write all those papers. So, really, it was a pretty balanced degree. I took a lot of philosophy, and I took a lot of literature. Also Electrical Engineering; Introduction to Transistor Theory. I really felt out of place there. The class was ninety-five percent Asian, and they're all like doing the homework problem sets together, and I really felt like I didn't fit in. That was *already* in 1977. Those courses are difficult. The same week I got my degree I came back to California and became Apple employee number 12.

Later when I was at Apple, I took electrical engineering classes at Stanford. But again the problem sets are a lot of work. The only way to really manage it is to get together. Later, I was in law school, and the only way to get through is to have a study group and divvy up the work. Same thing with electrical engineering at Stanford. You'd be in a study group, and they would divide up the problem sets, and one person would do each one and then share with the others. I wasn't part of a group. That's why I didn't pursue that all the way to getting a degree.

Bob - How long did you stay at Apple?

Dan - Eight years. Up through 1984.

Bob - So right around the time of the Mac?

Dan - We launched the Mac in January '84 and then that whole summer it was all about giving demos. We went to lots of trade shows. That was very exciting because I had never been to shows. Apple flew us around the country.

Bob - Why did you leave?

Dan - At that point I'd turned thirty, and I'd been working all through my twenties. I just needed a break. I went to Europe and traveled around Europe for three months. Which everyone should do in their twenties. Then, when I got back from Europe, I immediately started getting contract work; people asking me to design stuff for them. My first design was a physiological data acquisition card for the Apple][, for Greenleaf Medical Systems. It was for a sleep research company. The board would automatically read eight channels of EEG physiological data. Then I was off and running. For the next several years I had plenty of design projects, and I didn't really have any motivation to go back to work full-time. At that point I couldn't really see working for Steve Jobs anymore. I didn't really have a place at Apple.

Bob - Why not? Just because it had gotten so big?

Dan - Yeah, it had gotten big and I never really got along with Burrell Smith. Burrell's a difficult guy. And he was busy working on the...let's see, first there was the Mac, and then the Mac 512. Then all the sudden, next year, it was the Mac II. Or the Mac SE, that's where they put in hard drive. No, actually the next big project was the laser writer. I theoretically could have worked on that project. But I didn't get along that well with

Burrell, and I was kind of a non-person as far as Steve Jobs was concerned. Steve didn't leave Apple until late '85. Anyway, at that point, I had a girlfriend in Santa Cruz, and I was thinking of moving. I wasn't thinking about getting a full-time job at Apple.

Bob - What exactly do you mean you were a non-person?

Dan - Well, Steve wouldn't recognize me or talk to me. He felt betrayed by me because... there was a whole incident. Michael Moritz wrote this book called *The Little Kingdom*. And we were all given approval to talk to him for the book. Then, in 1982, sometime before that book came out, *Time* magazine was considering Steve Jobs for *Man of the Year*. I was like the fall guy. Michael Moritz called me up with a *Time* magazine writer on the line and said, "We wonder if you could just confirm for us that Steve Jobs has a daughter named Lisa." I didn't know he was denying that was true, He was denying that she was his daughter. I said, "It's not a secret. Of course he has a daughter named Lisa." *Uh-oh.* "Thank you very much Mr. Kottke," *click*. And that was the end of Steve being considered for "Man of the Year." He was denying his paternity.

I was the fall guy. Michael Moritz owes me a favor someday. Steve would never talk to me again. He didn't talk to me for fifteen years. I think he called me out in front of a whole bunch of employees in the Mac building. But I didn't really even know. I didn't know why he was so mad. I didn't know the story; I was basically set-up. Steve didn't really tell me, and I had the impression that he felt I had violated his trust somehow, but I wasn't really clear what the circumstance was. I didn't know about the *Time Magazine* thing. I would have profusely apologized, but I didn't know. He made it clear that he felt like firing me, but he didn't.

Bob - Do you think you ever would have gone the path of engineering if it weren't for knowing Steve Jobs and getting involved with the Apple-1?

Dan - Very good question, and probably not. Back in the early Apple timeframe, in 1979, before the public offering, my boss was Rod Holt, the

VP of Engineering at Apple. Woz never had people working for him, he didn't want to be a manager. He was always just a wing-nut off on his own, working with Randy. Rod Holt knew that I was Steve Jobs' friend, but he felt sorry for me because I didn't have a stock option. I wasn't eligible for one because I wasn't an engineer yet. So Rod had gone to Steve Jobs and said, 'What do you say, let's just give some stock to Dan Kottke. You know, I'll offer one hundred shares.' Which was a pretty small amount, but it was a nice gesture. He asked Steve, "Will you match that?" And Steve Jobs said "I'll offer zero, Kottke should be happy to have a job." And I never heard that until eight years later. Rod never told me. It really hurt my feelings.

But there was a germ of truth, which was, yes, I was lucky to have a job. Here I was, working at an exciting computer start-up, and I had zero background. Of course, neither Woz nor Jobs had an engineering degree, but they did have rich backgrounds. They had been doing electronics projects all through high school. So they knew what they were doing. I had no idea what I was doing.

Bob - Woz gave away a decent amount of stock to employees in similar situations. Is that true? Were you around for that?

Dan - It was called the Woz Plan. In 1980, what he did is he took a block of his stock of some thousands of share—fifty thousand shares—and decided he was going to spread it as an extra bonus to all the engineers, of which there were now one hundred. We had the Apple III project, we had the Lisa project, there was a lot going on. As an hourly technician, I wasn't eligible for a stock option, and I also wasn't eligible for the Woz Plan. The only people who were eligible were people who were already engineers.

Woz made a big list, and I knew I wasn't on the list. All the people I worked with were on this list. And I felt bad indeed. But of course Jobs was my friend, not Woz. That was the time where Jobs would not talk to me. Jobs did not approve of the Woz Plan. I was just left out in the cold. All this was before the IPO. At the last minute, I went to Mike Markkula and Mike Scott and just begged them to give me something. They did write me a stock option for one thousand shares, which was the standard option for engineers. So that was a nice gesture. The problem was at that point the stock had already been growing very fast for a year. And it split five times. Every time it split, it doubled. I got one thousand shares, but everyone else already had thirty-two thousand shares.

Then what happened was Apple went public at twenty. So if you had one thousand shares at twenty, that's worth twenty thousand dollars. That's a big bonus. Meanwhile, everyone else had thirty-two thousand shares at twenty. And then the stock price went up to thirty, which is a million dollars. When Apple went public there were one hundred millionaires. That's how that math worked. People who were fresh out of school all got one thousand shares. The more senior guys got two thousand or more. The stock options split five times, so the minimum people had were thirty-two thousand shares. Within a week the stock price went to thirty. So thirty-two times thirty, there were one hundred millionaires.

It was historic. And I had my little twenty thousand dollar bonus. And in those days, in order to buy the stock you had to pay the tax up front. You had to sell one third of it because there was a thirty-five percent tax bracket for capital gains in those days. Just to exercise the option, I had to sell one third of my one thousand shares, and pay tax up front.

Bob - Do you still have any of it?

Dan - No. The salary I was making at Apple just paid my bills. Being an up-and-coming computer person, I was buying electronics stuff. I have all the stuff I bought, but I never had money. I never had a savings account. I probably sold almost all of that first option within the next couple of years. I think I bought a synthesizer (a keyboard instrument).

Anyway, in 1981, not long before Woz's plane crash, Woz made a stock gift to me and half a dozen other guys who didn't have stock options. I wasn't the only one, there were half a dozen of us. And the list was Randy Wigginton, Chris Espinosa, Bill Fernandez, me, and Cliff and Dick Huston. Cliff and Dick Huston didn't have engineering degrees. They actually knew computers and they were doing good work. Randy and Chris were the high school kids. They didn't have stock options. Bill Fernandez had left the company because he found out he wasn't going to get a stock option and he said, "Screw this, I'm out of here." So, Woz was going to give a modest gift to all of us. Which, again, was only one thousand shares. It was worth fifty thousand dollars. And then what happened was he had a plane crash. He almost died, and nothing happened. We didn't know if we were ever going to get that gift.

Two years later, in fact it was '84, I finally got a call from Woz's dad, Jerry. He said Woz had amnesia, but Jerry was carrying out Woz's affairs, and the gift went through. I can say it made all the difference in my life. I wouldn't have had any money. The stock option didn't have anything to do with me leaving Apple. I could pay my rent easily by getting consulting work. But in 1986 is when that big house came along. And so I sold seventy thousand dollars' worth of the stock to make the down payment on this big house. And then, when I sold my share, later I made one hundred thousand dollars profit and that was my down payment for this house here, the house I live in now, which is worth 1.8 million.

It was the seed money of that stock gift that got me started in real estate. And I've made a lot more money in real estate than I've ever made in high technology. So, I'll eternally be grateful to Woz for that. And yeah, I think Randy and Chris Espinosa both stayed at Apple. I assume they also got stock options, but I don't know. I'd be quite certain that Randy got some kind of a stock bonus for having worked with Woz on the operating system. Bill Fernandez came back later to work on the Mac project. He probably got a stock option when he came back. I never did, because I was leaving Apple, and not coming back.

Cliff and Dick Huston both had Apple-1's and they sold them. They didn't invest in real estate, so they're kind of like hurting for money now. I helped both of them by writing a certification of, what do you call it, 'provenance?' Dick came over and had me write a certificate, "I was the first Apple employee and I can testify this is an Apple-1."

Bob - You said you and Jobs didn't talk for fifteen years. What finally made him come around?

Dan - Well, he didn't come around, really. What happened was—now we're talking about four years ago—in 2008. Albert Hoffman, the guy who invented LSD, was looking for people to donate money for LSD research. Albert Hoffman was a hundred years old, he's dead now. But because Steve over the years had made comments about how LSD helped his creative process, I heard through other people that Albert Hoffman had written a personal letter to Steve Jobs. This letter couldn't be sent to Apple. I don't know Steve's home address—I know where his house is, but I don't know his street address—and I volunteered to deliver it, thinking that, 'Well, at least I can help.' Albert Hoffman was a famous guy so I thought Steve might appreciate that gesture of getting this personal letter. I wrote Steve an email and I introduced him to Rick Doblin (president of the Multi-disciplinary Association for Psychedelic Studies), who put Hoffman up to writing the letter. So, anyway, that kind of broke the ice. And then, at some point, Steve replied to my email. A few months later he actually called me up and we had a little chat. That was three years ago. I kind of doubt he ever donated any money. But if he had, it would have been secret.

During the summer of 2012 , Kottke acted as a consultant for the Steve Jobs biopic starring Ashton Kutcher.

Bob - How was Los Angeles and the movie set?

Dan - Great. A great experience. Except Ashton wouldn't talk to me. He was in character. Steve Jobs wouldn't talk to me either. So I guess that was, you know, consistent.

Bob - There was an item on the official website about actually being at the house in Los Altos.

Dan - Yeah, they did filming there. I took them there the first time.

Chapter 18

Well-Kept Secret

We continued to try and catch up with friends of Steve's who worked for Apple in the house and garage. We were especially excited to speak with Elizabeth Holmes in July 2012 because we knew she had been the company's first bookkeeper. That meant she might recall Charles Ricketts. It was interesting to hear her story, but she wasn't able to help us regarding Ricketts.

Elizabeth Holmes - I arrived at Reed College in August of 1972. That's pretty close to forty years ago now. It was a different time and place. Reed was considered West Coast Ivy League. It was a small liberal arts college. A lot of remarkable people ended up there. And it's very small. There's like three hundred students per class; so there's about twelve hundred people on the campus. Well-qualified professors.

We were just coming out of the late '60s, into the early '70s, and it was a time of real cultural upheaval, particularly on the West Coast. Even though Reed is in Portland, it's close enough to the San Francisco scene where there was a lot going on. But anyway, the point is that Steve Jobs and I were from the same neck of the woods. It's now called Silicon Valley. But when we grew up there, it was all fruit orchards and farming communities. You know, my father worked for IBM, so there was a tech community there.

I was very familiar with it because I grew up with it. We had a modem in our house back in the late sixties and early seventies, because my father would work on the computer way over in San Jose, from Saratoga. Anyway, the point is I was very comfortable with high-tech because I'd grown up with it. Steve and I met on the Reed College campus when we were both seventeen-years-old. We'd both graduated from high school a year early. So we were with kids who were a lot older then we were, which makes a difference when you're in your late teens. And Reed tended to attract eccentric loners. They were wonderfully intelligent people, but they weren't always socially as adept.

It made for a funny kind of social atmosphere at Reed, because people were often into very unique and narrow interests. Also, it was a time of recreational drugs. There were a lot of recreational drugs being used on the campus. That was just part of the culture of young people in those years. And there was a lot of free love. There was a lot of sexual experimentation. I think, in some ways before the AIDS epidemic, there was a lot more casual sex. I think people became more aware of the dangers of that as the years rolled by. Friendships in that circumstance tended to be what young persons' experience now, which is your first experience of living away from home, and finding out what the world's all about. At the Reed College campus it all happened in an atmosphere of real permission to do...

Bob - ... An intellectual investigation?

170

Elizabeth - Oh, absolutely. In the Reed method of teaching, the classes were very small roundtable discussions, and there was a close ratio between the number of students and teachers; it was amazingly stimulating. They used, I think they call it, the Oxford Method, where they take the classic humanities—starting with Homer and the Greek tradition—and then they move forward through the Greek playwrights, into Shakespeare, and so forth. We had a pretty classic education in terms of the literature that we were exposed to, and expected to know thoroughly, in the humanities classes. You took basic courses, the basic undergraduate curriculum in the first couple of years at Reed. Then, go into whatever your specialty is, and write a thesis. All of which is unusual for an undergraduate program.

The sports palace on campus had just been built a few years before, which featured a beautiful indoor pool, and there was a dance and theater area. Of course, in other parts of the campus, there was a large calligraphy studio; there was a place to make ceramics; there was one whole dorm of former faculty housing that had been turned into art studios for the students. Each student had one of the old bedrooms in the house converted into their art studio. So creativity was highly encouraged. The art studios were cheek-by-jowl with the science buildings; biology and physics and chemistry.

I was a psychology major. The reason I chose Reed was, it was one of two colleges that I was able to find in the United States that offered Ethology—animal behavior studies—to undergraduates. I'd have to either attend Reed, or the University of Michigan. Reed was closer to home, and my parents were happier to have me nearby. So, that's how I ended up there.

I grew up in Saratoga, California. I used to ride my bicycle over to Steve's house during the summer that the computers were being made. I soldered the first chips on the first circuit boards because I had taken jewelry classes at Saratoga High School. I'd learned how to use a

171

soldering iron, and a welding torch, and the saws, everything. I'd polished gemstones. So, I had the fine motor skills, and I was sort of fearless about anything to do with technology. But that didn't last long, because after slopping a bit of flux around on the board, Steve said, "I think we're not going to have you do this, because I don't have any extra materials. If you make a mistake we're going to be in trouble, here. Let's have you do something else."

After the flux incident, Steve said, "How about if you do our bookkeeping?" It was a paper spreadsheet. I sat at the Jobs family kitchen table with a plug-in calculator and I'd tally the money that came in, and the money that went out. It was very simple at that point. For about a year after that, maybe two years, I came down on a periodic basis, once a month, or every two months.

I lived in Sausalito at the time, and I'd drive down the peninsula and come over to Steve's house. Of course I'd visit my family, and then spend the afternoon at his dining room table.

I was working in the summer of 1976. June, July, maybe a little bit into August in 1976 in Steve's garage. Let me just give you a sense of what it was like. This was a family home. Steve's nephew, Patty's son, was being bathed in the sink by Clara, by Steve's mom. His dad would be watching television, and Steve would come in and say, "Can we use the TV as a monitor, we need to check something." So, they'd unplug the TV and use it as a monitor. You know, it all happened in the context of a family.

We'd go into the Jobs family backyard, and we'd sit around, and Daniel Kottke would play the guitar, and we'd sing folk songs. Steve was very interested in alternative diets at that time. As I recall, there was a copy of Arnold Ehret's *Mucusless Diet Healing System* on the counter, about how to eat food that didn't create mucus in your body.

It was really family life. But Steve, and Steve Wozniak when he'd come in after work, would work well into the evening. I'd usually arrive late morning and leave in the late afternoon.

Bob - What was the personal dynamic of the group, from your perspective?

Elizabeth - Well, part of it was the gender difference. I really didn't understand what was going on there. Also I was a girl, you know, and it was kind of a boy's club. So, that, for me, made it difficult to really feel like I was part of the technology of it. That was okay with me, because my impression of what was happening at the time. The way I'd grown up, as the daughter of an IBM-er, I thought of computers as appliances. I thought that the work that my father did was making big appliances, like refrigerators. And I thought of the work that was being done there, in the Jobs' house as little appliances, like toasters.

Bob - Back then, calculators themselves were considered pretty exotic.

Elizabeth - Right, well, the calculator I used wasn't even one of the hand-held, battery operated ones. As I recall, it was one of the mechanical ones. My brother was really excited about the Hewlett Packard scientific calculators that came out in 1972, or 1973. Those were very elaborate.

Yeah, anyway in terms of the personalities involved, I knew Steve for thirty-nine years. We remained friends his entire life. We stayed in touch by phone most of the time. I was invited to major events in his life, his birthdays, and openings, and things like that. He shared the family side of his life with me. The things that made him smile. I made a decision early on that I didn't want to work for Apple. I recognized that Steve had a driven and sometimes abrasive personality. And I wanted him to be a friend, not as an employer. That was part of the reason that I backed away.

And in terms of the early personalities, Daniel and I were live-together lovers for almost four years. It's hard for me to be objective about his personality, other than to say that Daniel's an accomplished musician, and he has an amazing capacity for concentration. Those skills segued beautifully into working as a computer engineer.

Bob - He said he was good at that period, though not as an engineer as much as a technician. Later on, he had a better understanding of process and design, and he was able to move into things more fully.

Elizabeth - I'm sure that's true. He and I, just before we got to California that summer, had been living on the Upper West Side, 112th and Broadway in New York. He was going to Columbia University as a music major. We drove across the country and ended up at my parent's house. And that's how we happened to connect with Steve that summer, because Steve was only a few miles away. And as I said, I used to ride my bike over.

Bob - Dan indicated that he wanted to know what was going on, but he couldn't really understand Woz's thought process.

Elizabeth - You know, I can't speak to that. I will say that Daniel was a tinkerer, and he had amazing powers of concentration. He'd observe something until he understood how it worked. That served him well in terms of being able to observe and learn. Also, you need to understand here, the difference between being twenty one, which is what we were, and Woz who was maybe twenty-three, and at that point had been in the work world for many years. I was used to my dad coming home from IBM every day, and Steve Wozniak seemed like somebody close to my age who was in the high-tech world. So I was comfortable with him on both levels; in that he was a peer, and also in the more formal world of high-tech commerce in Silicon Valley. He seemed just way more professional, and way more focused.

Bob - Back to you, did you follow up on accounting as a career thing?

Elizabeth - I did. Early Apple was my first exposure to bookkeeping. You know, I mean there's nothing quite like having the first thing that you do turn into something amazing. Steve said something to me about six years after that. It was probably the early '80s, maybe '82. I was visiting him in his home. As we were parting company, he leaned across the hood of his car and he said—I was working in the Pyramid Building in the financial district in San Francisco for a big CPA firm at this point, and I was talking about what it was like to be in business—and he leaned against the hood of the car and said, "You know, business is a well-kept secret. I had no idea it was going to be this much fun." So, he was having a ball. On some level, he'd entered a world where he had opportunities and influence, and was able to express his creativity in an amazing way.

Bob - How do you evolve from a bookkeeper to a voice artist, doing books on tape?

Elizabeth - Have you ever seen the movie *The Producers*? Remember the scene at Whitehall & Marks, with all the people toiling over their desks, singing the song "Unhappy, unhappy?" There's a certain repetitiveness to the kind of work that I do. One of the ways that I've coped with that is to listen to books on tape. Now, of course, it's audiobooks on an MP3 player. But the point is, I've listened to over a thousand of them, and at some point I thought, 'Okay, maybe I could do this, too.' I started looking in to that about four years ago and never looked back, and now I'm doing that as well.

I have another detail to suggest about something you may not know. When Steven and Daniel came back from India, Daniel came pretty much straight home. Steve went through Switzerland to visit Marcel Muller, who was a multi-millionaire; his area of expertise was metric nuts and bolts. I think he pretty much cornered the market in Europe. Steve's exposure to people like Marcel, and our friend Robert Friedland, from Reed College, influenced his ability to see the bigger picture in terms of something everyone would use, and make it available. My point is, he didn't assume limitation. He'd seen things on a large and successful scale, so he had the ability to imagine that possibility.

175

Another thing that used to happen after our work day, we'd drop our tools and go over the Zen teacher Koben's studio, and we'd sit and meditate with him. And that was very much a part of it. Our spiritual practice was very, very important. (In fact, that's why I left. I left to join a religious community.) We'd spend an evening or an afternoon sitting in meditation. With Koben. Koben was an accomplished Zen Buddist practitioner and teacher. I'm not sure what his title was, I'm not sure if he was a roshi, but in any event he taught us. He'd sit on a dais, a few steps up from us, and we'd sit on the floor on cushions. It was part of the way that we refreshed and regrouped, because that work involved tremendous long hours of concentration and frustration.

I do remember, early on in the production of the computers, that Steve wanted to put wooden consoles on them, and he was looking into getting Hawaiian Koa wood. Again, it's like, when this stuff is happening, you don't realize where it's going. This was a summer job when I was twenty one. Think back to *your* summer job when you were twenty-one. The details of it stick in my mind only because of the people who were there and relationships I had with them.

Chapter 19

The Loan

Allen Baum was there in the very beginning, a high school classmate of Wozniak's. Also, we hoped he might know of Ricketts, especially since his dad loaned Apple their first funds to get the company going.

Allen Baum - I met Steve Wozniak when I was in high school, and he was two years ahead of me. I think his homeroom was the library. I was in the library one morning, and I saw this guy drawing these weird pictures on a piece of paper. I went up to him and said, "What are you doing?" He said, "Oh, I'm designing a computer." And he had pages full of *nand gates* and things, and that's literally what he was doing. He had a manual for a Verian 620i; I have a copy of that manual right here. And he was using that to try to essentially replicate it with whatever IT he thought he could get a hold of, mostly simple nand gates and things. And I said, "Wow, that's really cool. I want to do that." Which is why I ended up designing computers.

Nobody was thinking about computers in those days except for Steve Wozniak. There wasn't any access to computers. They did put a timeshare terminal at the high school, and I was signed up to use it. I taught myself *BASIC* real quick. And then the seniors just dominated it, and I never got a chance to play with it. It was there for like a week or two. I think the seniors used so much computer time that the school yanked it out. I didn't even go looking for any other people that were interested in computers. I certainly didn't know any others.

After that, somebody's father arranged for a bunch of students—it might have been as many as eight—to come to wherever they worked to use the computer there. I believe it was an IBM 1620, so I programmed my first little *FORTRAN* program. And then even later, somebody's father arranged for Steve Wozniak and I to have access to an IBM 1130 at Philco in Sunnyvale. They were a defense contractor. We got permission to leave school once a week to go over there for a few hours and play with computers.

Now Steve Jobs, I have to remember exactly... It was either Steve Wozniak or Bill Fernandez that introduced us. Bill Fernandez lived across the street from Steve Wozniak. I was trying to fix my car, I had this weird car. I needed to take the steering wheel off, and I needed an inch-and-a-quarter socket. And it's like, 'Where the hell am I going to get an inch and a quarter socket?' That's not a standard size. Bill Fernandez or Wozniak said, "Oh, I have this friend and his father rebuilds cars for a hobby. He'll have all these tools." So I went over there and he lent it to me, and that's how I met Steve Jobs.

Was I a sophomore or junior? Another interesting connection there. When I was in at school, I wanted to get a summer job, so I applied to HP. At the same time there was this co-op program at HP that I applied for. What happened was I got a summer job offer from HP, and I said I want to hold off because I wanted to see about the co-op program. And then I got an offer from HP for the co-op program, from exactly the same group. So I went to work for HP labs. My first job was to programming the HP Micro45 Calculator, microprogram it. I was hired by Tom Whitney, who went on to become engineering manager, or something. The next summer when I worked for that division, they were still doing calculators, but now they were sort of a calculator division. I worked for them for the summer, down in Cupertino. That was in one of the buildings that Apple has now bought, by the way. I mentioned I knew this guy who designs computers, and they said to pass him over this way. So that's how Steve Wozniak got his job at HP designing calculators. Tom Whitney was then later hired to be engineer manager at Apple, I guess because Steve Wozniak knew him.

I was at the People's Computer Company. I dropped by there because I'd heard about it and it sounded interesting. And they had a whole book shelf of science fiction, and I was a pretty avid science fiction reader. They had one particular book that I wanted to read, so I sat there and read it. I then recall seeing a flier on a telephone pole, which was right outside the PCC building. It said, you ought to come to this Homebrew Computer Club meeting. I told Steve Wozniak about it, and said we should go to this. And that's how we ended up there.

Bob - So your dad lent money for Apple to get started, was he the type of guy who'd normally do that kind of thing?

Allen - Nope. Absolutely not. He was out of work, too. He was just not doing anything. He had the money, and I asked him if he'd lend it. I actually don't remember if we both lent them the money. I think we both did. It was an outrageous interest rate. It was like ten percent. I think that was high at the time. I had a house loan just right around then, and it was like seven and a quarter percent. So, I guess it wasn't too outrageous. It wasn't supposed to be a short-term loan. As it was, they repaid it very quickly. Rather than in a year, they repaid it in a couple of months.

Bob - Did you consider the loan risky?

Allen - Somewhere in between. We expected that they'd sell all the computers, and we'd at least get the principle back, if not the interest. I don't know what my father was thinking. And I was, of course, young and naïve. I was a Homebrew Computer Club member, so I thought this was like a no-brainer.

Bob - Was there an option to convert the loan to stock?

179

Allen - No. I'm not even sure there was any stock. There was no Apple Computer, Inc. then. No corporation. Just a couple of guys in a garage. For the time, five thousand dollars was a significant chunk.

Bob - You have an Apple-1. I don't see you on the registry list of current owners.

Allen - No, probably not. It's been sitting in a closet. It was actually probably my father's. My father, who was an engineer, was Apple employee number 34. He should've been Apple employee 12, but he waited for six months and worked as a contractor before he actually became a full-time employee. This way he could say that he had no preexisting conditions. So, he was there really, really early.

He had health problems. He'd had a heart attack, and was laid off from the company he was with. When he finally got a job with another company, the first day on the job he got appendicitis. And he was laid off from that. So, he was just, you know, frantic and bored. He approached Apple, and said, "Hey, you guys. Need any help with anything? Let me know. I'm not doing anything."

To his surprise, they actually hired him. He wasn't expecting that. He was basically doing technician's work at Apple. A lot of testing.

One of his bosses said later on, "Hey, you have a job here for the rest of your life." He was sort of a father figure, he'd been there longer than just about anybody. And he was the oldest employee except for perhaps one other person. Basically, John Sculley gave him his fifteen year pin on his deathbed. He got to work for the rest of his life. He got to work with a bunch of young guys... I mean, he would have died a lot sooner if it weren't for that.

Bob - Wasn't there a time when you, your dad *and* your brother all worked there?

Allen - Yup.

Bob -You started at about the time that Steve Jobs left, and your term ended at about the time he came back?

Allen - Yeah, I was actually offered a job at Apple way in the beginning. It was the guy that hired me at HP, whom Apple hired to run the engineering division, but I didn't like the offer. What I didn't like is, Steve Jobs said, "Oh, yeah, you'd get this much stock." But when the offer came in, it wasn't anywhere near that. So I was just, '*Ehhh*.' I stayed at HP. My interest was designing CPUs, and that's where I could get to do it, at HP. I couldn't do that at Apple until I actually joined them at a later date, which is the reason I ultimately joined Apple.

My brother Peter was also an engineer, and he worked on the Apple][e. Eventually, he became a developer and tech support guy. He taught developers, and how to design memory cards and things. We actually had a little consulting company, and we designed memory cards for the Apple][e, which was the most popular one there was, I think. He worked there until *he* had a heart attack. He's now permanently disabled. He has no short-term memory. So, he just can't do that work anymore. But he's on sort of permanent disability from Apple.

Bob - Back to your Apple-1 that was your dad's, you have a friend that got one from the trade-in pile?

Allen - My father may have gotten this one from the stack, also. I'm not sure.

Bob - To the best of our knowledge, the only Apple-1's that are numbered in any way were sold by Byte Shop.

Allen - This one does have a number written on it in felt pen.

Bob - Do you remember what the number is?

Allen - I can go look. I think the one that my friend in Palo Alto has, also has something written on it. I gave it to him because I thought, 'What am I going to do with two of them?' So he has it. He had it in one of those wooden storage sheds in his backyard, in a box. He went into the shed and realized, 'Oh, my God, the rain's been in it.' So, he got it out. It was still in the original box, which was a bit damp. It was in a plastic bag *in* the box, so it was completely untouched. The transformer that it came

181

with—and probably the capacitors, I don't remember if they're mounted—no, I think it's just the bare transformer. It was very corroded. But everything else looks just pristine and new. His was an unloaded board. And the one I have is partially-loaded. But I may have done that long after the fact. The one I have didn't come with all the hard-to-get parts. The ROMs, the clock driver. Well, it certainly has everything else.

Bob - Was there some reason to take parts off of the trade-ins?

Allen - (Referring to his board) Wait a minute, what doesn't this have? Where are the ROMs on this thing? Maybe I just plugged them in there. I have a set of program ROMs now. There's a piece of tape on this with the numbers 4062. I don't see any numbers written on the back. Well, my retirement project, one of my *many* retirement projects, is to get it working.

Bob - I recognize that 4062 number. There are one or two others that have that same number.

Allen - By the way, there's another little taped-on number on the back of this one, just two digits... *82.*

Bob - Yup. There's other ones that have that number also.

Allen - Also have 82?

Bob - Yes, that's funny.

Allen - I see a little rubber stamp, like a quality check or something right next to that. Where'd it go? Yeah, there's a little round rubber stamp. And there's another one on the front, as well...somewhere I think. Yeah, a little rubber stamp right next to the power supply that says 6. Right next to the voltage regulator.

Bob - I think there's one or two that have that have the 6 or 7 like that, too.

Allen - I certainly can't see anything else.

Bob - So you originally had two, and one went to your friend. Would both have come from your dad?

Allen - Yeah. That's the only place they would have come from.

Bob - Because the only ones we've ever heard about coming from the trade-in pile were from the Huston brothers.

Allen - Oh, Dick Huston?

Bob - Your Apple-1 isn't in a box?

Allen - Oh, no. It's a bare board.

Bob - And the same for the one you passed on to the friend?

Allen - Yeah, that was also a bare board. His was an unloaded bare board.

I did have an Apple-1 that I actually used, way, way back when. That's how I developed the disassembler. This (the computer Baum is examining) might actually be one that worked.

Bob - Was that the Apple-1 you retained?

Allen - Yeah. It's been so long, I just don't remember. But I'm pretty sure I got this from my father.

Bob - So, you mentioned the disassembler and mini-assembler. Would Wozniak or Jobs have known you were good at that type of work?

Allen - Well no, actually. I was playing around with it, and I got frustrated trying to type in the hex, and not knowing if I got it right. I'm not as good a typist. Woz was an amazing typist. God, he was unbelievably fast and super-accurate. He'd put any secretary to shame. Oh, yeah. He was amazing. He could've been the best secretary in the world, because he typed faster than anybody I've ever seen, and more accurately. He used to sit at Homebrew Computer Club, during the first part of the session, and he'd type in *BASIC* from the hex. And that's, you know, 4K of hex or something. By the time the first session was finished, he was all loaded and he could demonstrate it. He could only do that because he could type that fast. At that point, there was no little cassette boards or anything. That's why he did the cassette board.

Bob - When you were working on the disassembler, you had the Apple-1?

Allen - Yeah. I was playing with the thing, and getting frustrated. So I went over to Steve's apartment and we looked at it, and he, of course, worked it over and saved a bunch of bytes: 50 to 56 bytes. A little bit later I said, "Well, why don't I just do an assembler?" The way I did the assemblers, I just tried every combination and ran it to see if it popped out with the same answer, and then I'd say, 'Okay, that's right.'

Bob - You did that at the garage or at your house?

Allen - I did that at my house. And then at Steve's apartment. I think that was the Valley Green Apartments.

Bob - And was that initially done on the Apple-1?

Allen - The disassembler, I'm pretty sure was the Apple-1. The assembler may have been done on an Apple][. I was not being paid for it. I was helping them out because they were my friends.

Steve Wozniak figured out all sorts of ways to squeeze out a byte here and a byte there so it all fit into 256 bytes, which was kind of a magic thing for a 6502.

Bob - They gave you a challenge and you said, 'I'll give that a go?'

Allen - No, it was mostly self-directed. I remember playing with it at home, and the display I was using was a GE nine inch black and white TV that Steve Jobs had drilled a hole in the back. He'd stuck in a BNC Connector, and wired it up to the right place on the TV to turn it in to a monitor. I think it was my TV. I bought it and brought it over there. He drilled the case, screwed in the connector and wired it into the right place on the TV, the inject signal.

He'd done that for a few GE TVs, because I guess they came with a schematic, and he could figure out where you could do it. He figured that out, or Steve Wozniak figured that out. But Steve Jobs was not afraid to use a soldering iron. He couldn't solder like Steve Wozniak, but nobody I know can.

Wozniak was an unbelievably good technician. I mean all the early boards were just hand-wired and soldered by hand, and they were works of art. They were amazing. If you look at his prototype boards, they're just gorgeous. Oh, yeah. They're just neat, clean, the soldering joints were perfect.

I was drawn to him because he knew how to design computers.

He was also really athletic. You wouldn't want to play tennis with him, that's for sure. He was a really good tennis player. He was quick, and really strong; he's built like a gorilla. Just all solid muscle. He'd break rackets when he hit the ball. Metal rackets even. He'd break the welds. If he hit it like on the base instead of on the strings, he'd just crack the welds.

He said he did pole-vaulting in high school, but he never practiced like the coach wanted him to, so eventually they just wanted him to go away.

Chapter 20

Byte

The Byte Shop computer store started with one location in Mountain View, and founder Paul Terrell grew the chain to a group of stores around the United States. Paul's order for fifty computers is considered the catalyst for the start of Apple. We spoke in September 2012.

Paul Terrell - Jobs and Wozniak had brought to the Homebrew Computer Club their Apple-1 circuit board. Originally they were just trying to sell the circuit board to all the hobbyists there. We were at the

Stanford Linear Accelerator auditorium, and just outside there was a little area there where people could set up, plug in things, and show them after the meeting. They had a prototype unit that they'd built up, and had it on display. So that's when I first approached the Steve's and saw the product. At that point, Jobs wanted to come over to the Byte Shop.

He came over the next day in the morning, and we sat down and talked about it. Basically, what I said was I want them assembled and tested. Because they were just trying to sell the boards to hobbyists. Quite honestly, I had computer kits coming out of my ears. I was really looking for something that was finished. There was a lot of interest in those days from the programming community. Guys that were into writing code and having something that worked. Unless they had a buddy of theirs that was an engineer that could build the hardware, they were out of luck. So, anyway that was the big thing, and the deal is that the two Steves were going to have to assemble and test the things, and deliver me completed circuit board units.

I don't remember ordering more than those fifty. What was happening at the same time is that when I first started the Byte Shops, I started them as a dealership program; it wasn't actually a franchise. So when I was signing these different stores up, they had the ability to purchase directly from suppliers as well. There wasn't anything like franchise requirements that require that you buy from them and so forth. The interests of the people that were opening these stores were so varied. Some of them were programmers, some of them were engineers, some actually left their jobs and went full-time into the store business, and some of them kept their present jobs and hired staff for when they were off working.

Probably what happened was, on the first fifty computers, we had enough units to sell to the store owners. And then the individual store owners—particularly the ones in the local area—were buying direct from suppliers as well. The other thing that was happening was that the manufacturers couldn't build their products fast enough. They actually didn't have the funding. All of those businesses in those days were just being bootstrapped, and getting your hands on inventory was a tough thing to do. You know, you'd show up at somebody's loading dock with cash and you could literally buy somebody else's order. That was something we used to do all the time. I had a van, and we'd just run over to the different companies, and the company wanted cash. It was better for them than waiting for a COD check to clear through UPS or whatever.

Like I say, I think with the fifty Apple-1's, they didn't all come in at once. They had to stagger it some. Since it was COD, I was paying them cash. Cash was king in those days. I don't recall any significant second order sort of thing. We just had one company-owned store, in Mountain View.

Bob Moody was the manager of the Byte Shop in Palo Alto, which was the next one north of me. He was actually closer to where Jobs and Wozniak were. He'd buy product direct from them. And as a matter of fact, he was one of my guys that found us a source for cabinets. There was somebody that was building them out of wood—they were kind of nice— walnut cabinets that we could put the circuit board, transformer, and keyboard into. There was a lot of that kind of thing back in that day. I'd have monthly meetings where I'd have all the Byte Shop guys get together, we'd get a conference room in a hotel, and we'd all come in and talk about what was going on and how things were going, what trends they were seeing, and so forth. They'd say, 'Hey, I found a great guy for keyboards,' or 'I found somebody that has black and white monitors,' because we were all on the phones trying to source products and all of this kind of stuff. That was the reason I made it a dealership rather than a franchise. I was getting as much information as the store owners. It wasn't where I was the biggest help at being able to source product, and get volume discounts for the group. Some of these guys would actually take a liking to Southwest Tech's 6800 base microprocessor product, and they'd be carrying that, be dealing them direct. I couldn't carry inventory for everybody under the sun. I was trying to be focused with people like Apple, and MITS, and Altair and the IMSAI.

Byte Shop number two was in Santa Clara, Byte Shop three was in Campbell County, California. Number four was Palo Alto. Then I was in Mountain View. So, we were all in vicinity, within miles of each other. I was actually warehousing inventory. I had an office in a warehouse space. We incorporated Byte Shops into Byte Incorporated, and Byte Inc. was headquartered on 1st Street in San Jose. And, so we would inventory the computers there, and ship to the different stores. I didn't sell to other retailers, like, for instance, Computer Store, or something like that.

I'd say that I sold maybe ten or fifteen Apple-1's out of my own store. It wasn't anything big. The next thing to happen, basically, was that Jobs and Woz showed up in the Mountain View store with the prototype of the Apple][. We had things in our store that they couldn't get their hands on, like our color monitors, so they'd actually come into our demo room for access to equipment that they couldn't afford themselves. A peripheral attachment, or a floppy disk drive, or something. They'd come in to the store and actually run tests, and work with my guys. So I knew that the Apple][was coming; I didn't want to get stuck with a bunch of the Apple-1's.

A lot of the follow-on developments for the Apple-1 had been done in the store there as well, because we had some of the peripherals and attachments, they could just hook up and make sure things worked. I remember that they were always tweaking things like their cassette interface; they'd micro-coded that, so Woz had to get access to different cassette recorders. Before Radio Shack got into the computer business, we were buying Radio Shack cassette recorders to run with these cassette storage computers. So, at any rate, yeah, we could see that all of the sudden the two Steves were coming in and they weren't putting together things to attach to the Apple-1 anymore. There was this new box, and it was the Apple][. And they, of course, were excited about it. Los Altos based Cromenco, actually, was the first to introduce color to that hobbyist community with their Dazzler card. The S-100 bus plugged in to an Altair and IMSAI. Jobs was very tuned-in to how attractive the color was to everybody, hobbyists as well as everyday people.

The best seller was not the Apple-1, it was the MITS Altair 800. The principle reason for that was that Bill Gates and Paul Allen had written the 40-K *BASIC*, and then the follow-on 8-K *BASIC*, and of course everybody at Homebrew was knocking it off. MITS had put a real high price tag on the *BASIC* software. That's one of the things that fed the piracy, everybody felt like they were being ripped-off, so it's okay to go ahead and make and distribute copies of the product.

Bob - You mean if you bought the machine, you'd get the software with it. But if you wanted it separately, you had to pay a premium for the software?

Paul - Exactly, that was their strategy at the time. That came back and bit them in the ass, I think. Eventually Gates conceded that, 'Hey, we've got to do something about this.' He was in Albuquerque, working in the back of the MITS facilities on a PDP-10 timeshare system. That's how they developed the *BASIC*. When I went down for meetings with MITS, I first met Bill and Paul, and saw what they were doing. Bill would write a little software article in the newsletter that MITS would distribute. They put out this little newspaper once a month. See, I was the exclusive sales rep for the MITS Altair in Northern California, Oregon, Washington, and Idaho.

That's why I was at the Homebrew Computer Club meetings. I was there telling the people what was going on at Altair and MITS, and what was going on with Gates and *BASIC*; all the developments. They'd ship me those newspapers, and I'd hand them out to people, put them on that table where the Apple-1 was being displayed, you know, that kind of thing. A part of the meeting was called 'Random Access,' which came from a term in memory devices. Lee Feldenstein usually directed the meetings from the auditorium stage, but they'd go into this 'Random Access' mode after he'd given his talk. And 'Question & Answer.' Everyone walked around and got together in little groups of twos and threes. If somebody got up and said something of interest, you'd go over and talk to them, and so forth. It was that kind of atmosphere.

Bob - Did you put inventory numbers on the back of the Apple-1 boards? There are numbers, in sequence and put on by a black marker, on some of the surviving boards and everybody seems to think they were put on by the Byte Shop as an inventory system.

Paul - No, that wasn't anything that I was involved in. That might have been in the manufacturing process. My suspicion would be that it was something they were doing before they actually shipped the product, keeping track of what was where, and what was going on. Or, even whose order they were building them for.

Bob - Everybody we've spoken to who was associated with Apple at that time says that they didn't do it, but it never occurred to me that it could've been the board manufacturer. The guys at Apple may just not have paid attention; the markings are nondescript. They're in sequence, and run from 01-0011 up to 01-0060. Obviously, *someone* intended it to be an expandable system.

Paul - Quite honestly, I'd *like* to say that I was that sophisticated, in those days, and had some kind of an inventory-control system in my warehouse. But like I said, as soon as you got these things in, they're gone. There were guys waiting with their hands out for the next shipment. And so, new product would just bounce off my floor going out to another store.

Bob - Would there be any kind of surviving sales record?

Paul - No, again, we weren't that sophisticated in what we were doing. We had no *point of sale* systems. I actually had a Scientific Data Systems 940 mainframe computer on display, a huge thing sitting over in the corner. And my cash register was an antique that didn't even print paper. It was *cling* and *clang*, and so forth. We just used those little pads of receipts, fifty to a book, and that's how we were running the business. So they'd have receipt in their hand, walking out the door. I'm sure that I have no records of that.

You know the one guy that would know something in terms of the Byte Shop and Apple relationship was Bob Moody. He was a originally a neighbor of mine, in San Jose, and our families were friends. I hired Bob when I started the Byte Shop, to manage the first store. He managed Byte Shop number one. Then a guy from Lockheed wanted to open a store. He was pretty high-up in management in Lockheed Missiles and Space, and he didn't want to give up his job. He wanted to retire with Lockheed, but he wanted a store. I introduced Bob Moody to him, and Bob left me. I hired another guy for the Mountain View store, and Bob opened up the Byte Shop in Palo Alto for this guy from Lockheed.

He was probably the first guy—my Byte Shop people—that was sourcing directly out of my warehouse. And it was with the Apple guys. He was so close to Apple in Palo Alto. He was the one that found the guy that would build the wooden cases, and then I was buying them.

I'd think Moody would have more of that direct contact type of thing. As far as I was concerned, I was more into expanding the stores, and building a franchised operation, than I was in actual contact with customers. I actually spent a lot of time at the Mountain View store, and I met a lot of people. A lot of these guys would kind of hang out there. Stanford only let us have the auditorium once a month, so they needed other places to go.

I used to go to all the trade shows, the National Computer Conference and these big shows. One of the statements I made at the time was, "Hey, this Byte Shop thing, this is a trade show that's going on three hundred and sixty-five days a year, right in your town." That's what these computer stores represent. So, people would come by the store and they'd want new products, they'd buy the magazines, because you couldn't even get a *Byte Magazine* on a newsstand. We became the focus in the community for any computer interest, whether it was from the university, or business types, or whatever. Though, those machines didn't do much for business until the Apple][came out, and they put *VisiCalc* on it, and then we started to get more serious. Up until that time it was more of a hobby deal, of course, with video games as well.

Bob - Was the magazine yours?

Paul -It's interesting you say that, because that's exactly why I called the Byte Shops *Byte Shops*. I'd gotten a copy of *Byte Magazine*, the first issue that came out, and I was reading this thing. I said to my partner, Boyd Wilson, "Boyd, this thing is going to be big. This *Byte Magazine* deal." I said I think we ought to do some stores, and we ought to call them Byte Shops, and everybody will think that we own the magazine, too. We had named our corporation Byte Incorporated. Downstream, years later, we finally did have an issue with McGraw-Hill and Byte. McGraw-Hill had bought them. We'd had a really good relationship with the original owners.

I displayed *Byte Magazines* in my store, and I was talking about them being the family jewels behind glass, so they did an ad that they ran in the magazine. What I did every month, after the current issue was out of print, was jack the price up a dollar. So, you were paying more for the older issues than for the current issue. And they thought that was kind of clever. They did an ad that said "Hey, you ought to buy our magazines because they're going to get nothing but more expensive."

At this point, I mentioned that Joe Copson had purchased his Apple-1 from the Byte Shop and it had been shipped to him.

Paul - An interesting sideline to that, was that I actually did mail a computer to an individual from the Byte Shop. I think I might even have that photo, I'll have to go back and see if I've got that, and see if that was his name. Because my lawyers wanted me to have proof of use of the mark *Byte Shop*. I shipped somebody a computer, and took a photograph of the box and label as proof of the Byte Shop mark. That's how we registered our trademark.

I put that photograph on a piece of cardboard, and later somebody wanted it. It might have been when they were doing the *Apple][Forever* theme at the Moscone Center, when they launched the Apple][c. I got a call from Jobs, and he wanted me to come down to the Mac building, and have an interview with me and Wozniak. The marketing people were putting together this big launch. They did a film on the old days. I lived right there in Saratoga, so I drove on down to Cupertino, and the three of us got together in this room. The most memorable thing for me from that meeting, was, you know, Steve had quite an ego. So at any rate, it was funny that in this meeting on tape, Steve Jobs actually admitted to me that if I hadn't forced him into assembling and testing the Apple-1, that they would've never have made it. It wasn't his idea, it was mine...and I was pushing him to do it. And of course Woz was right there. You know, you might not think of it at the time as being such a big deal. But I obviously had my own agenda. Here I was, the exclusive sales rep for the MITS Altair, and that was coming to me in a kit form and pieces, and I was desperately trying to get assembled and tested stuff.

My sales rep was calling on the Department of Water Resources in Sacramento, the ramp controller guys over there, and the transportation department. We're looking for some serious microcomputer applications, serious computers were needed. And these guys kept sending us *kits*. So we had a little manufacturing operation going on in our demo room. Customers would come in, they'd buy something, and then all the sudden—they were a technician over at National Semiconductor, or something—now we're putting them to work in the evenings.

As I said, the Byte Shops became hang-outs for people between Homebrew Club meetings. Well, this was the other thing that was going on. We had guys there actually doing the assembly because they *were* technicians, soldering stuff in the demo room and, you know, the whole thing. Things were being built, demonstrated there, and engineered there. Woz and Steve Jobs came down quite often to that environment, to get their hands on peripherals and stuff that we had that they didn't.

I brought up the subject of boxes for the Apple-1.

Paul -They were in so many shapes and sizes. One of the things that I really hadn't thought about when I made my demands on Steve, when buying those first fifty units, was the fact that the power transformer and keyboard were not included in it. We had to go out and source those things as well; a lot of the store owners took that on themselves. I believe it was Keytronics was the company that made the keyboard. When you bought an Apple-1, you had to buy the power transformers, the keyboard, and you had to source a case.

It was still a kit. It was for programmers. And all of the sudden the first Apple delivery shows up, and I said, "My God, what have I done?" I've got to do all of this. And once again, it was one of the things that kept my relationship with Steve going, was because, "Jesus, now I've got a real problem. Twenty-five thousand dollars' worth of these things showed up, and I paid you cash, and I can't sell one of them without buying keyboards and transformers." I remember having that conversation with him. It was kind of like, 'I got you!' Okay.

Bob - You paid five hundred dollars each, how did they end up priced at $666.?

Paul -I told Steve my deal for the Altair MITS computer, was the dealers were getting twenty five percent off from Altair MITS. Then what happened is—when I talked Ed Roberts into doing the sales rep thing, and he started hiring reps, we got five percent on top of that. So basically, the discount needed to be at least thirty percent. So that's what I told him that we were gonna do. I said, I've got to have some markup in here. In my case, it was a two-step distribution. I was the wholesaler for them, so I wanted to make at least five percent, and the retailers, the store dealers, needed to get twenty-five percent. That was my instructions to him in terms of pricing and what we were going to do.

Then, I cut my purchase order to him for five hundred bucks apiece for fifty of them. And so, that's what we did; that was the Byte Shop program. I've heard stories too, about, 'it was in integer thing...' I've heard all these different variations. But the conversation between he and I was very clear cut. It was "Steve, here's what I'm going to do, okay?" And, I'll give you five hundred bucks for these things assembled and tested. I also had to consider the other computers that I was carrying. Not that a 6502 microcomputer was necessarily a competitor to an 8800, or you know, an Intel chip, but that was where we established the pricing. Those were crazy days.

The other thing, of course, was the store guys. The different Byte Shops, they'd have established their own pricing. Once again you had to source a case a transformer, the whole deal. As I was telling you before, with these other kits, we were buying these kits by Altair, and putting them together ourselves in the stores, you know, and having to say we could deliver an assembled, tested unit. Whatever that markup was, you negotiate according to that customer.

Some sort of uniform retail pricing wasn't on anybody's mind, whatsoever. I think probably most of them that we sold were probably like $999., or something like that, out the door. You know, in a case, with a cassette of the *BASIC*. Because we were trying to do *systems*. Really, in those days, by the time you put a computer together so that you could actually use it and program it, you were looking at over a thousand dollars. Nobody was producing anything under a thousand dollars by the time you got done with a monitor, keyboard, and cassette, you know, everything you needed to actually run the thing. That's why Commodore made such a hit with their Commodore PET, at the price point of five hundred bucks. Like, *wow*, this is incredible. So, obviously Apple had to have some number for just the PC board itself. What they were shipping and the price listed in their ads.

Bob - So that's where the $666. came from.

Paul - Yeah, and how Jobs derived it, whether he was going off of my mathematics, or whether it was some kind of a magic number... I think I even heard that it was Woz's number, or something. It wasn't necessarily Steve's.

Chapter 21

Sputnik

An Apple-1 computer showed up for sale on eBay in December, 2011. The eBay listing read:

"Original Apple-1 Computer made and purchased in 1976. A keyboard that was used with it will be included. Also, a copy of the owner's manual signed by Woz. Special courier delivery and payment arrangements - contact by email through *eBay*. No shipping fee. Joe Copson nameplate for viewing - not included in sale. Will provide a copy of his resume with Apple, if requested. There is a serial number on the back of the computer

01-00##. In answer to all of your questions, it is a real original Apple-1 computer. Joseph Charles Copson worked for Atari and Apple as a programmer and troubleshooter. He worked with Michael Kisor, who was a senior software engineer with Apple - he collaborated with Joe on the diagnostic software for the Macintosh. Joe also worked on the Cray supercomputer. He loved technology and served his country in Vietnam, which may have eventually caused his death from cancer on 3-5-2003. He wrote the program for Atari games such as Star Raider, Spitfire on the Silver 1. Look up his name on Google under Atari Age. I would like this Apple-1 cared for as an American technological historical treasure. Not to be used but to be cared for. To remain in the United States. In that way it would truly honor Joseph Charles Copson Army USAR Control group - Fld Radio Mechanic 1971."

The seller had substituted "##" instead of providing the actual number sequence from the backside of the computer. The starting bid was listed as one hundred seventy-five thousand. It's usually better to offer an item on eBay with a low starting bid, because bidders like to start low. I believe it didn't sell because the starting price was too aggressive. Also, the seller did not give an explanation as to he or she was. Since Mr. Copson had passed away, who was now selling the Apple? When you're spending a couple hundred thousand dollars, it's nice to know who you're dealing with.

So I got in touch with the seller, and she turned out to be the ex-wife of Joe's brother. Brother Bill was proud to share the story of his older brother Joey:

Bob - Did you and your brother Joey have different interests?

Bill Copson - Oh, yeah. One hundred percent. Except for the college I went to, and the photography I got interested in, I probably learned more from him than all my schooling combined.

Why was he so intelligent? Who knows? I'll tell you, it's funny. Nobody ever even questioned that. Even when he was a kid, it used to blow my mind because adults would listen to him. You know, even though I was five years younger, I'd notice all these adults listening to him, to essentially a kid. It was unbelievable. Did I tell you the story about the first satellite going over?

Joey was nine or ten. I think it was 1957, and I'm pretty sure it was a Russian satellite. My brother knew about it when this stuff was happening, and it just happened that the satellite was passing over the part of Oregon where we lived. And so he spread the word around the neighborhood. "At such and such time, you've got to be outside to see it." The kids spread the word, and friends of mine told their parents.

And they said, "Well, how do you know this?"

"Well, Joey told me. Joey Copson."

"Oh, we'd better be out there."

And I remember standing—I was four, five years old—I remember standing there and thinking, 'How does he do this?' Here's a group of thirty people that are out here just because of something he said. And right to the minute, he goes, "There it is." I remember looking up and I'm thinking, 'Oh, my God, it's true,' and this bright object with no blinking lights goes shooting over, you know? I'm standing there thinking 'This is unbelievable.' I didn't *disbelieve* my brother, never.

After the satellite goes over, they're all asking him questions and he's answering them as best as he can. And then everybody goes inside, and that's a moment in time.

Joey was interested in any kind of esoteric subject. His interest in astronomy lasted pretty much his whole life, but he also got into chemistry and electronics. He would get into something and learn it, and

198

then move on. It was phenomenal. When I was a kid, I remember my mom would take him to the library. He'd drop off three to five big books, pick up three to five more, and that week at home he'd read all of them, and mom would take them all back the next Saturday.

He did that for like a decade. His brain could absorb so much stuff, it was just spooky. That started when I was a little kid in Portland, before I was even five, and it continued when we moved to Palo Alto. He might get an off-the-wall book sometimes, and say, "I just want to read this." Like when he was studying about electronics, they were electronics books. And he always would pick up something on astronomy.

It was a huge hobby for him. He was interested in astronomy all the way 'til the end. I mean, my dad took us bowling, but as for Joey's hobbies, he was into astronomy and chemistry. Well, to other people, that would be *learning* about something, but that was Joey's *hobby* for years. He didn't like going off and throwing darts. He didn't play Ping Pong. The bowling we did because we were little kids and our dad took us. All his hobbies had to do with learning more about stuff he just dug. When he first got into chemistry, he learned so much about it, it was unbelievable. Do you know what he did? He wanted to make little things *go boom!* And not just with the regular old fashioned ways of gun powder and stuff. Now, was he a terrorist? No. Did he like to blow some little shit up? Oh, yeah. But that's what got him into it, and he was into it for years and years. He went far past the spectrum of learning how to blow things up.

Moving to Palo Alto was a huge blessing, because the schools up in Portland weren't anything like the schools in Palo Alto. In Palo Alto they were teaching kindergarteners how to read.

My dad was in sales his whole life. He generally had two jobs, just to be able to afford to live where we lived. We weren't rich or anything, but he wanted us in a good neighborhood. Not that Portland wasn't, but Palo Alto is *Palo Alto*, you know? We didn't live in one of the big houses. I was in second grade when we moved to California. Joey was in seventh. For high school, we went to Palo Alto High. 'Paly.' He graduated the class of '69, and I graduated the class of '74.

Around seventh or eighth grade, they took Joey and the other 'brainiacs' in his class to a company in Mountain View called Spectro Physics. They got to build a laser with parts the company couldn't sell, but that could still function. So, Joey built a functioning laser, which was a big deal back then. I remember there were gas vacuum tubes, and there were these little tiny reflective mirrors on a round glass about a quarter-inch thick. The surface had to be perfect. Their quality control department looked at it with a micrometer. If there was one piece that wasn't perfect, then the company couldn't sell it. So, they used it with these kids, who had an instructor. I used to go over there. I went inside twice, and there was one room where they tested the lasers. They'd screwed up once and the laser ray had made actual holes in the wall. It was neat.

Chapter 22

Star Raiders

Bill Copson continues with his story about the life of his brother, Joey Copson.

Joseph Charles Copson's "Job History" from his resume:

U.S. Army, USAR Control Group, Field Radio Mechanic, Technician Jan 1970 to October1974, Vietnam tour of duty

Commodore Computer, Technician Calculators, November 1974 to December 1975

Programmed Power, Technician, January 1976 to February1979

Vindicator Corp, Programmer, March 1979 to March 1981

Atari Corp, Programmer, March 1981 to March 1984

Macromind, June 1990 to September 1990

Apple Computer, October 1990 to December 1991

Bill Copson - When Joey was eighteen, everybody was getting drafted right out of high school. So he got his numbers. I'll never forget that day. Oh, God, did that suck. He was 1-A, you know? And if you don't know what that means, that means you're going in. You're going in unless you only have one leg. The Armed Forces got all these results from high school. Remember when we were in high school, and they would do tests in gym class? How many pull-ups and how quick? Everybody's results were recorded, but they didn't seem to go anywhere. That's what went to the military. It would let them know what these boys and girls—well, *boys* back then—what they could do. You know, that's how they knew all that stuff. My brother told me, if they ever do that test at your high school, do really shitty. They came up in my junior year or sophomore year, and my coach just goes, "What the hell, three pull-ups? What's wrong?" And I said, "Ahh, I just don't..." "Four sit-ups?" Like, I ran the mile in twenty-one minutes.

When he got the draft notice, he just went in the bedroom and sat down. I looked at his face, and I was like, "Oh, shit. What's wrong?" And he just handed it to me. You know, he knew it was coming. All the guys were just scared as hell in those days. I mean, I just missed it by a little ways, thank God.

He went and talked to my dad. My dad and he weren't always really close, but when he needed my dad, he wasn't scared to go talk to him. And my dad's best buddy was retired military; he was an attorney for the Army. So my dad calls him up, and says, "Hey we need to ask your advice, my son just got his notice and he's 1-A." So, his friend said, "Does he want to go, or does he want to leave the country?" I remember my dad saying, "No, he's not going to Canada." A third of the people were. "He wants to go," and my dad's friend knew how smart my brother was. He said "He needs to go in and enlist." Because if you enlist, you'd get all kinds of advantages.

So, he went and enlisted. In boot camp, he was in charge of ten guys. Just because he enlisted. He had a great time in boot camp. He had a blast. I mean, he got tired, but he'd send me letters and call, and *Oh, my God*, they were having fun. But they busted their butts. And then, when he got out of boot camp, he stayed stateside for twelve more months, going to specialized schools for the military. And when he got to Viet Nam, as soon as he put his foot on soil, he was E-5 with combat pay, even though he wasn't a fighter. He was in an air-conditioned office. He worked something called Tailboard Controls; the helicopters would take off... (makes whirling sound effect) then they'd radio to him and give a password. He'd open up the safe and give them their orders. You know, exactly what they were supposed to do.

But he never could tell me more than that. And, he told me everything, so it was weird. The military got to him. It was on a 'need to know' basis with him.

I know he was exposed to Agent Orange and it later contributed to his death. Everybody in that whole region was exposed. My God, I mean the helicopters flew out of there to disperse it, you know? It was everywhere, even though he wasn't crawling on the jungle floor. Now, they might have been out in the jungle getting drunk and having fun, you know? And believe me, they got to have a lot of fun when they were out there.

And so Viet Nam gets over. And he left two days before they took over the Embassy, so everything over there was crazy. And his CO says, "Okay, you've got to go over to this base to get your records." Joey goes, "Well, why can't they just send them over?" Everybody's excited, "This is it! We're leaving!" My brother had to hitchhike over to this base and they gave him all his papers, *everything*, not just what they would've forwarded. He had twenty pounds of papers, you know? They just said, "Here, take it." Everybody was packing up and getting out of there.

So my brother comes home. He's got a month off. Well, a month goes by. My dad says to him, "Hey, wait a second. You're supposed to go back." Joey goes, "Ah, I don't think so." My dad's like, "*Whoa*, you can't do that." He collected pay for three months, going over to the base in Oakland. Then, finally, one of the guys at Oakland, a real cool dude, says, "Don't come back in here." So my brother said, "Okay." My brother was home for, I think it was nine or ten months, and his hair's getting longer. He's starting to get ready to look for a job. And I remember, we were eating potato chips and watching stupid afternoon TV. Then, there's a knock on the door, and I went towards the door. I look outside, and there's an MP Jeep. Then I head over to the front window and on the porch there was an MP with a rifle over his shoulder. I'm like, "Oh, Joey..." And he goes, "Well, open the door. Open the door."

So they come in. And they're real nice, and they go, "Are you Joseph Copson, blah, blah, blah..?" And he goes, "Yes, I am." And they say, "You've got to come with us." And he goes, "Yeah, no problem. Can I get my shaving kit?" Because if you're in the military, that's your one sole possession you keep around. And they go, "Yeah." And he gets his Army coat and he walks out the door. They don't handcuff him or anything. And he says, "You tell mom and dad that when I can, I'll give them a call." And I'm thinking, 'Oh, my God, here he's gonna be gone for twenty years, who knows?' I mean, like *right now*. I'm like freaking out. And mom and dad get home—of course, this is before cell phones—and I tell them, and I'm like, '*Oh, gosh!*' It was three weeks later when we got a call from him.

And Joey says, "Well, it's not *too* bad." And we're all like, "What do you mean? Where are you?" Well, all they did to him was put him at Fort Ord in Monterey Bay, for one month. And in the military if you're bad, they take money out of your paycheck, they scold you financially. And he did shit work, I mean absolute grunt work for a month, and he got a forty dollar paycheck for the month. He went to some base in Texas for the rest of the months he had to serve, and he got out with an honorable discharge. He had full benefits. So why would they allow somebody–a 'brainiac,' and also a big pot smoker and stuff–why would they treat him like that? I just wonder, *what did he know?*

Bob - I know Joey was self-taught. Did he use his military benefits to go to school and study computers?

Bill - Not one bit. No, he hated school. Let me explain it to you this way, one time he said... He kind of worded it like this, this was long time ago. I asked him, "Why didn't you go to more college?" And he said, "For me going to school, it's like, okay, this whole class teaches you how to swim, and after a half a day I'm doing laps. And now I've got to sit here for the rest of the year just to take these stupid tests to show that I know it." So, school was too slow for him. It was like reading the same comic book that you never even liked, and it's the fiftieth time you've read it. You know, it was something that if you had a choice, you wouldn't do it. That's where he was at. He didn't really even get fantastic grades because he never did his homework. And he'd take these tests and get perfect scores. The teachers hated him. They're like, 'You put no effort out.' So, he passed everything, but he wasn't a straight A student. Now, some teachers would realize that he was real smart, and liked him, and he liked them. But the other teachers, they just couldn't handle that crap. You know, 'You're not doing it the way that you're supposed to.' Well, screw that.

Bob - Do you know where he bought the Apple-1?

Bill - Yeah! He got it brand new from a shop down in San Jose called the Byte Shop. That's who he bought it through, but I'm almost sure it came to him via the mail, through a package, you know what I'm saying? I was there the day he opened it, and he was all excited about this green board with black chips. He's opening it up and I'm going, "Wow, this has got to be something really bitchin'." And he opens it up, *oh, wow!* But to him, he's almost bowing down to it, and I'm like, "What are you so excited for?"

It was something else! He was like a kid opening up the best present he ever got at Christmas. It was as if you got the BB gun you always wanted. I tell you, it was unbelievable.

I remember when the Apple][came out, and he was sitting there saying—and we were partying or something—and he was going, you know, "They'll give me a big discount if I trade in the Apple-1," and he goes, "No, I'm not going to." He goes, "I don't care, I'm keeping the Apple-1."

205

That's how come there's not as many Apple-1's. Apple did the typical thing they would do to this day. Bring in your Apple-1, we'll give you this much off your Apple][.

I don't remember what the dollars were, but my brother said, "Well, that's not worth it. Hell, I'll just go and buy an Apple][."

Bob - What do you think his motivation was to keep it?

Bill - Because he knew how unique it was. It's such a cornerstone of technology, you know?

Joey gets credit for being the Atari programmer who did the games Star Raiders *(Silver 1, 5200 System, 1982) and* Spitfire *(1983). In 2007, Star Raiders was named one of the ten most important video games of all time.*

Bob - Do you remember when he first went to work for Atari?

Bill - Oh, I remember. I had my own pass! I went there all the time! I met all those guys. See, how it would work is the building he worked in— at that time I think Atari had like eighteen big buildings right in Silicon Valley—and to this day, some of them are still vacant, because of the economy, I guess. And, I would go into the building, and the girl would say, "Hey, Billy," and I go, "Hi," and she would give me my badge. And I had a badge with my name on it, *Visitor Billy.*

You'd walk in the very front, and it was all three-piece suits. You get fifty feet further and all the ties are off. You get back another fifty feet, and now you see some guys with cut-offs. You go back another hundred feet, and you could even smell marijuana. I'm telling you. And all of the suits told everyone, "You don't bug the programmers. They can do whatever they want." And, no kidding. I remember one time going to my brother's office and there were six of the designers sitting in a circle and passing a joint, talking about the problems they're having with their particular situation. They were trying to make the arcade game fit into the Atari home version. Well, the arcade game had a mile of memory, and

206

the home version had one foot of memory, and they have to make that game interesting, and *they did it*. Son of a bitch if they didn't do it. They'd all brainstorm to help each other out. And they'd go, "Shut up, sit down Billy," and I might have to sit there for a half an hour.

They had a big room in the very back with all the arcade games, you didn't have to put quarters in them. It was for the guys to go play, like, 'Okay, I'm running into a problem here.' They had the games there so they could play as much as they wanted, to kind of refresh their memory. So I could go back in there, and I'd go in for hours at a time, and just play these friggin' games. It was fun, man. And nobody else's kid brother went in. I was the only one. It was weird.

Bob - Why?

Bill - Because I dug my brother, and all of the guys liked me. See, I was like six feet tall at a very young age, and everybody caught up to me. When I was in fourth grade, I was the tallest kid in the school. I was taller than most of the teachers. And then, later on in life, I looked older than I was. I could hang around with my brother's friends because they were all five years older; I wasn't a stupid little giggly kid. That's how come. I used to say to some of the other guys, "Don't your brothers want to come in and do this?" "No, they're not really interested," and I said, "*Wow*." I saw the value in it, of going and having fun over there. And plus hanging with these guys was exhilarating to me, anyway.

Bob - You told me you'd sold some collectibles that were owned by Joey. Did any of that have to do with Joey's career?

Bill - Well, we put up four Atari games on *eBay*, four games that are signed by the writers.

Bob - And those were guys that he worked with?

Bill - Yeah. Those were all his buddies. What's a bitch is I have one of his games, but he never signed it. He didn't think he was gonna die, you know?

Bob - You said Atari staffers could get a bonus if they'd done something that was a big success?

Bill - Oh, yeah. I remember years ago, what happened was Atari and these big companies were paying these guys pretty much shit pay, and then they were making millions and millions off these completed programs. And so these writers started saying, "Well, screw you, I quit." And that's how all these *other* places (start-ups) came to be. Hell, that's how Apple came to be, because designers got tired of being ripped-off. And finally Atari says, "Wait a second, we've got to start giving them a percentage." I think it was in the area of one percent. Well, his good buddy did *Centipede*, and he got a million dollar bonus. This was back in the '70s, dude. We didn't see him for a week, but he didn't quit the company either. He was very happy. That was when a million dollars meant something, not like today, you know?

Yeah, here you give a twenty-three year-old kid a million dollars—that's a brainiac like Joey was—and you know, and so that goes around, and that pumps all the other guys up. But then Atari went belly-up. Joey was supposed to get a pretty substantial bonus, but he got screwed. Yeah, so be it.

I think he even did some work at home. He wasn't even on the clock, it was just a challenge to him. My brother invented a really great astronomy program that was better than anything else at the time. It took so much memory to use, he'd have to go to NASA, to NASA's database. Then, his computer could handle the rest of the program. And I always used to bug him and say, "Dude, why don't you sell it?" And he goes, "No, no. I don't even want to sell it. I'm just making it for me. It's an achievement." Well, one day he finally told me, "Billy, I can't sell it." And I said, "Why?" He goes, "Because I got the idea while I was working for Apple. "That's why I can't." Because I knew he signed something. They all signed a proprietary agreement which said that anything they thought of while they were employed by that company, was owned by the company.

208

Bob - Do you know how he first started working with Apple?

Bill - I don't know exactly. It could have been the headhunter, or word of mouth. Because even though Silicon Valley is rather large, every industry is small in itself, when it comes to people that know people around in that industry.

When he worked for Apple, he worked for them a number of times through a headhunter. My brother's big thing was they would hire him to de-bug new programs that their in-house people had put together. The programmer did that normally, but that was my brother's forte. He figured out where the glitches were and then fixed them.

Joey was real funny. All of Joey's friends know that they couldn't say, 'Yeah, I bought a program and made a copy, you want one?' My brother would kill them. 'You don't copy that stuff. You go out and you buy it. And you pay the people the money that invented it.' My brother would... It was like, my brother didn't have that kind of attitude with anything except for when it came to programs and stuff. You don't short the system on this, you buy it like you're supposed to.

If he was around now, he wouldn't bootleg any music off the Net. He'd pay for it. Because he goes, 'That's stealing and that's just wrong.' My brother, in his own way, was one of the most honest guys in the world. He wouldn't do something he could get away with just because nobody was watching. He wouldn't do it, because he knew it was wrong. That's how we were raised.

You know, it's funny. I'm five years younger than he would be if he was still alive. I remember when he came home one day with this big thick manual, because he was all excited because they were going to let him work on the Cray computer that they had, right? He brought home this like four-inch thick book. I'm sitting watching TV, and he drops this book on the table, and it's like a phone book, right? And I go, "What the hell is that?" And he goes, "This is the *condensed* version for the operation manual to work on the Cray." Which he was all excited that he was one of the ones picked to work on it. And I go, "What's a Cray?" Well, that's when I learned. He told me, it's a supercomputer, it does this, that, you know? And I'm looking at this book, I go, "How are you going to read the thing?" "Oh, I've already read half of it." I'm like, *oh, Jesus*, you know? Whatever he read, he remembered, man. It stuck in his head. It was amazing.

Bob - Where was the Cray?

Bill - At Apple. Yeah, exactly, the Cray was at Apple. As far as I knew, back then, Apple was the only company that even had one of them. I have his Apple insignia with the name *Joe Copson*. They'd Velcro them on his office door in a plastic sleeve. He ended up keeping that, and when I came across it going through his things when he passed, I kept it. I kept anything. I got business cards from when he worked at Atari saying he was a software engineer, and I got tablets that say Atari in his name, and I think I have some that say Apple, because they always supplied that stuff for him.

When Joey went into the hospital, he didn't think he was going to die. Dude, when he drove himself to the hospital, it'd be like you going in to have your tires rotated, and then the mechanic tells you that your engine is blown. You're like, 'What?' He never got out again; he was in a coma thirty hours later and never spoke to anybody again. So, he went down feeling bad; he didn't know any of this stuff was going to happen.

The VA (Veteran's Administration) had diagnosed him a decade before with Crohn's Disease. But he never had Crohn's Disease. He had cancer, and they treated him for Crohn's. That's why the cancer spread through his entire body.

Even the doctor told us, me and my mom—bawling next to me— "We're sorry, you know, but we misdiagnosed him." You can't sue the VA, otherwise I'd have taken them to the friggin' cleaners for taking away my brother like that. I wanted it to end, and not prolong the pain my mother was going through. She aged twenty years in one day.

It took me three weeks to take care of his stuff. My boss said, "You don't worry about it, Bill. Your chair's open here, you just take care, do your stuff." And when I left, I started calling my mom every day, because her memory, she couldn't remember shit. And it was about one year to the calendar day of him dying, all the sudden she popped out of it. She was better. It was unbelievable.

When a parent buries a kid, I couldn't even imagine that. I've only got one kid. I can't even fathom how bad that would be, you know? Joey had one best bud. He had a lot of friends, but he had one best bud, and his name is Mike. Well, what Mike does, he can't really talk about. He's a genetic engineer. He used to work in a building that had no windows. But Joey and him, they had a grease pencil board out in the carport of his back yard. And they would do equations like Einstein. Sometimes it would take them a year to get through one. And we're sitting there one time, getting stoned or something, and all of the sudden, I remember Mike stood up, he goes, "No!" then he erases this…and writes another line and a half of all these equal marks, and parenthesis, and God knows what, 2 with another 2. And my brother goes, "Why didn't we see that?" And then they stare at *that* for three more weeks before they can figure out how to go forward. Dude, I don't get any of that shit.

To me, it's Chinese. Mike loved Joey; they were best buddies. Mike would go eighty miles out of his way to pick up Joey's mail when Joey was in the hospital. Only true friends do that, you know?

Joey lived in a tiny cabin shack in the Santa Cruz Mountains. It wasn't like a shantytown shack. It had a bathroom and a living room, the kitchen was part of it. You'd walk down a short hallway, and that was his bedroom. And that was it. I mean it was maybe five hundred, six hundred square feet. It was heated only by a potbelly stove. It's up on Scotts Valley. You get to by the way of Highway 17, and he lived on Summit

211

Road. As long as you went off-hours, it wasn't that bad of a drive to commute to Silicon Valley. If it was during traffic time, it could take an hour. That was exactly how he did it. And he'd come down and visit my mom three or four times a week, you know, in Palo Alto, which is just another hop, skip, and a jump going north.

Bob - Did he ever marry?

Bill - No. No, it would have been a special woman to fall in love with my brother. You know, he was, I don't know how to say it. I mean, he wasn't extremely handsome, he just grew long-ass hair and he had a big bushy beard. He wasn't real clean and neat as far as his house went. Now I know he had some girls that he knew that were *friends*, but... No, it would have been a special kind of woman to have fallen in love with my brother and he never came across her. Which is too bad. He wasn't afraid of women. He just was a geek.

Bob - When he passed away, was he still living in the shack?

Bill - Oh, yeah. It took me three weeks to clean it out, empty it out, get it right.

Bob - And the Apple-1 was in the shack?

Bill - No. He'd lived there for over twenty years. He got out of the military, and then he lived with my mom for a while, because my dad was dead, and, you know, he helped her out. Then he found this place, and I remember the day he found it. He says, "It's way up the Santa Cruz Mountains," and I just knew he was going to move there. His eyes were glazed over. And, he was like, "This is too bitchin'. As long as the clouds don't come in, I can see the stars like you wouldn't believe." That was big deal. That was because astronomy was always one of his hobbies.

Bob - I don't mean to focus too much on the difficult time when he'd just passed away—but when you cleaned out his shack, did you have his most important assets in mind? Were you thinking about the Apple-1?

Bill - Well, no. When he died, I hadn't thought about the Apple-1 for years. It was already down at mom's house, stuffed in a closet. In the shack, he had a Dobsonian telescope with a twenty inch mirror, and a Celestron A. Then he had his big binoculars that he'd search for comets with. I ended up with those.

Bob - So he'd stuffed the Apple-1 into a closet at your mom's house?

Bill - Yeah, that's exactly what happened. He brought it down. He was thinking of selling it, and he didn't get any real bites on it. This was decades ago. And then my mom said, "Leave it here." When my mom died four years ago, I cleaned up her assets and came across it. I thought, "Oh, fuck, the Apple-1!" I'd forgotten about it!"

Bob - So you're cleaning out a closet and you come across the Apple-1?

Bill - I came across it. You know, if I'd emptied everything out and not found it, at some point later in life I would've gone, 'wait a second.' It would have popped up in my mind, like, *oh, my God!* What happened to it?

Bob - And you knew at one time he'd considered selling it anyway.

Bill - Oh, absolutely, yeah. Exactly. I think somebody gave him an offer of seventeen hundred dollars. And he was working, and he said, "No. It's worth more to me to have it." If he'd have lived until he was ninety, he probably never would've sold it. Unless he really needed to, he would have hung on to it, because that was a prized possession.

Chapter 23

Star Trek

Wendell Sander is an active enthusiast of the Apple-1 today, and his machine is housed in a beautiful plexiglass case of his own design. But Wendell's history goes way back to the beginnings of Apple Computer. We first spoke in October of 2012.

Bob - I spoke with Steve Wozniak a few months ago, when he was in Washington, D.C. He came to see Mike Daisey's play *The Agony and the Ecstasy of Steve Jobs* and my Apple-1 was on display in the theater lobby that evening. When Woz saw my machine, the first thing he said was, "Oh, I know the guy that can get that running." And of course, he was talking about you.

Can you tell me the history on your Apple-1? Did you purchase it from the Byte Shop?

Wendell Sander - Yes. I still have it and I'm still fairly active. I bought it new around June or July of 1976, and I bought it from a Byte Shop. At the time, Paul Terrell had franchised out a lot of Byte Shops.

Bob - Were you familiar with Apple? Did you know about their computer, and that it was being sold by the Byte Shop?

Wendell - I had no familiarity with Apple at the time I bought it. There were so many companies making hardware at that time. It was really all a hobbyist's world; company reputations weren't that significant. I knew of the Homebrew Computer Club meetings, but I'd never actually been to one at that time. A technician I worked with had been to several of them, and talked about them frequently. I did go a little later, after I'd gotten my Apple-1.

There were a number of Byte Shops around at the time. I was curious about these personal computers. It was a field of interest, so I'd go to different Byte Shops and look around and see what they had. So, I'd been to the one in Mountain View, the home base location. There was one in the Cambrian area, and one in South San Jose where I'd go and look at the different computers.

At the time, I was the director of the memory research department at Fairchild Research & Development Labs. We were developing a bi-polar DRAM at that time. So I was interested in usages for that. The Apple-1 was attractive because it used DRAMs, and I knew if I got it, I could adapt the circuitry of my DRAMs and make a larger system. I saw the Apple-1 at one of the Byte Shops, and what triggered my interest was you could get a complete computer inexpensively. Also, I thought, 'Oh, if it uses DRAMs, I can adapt it,' because I was interested in making sure the DRAMs operate in a real environment. So I bought it for that purpose, because it met both of those conditions. I happened to be in a Byte Shop, and they had one, and I purchased it.

I'd had an interest in hobby computing for quite a while, and I had teenage kids. I'd at times gotten on timesharing systems; you could rent a terminal and get computer access and learn to do *BASIC*, and the kids could learn stuff on it. So I was interested in getting one.

I had four teen-aged boys at the time, so I was writing a lot of games on it. You transferred them from the *101 BASIC Games* book. One of the games I did was an adaptation of *Star Trek*. But it used more memory than the normal 16K bit. I got in touch with Steve Jobs, because his was the only place you could get copies of the updated software. When I first got it, the *BASIC* didn't even have an input statement. So, I contacted Steve, got updates, and I mentioned I had the *Star Trek* game. One of my kids had made some copies, and we tried to sell some of the tapes, but man, the tape was pretty flakey, so it was kind of tough.

Bob - In the *Apple-1 Registry*, it says you purchased it in August of 1976.

215

Wendell - I don't recall exactly, it was July or August. One of the reasons I know it was at least that early was as follows. When I got the Apple-1, of course they gave me a copy of *BASIC*. That copy of *BASIC* was very incomplete; it didn't even have an input statement in it. I know from the literature that, later on, there was a conference where they showed the Apple-1 on the East Coast (the Atlantic City Personal Computer Festival, held on August 28th, 1976). And that was the point at which they rapidly brought the *BASIC* up to date. So I know it was prior to that conference that I would have bought it.

Bob - Have you looked to see if you might have old records in your files, which might identify that date?

Wendell - No, I don't have any. I must not have kept the paperwork. I don't have perfect records, and unfortunately I lost track of some of those early records a few years ago.

I don't recall exactly when the first ones were sold, but I would guess it would have been within that first month. I'd gotten quite a few programs done by the end of that year. I had a large amount of memory, so I could do it. I wrote the *Star Trek* program, which I demonstrated to Steve Jobs. And that would have been in the fall.

Then early the next year, in '77, Apple started in their first corporate shop. They got a hold of me and wanted me to import that program to the Apple][, which I did.

So that was my introduction. My background, I have a Ph.D. in engineering. So, I worked at Apple for about five years, and semi-retired after that.

Bob - Have you had the Apple-1 in use the whole time, over the years?

Wendell - Not really. I had it, and shortly before I worked at Apple, I switched over to standard DRAMs and mounted the board to 32 DRAMs, which is the way it's set up right now. At one point, I built a new house, and I had the idea of making it a wine computer. I actually put a terminal program on it, and put it in the wine cellar. It was in the wine cellar for about twenty-five-years. I figured a *vintage* computer was appropriate in a wine cellar. It essentially worked the whole time, but it wasn't used much. It kind of got in some disrepair and the mice got into it, and I had to kind of clean it up and get it working. About three or four years ago, I decided to check it out, and restored it back to being a normal computer.

Bob - I know yours has the number 0100-24 on the back of the board. Today, those numbers are always referred to as "Byte Shop numbers." When we talked to Paul Terrell, we asked him about that and he said he never put those numbers on there. He didn't know about their origin.

Wendell - I really don't know of the origin of those numbers either. Steve Jobs was asked once, and he said Apple didn't do it. I have no other knowledge on the numbers, I was never privy to it. When I was first at Apple, they had an Apple-1 that was still running. They sort of had me be responsible for maintaining it. But quite honestly, I never took it out of the case to see if it had numbers on it. I think it was kind of an unusual one, because you always saw the classic Apple-1 in the wooden mahogany case, and this particular one was in a metal case that was almost exactly the same shape, and it was blue and white. It had a perfect cut-out for the keyboard. Somebody had obviously very carefully built that metal case for it.

I don't know what happened to it. The only thing I can conclude is it's probably at Stanford University in their Apple collection. You know, Apple gave them a big donation of material, and I expect that the computer ended up there, on display in one of their buildings. I'd sure like to get to see it, but it's almost impossible.

Bob - Was the board inside the metal box?

Wendell - Yes. It looked almost exactly like one of the mahogany cases, but it was of metal. It was exactly the same shape.

Bob - Mine is in a metal box, but it's a definitely a different design from your description. My metal box is a standard bent or pressed metal box of the time. It has a Plexiglas panel on the top of the box, so you can see the board. The keyboard is separate and it's in a wooden box.

Wendell - Okay. Yeah, that's quite a bit different. This one, as I recall, you know you sometimes see these pre-made metal boxes that are sort of bent and sloped like that? This one is much like that, the base was bent up on the sides and the white top sort of fit into it. It was a one-piece design. That was at the time I joined Apple. That was Apple's Apple-1, you might say.

Bob - Did you know Joey Copson, who later worked for Apple? He also purchased his Apple-1 from the Byte Shop.

Wendell - I didn't know him, though I've seen his name before.

Bob - His Apple-1 case is similar to the case of an IBM Selectric typewriter. It's like a clamshell. If you want to open it up, it's hinged. Copson's brother told me that Joey put it in that case when it was new.

Wendell - They made up those mahogany cases that were sold; that was kind of the only real case that was made intended for the Apple-1. Anything else was pretty much whatever somebody could figure out.

You know, when I went to the Byte Shop, it was this small place, and I don't think the guy stayed a Byte Shop, I bet he wasn't in business for more than six months. But when I bought the microprocessor, the only keyboard he had available was an old DECWriter keyboard. I used it for years.

Bob - There's interesting opinions about the $666. price point.

Wendell - I think they gave me a discount.

Bob - When we talked to Paul Terrell, who started the Byte Shop, he gave us an explanation for the $666. pricing. He said that when he and Jobs set the terms, the rule of thumb of marketing involved marking things up a certain percentage. But he also said, "When these things went out the door, we usually sold them with a bunch of extras, so the entire package was closer to a thousand dollars."

Wendell - I think mine wasn't much above that for everything, including a keyboard and transformers. What I got was basically the keyboard, the transformers, and the board. I think I might have gotten the cassette board at the same time. Although, the cassette interface came out a little bit after the main board.

Bob - The machine I have was bought new by Charles Ricketts. I wonder if that name rings a bell for you? He lived a mile from Jobs. People recognize his name, but no one seems to know anything definitively.

Wendell - I've probably seen the name, but I don't know him. It's interesting that Ricketts' Apple-1 was purchased directly from Apple as opposed to from a Byte Shop. That implies that Ricketts must have known Steve Jobs.

Bob - Well, when I first got the computer along with the original cancelled check, I looked up the address on the check. I went on Google Maps and saw they lived four miles apart. Wozniak told me the name was familiar. Other very early Apple employees have said they recall Ricketts and think he had big plans for the use of his Apple-1, but we've never specifically figured out who he was.

Wendell - That's interesting. I talked to Steve Jobs five or six years ago. I mentioned that I was getting my Apple-1 running. I did some demos at Apple, and let him know. He made some comment, such as, 'I think I may have an Apple-1 in my stuff.' The way he said it, I have a suspicion that he had at least one Apple-1 in his collection already. Or he did have one. Quite honestly, Jobs was never interested in the old stuff. He had zero interest in it. Zero.

Bob - Well, it fits what I've always heard about him. Like, it sounds lucky that the archive went to Stanford and didn't just go to the dump.

Wendell - I don't believe that was in Jobs' era. Or if it was, it was right after he came back.

Bob - I read it was right after he came back and was cleaning house.

Wendell - Well, actually, I'm not surprised at that. That was his style, to donate that stuff to the university. He would do that. It's just he wouldn't spend any time thinking about the old stuff. It wasn't that he wasn't interested in history to some extent, but he was totally uninterested in working on the old stuff. When I would text him and say, "I'm having an Apple-1 demo in one of the cafeteria areas at a certain time," and "Let anyone know that might be interested in seeing it." I'd get no response from that whatsoever. He just wasn't interested.

Bob - What was he like in terms of your working with him?

Wendell - He was very sharp, attentive. I mean, he just didn't have time to fool around. Everything was just very brisk, quick, and serious. That was sort of his style. Although, he had some sense of humor. But business was business. He was always highly focused and the focus was on "What's the next thing?" Never looking back. Once it was done, it was done.

When the Apple][was done and he was focused on the Macintosh, the Apple][didn't exist. He had almost no consideration for it. There were two senses to it, he had almost no technical interest in it, and on the other hand there was a period of time there, of course, where the Apple][was paying all the bills, to develop the Macintosh, and the Lisa, and all that stuff; they weren't making any money. So, the Apple][was a seriously important product. I think he recognized that from a business perspective. I know he made some moves and decisions that were important for making sure that the Apple][stayed successful. He wasn't dumb in that way. It was just that if you wanted to tell him about some new feature on the Apple][, he wasn't interested. That wasn't his world. He was strictly business.

You see, I met Steve during the Apple-1 era. Like I said, the *BASIC* was really primitive, and I knew it needed upgrading. So I called him and asked for new copies of the software. And so he'd say, "Okay, I have a new version now." and I'd go down to his house and pick up the new version of the tape.

One time, one of the chips failed on my board. I went down there and he just replaced the chip, you know, and got it working again. I'd talk to him occasionally; I let him know that I had this *Star Trek* program, and he was interested because nobody else had that. Then early in 1977, when they were working on the Apple][and they'd done the West Coast Computer Faire, they wanted me to port that program on to the Apple][, which I did.

I went in to Apple in March or April of '77, when there were only like five employees in place, and would sit there on weekends, and spend some time working on my programming. They eventually gave me a prototype Apple][to use, they loaned it to me to use for development. From the time they started shipping the Apple]['s, they were shipping a copy of that *Star Trek* program. That was shipped with some of the early Apple]['s. It started as an Apple-1 program, and it went to the Apple][.

Bob - Were you initially doing that as a contract job?

Wendell - No, I was just doing it on the side, because I was interested. By then I was kind of interested in, and getting involved in Apple, anyway. My background was in working in semiconductors from a device design viewpoint. In my last job, I was managing about twenty people, and had my own FABLINE and everything at Fairchild R&D Labs. And so I was doing a lot of stuff, but I was interested in getting back into systems again. I was definitely intrigued by the concept of personal computing.

So I was interested in joining; I thought these guys were good. You know, by that point of course, Mike Markkula was in there, and it was Jobs and Woz and Markkula. That was before Scotty (Mike Scott) had joined. And Markkula was a very impressive guy, I kind of knew of him; he'd worked at Fairchild years ago.

So he knew who I was. I looked at it as being a very interesting and creative environment. It was obvious Woz was a very creative guy. That all made sense, so I was doing it, and figured, 'Well, eventually I'll join,' which I did later in August.

Bob - So when you were first doing the *Star Trek* stuff, were you paid?

Wendell - No. I just did it for the fun of it.

Bob - In the beginning, when you'd stop by Jobs' house, what were the dynamics of that? I mean, you're going to somebody's home, but they're running a business out of it.

Wendell - They were in the garage. You know, literally. So, it was like going to a garage shop. By that point, even then the garage was pretty fully occupied by the Apple-1, so they were doing burn-ins, and all.

Bob - Bill Fernandez told me that, at one point, only three people could fit in the garage.

Wendell - When I did the demonstration of the *Star Trek* program for Jobs in the garage, Randy Wigginton was there too. I remember Randy. And my son was along, too. At the time he was fourteen or fifteen. He is now director of iPod hardware at Apple. How's that for interesting? So, he got to see it from the ground, up.

Bob - When you ultimately joined the company, which building were you in?

Wendell - In the ones on Stevens Creek...

Bob - Bandley?

Wendell - No, this was before Bandley. It was well before that. On Stevens Creek Boulevard there was a set of offices. At the time I first started, they had one office, and they were just adding a second office. They didn't have much square footage. They didn't even have two thousand square feet—it was pretty small. Then they expanded into that for a while, and then they leased the Bandley space. We moved in January 1978, just about the beginning of the year is when we went to Bandley.

My Apple history was, roughly, I joined in '77 in August as the sixteenth employee. I was there for about five years. I worked on most of the early peripheral cards, almost all of them; language cards, a ROM card, and all. Then, I was the principal designer on the Apple III. They

222

went public, and I was basically semi-retired for a few years then. And started another company called the Engineering Department, which did a lot of contract work. There were several of us early Apple guys who did a lot of contract work for Apple. The Huston Brothers were part of that. Dan Kottke worked there for a while; different people. And I worked at a lot of different start-ups.

I worked at a company called General Magic (working on a hand-held communicator; the precursor to the smart phone), historically one of the interesting start-ups, which was started by Andy Hertzfeld, Bill Atkinson and Marc Porat. General Magic was really a high-flier type start-up, no two ways about it. And so I was there, and so was my son Brian, who was sort of the engineering manager there. One of the young employees was Tony Fadell. That's where Tony started out. So we got to know him there.

And a little after that, Brian and I were with another company called Tropian, and that was interesting because it was actually located in the same complex as the original Apple building. It was doing RF (radio frequency) work; cell phones. It started out with some stuff I'd developed for techniques for cell phone transmission chips. One thing it migrated into for a while was actually doing custom cell phone design work for Taiwanese companies.

Tony Fadell then went off to Apple, and he was the one who started-up the iPod. He basically built that operation. Brian knew Tony well, and he decided to go over there. As that got started, and then when they decided to go do the iPhone, well, Brian knew all these guys who were cell phone designers. So, many of the key players for the iPhone design—even currently— originally started at the Tropian company, in the same complex that Apple started in. So it got to be a very winding thing. Anyway, it's an interesting thread. Then I joined him, and I worked on iPods, and other related products at Apple.

Bob - You went back and were an employee of Apple again?

Wendell - I went back to work at Apple about seven years ago, and stayed for another five years. My son was working there, on the iPod, so I worked on the iPod for about five years.

Bob - When Apple went public, were you there?

Wendell - Yes. I was there a couple of years after that.

Bob - So, did you benefit from the public offering?

Wendell - Oh yeah.

Bob - So that worked out well for you?

Wendell - When I went to work at Apple, I took half salary. I cut my salary in half, and took stock options. That's how you play the game in Silicon Valley.

Bob - So, that paid off, then.

Wendell - Yeah. When Apple went public, they made more millionaires in one day than any company had made on an IPO; it was one of those deals. There were a lot of people that were wealthy that day.

Bob - When you joined the company, the Apple][was carrying the company. Steve Jobs was not excited about the Apple][, but he recognized that it was what was paying the bills. Was that similar to when you joined the company, in the sense that they were still actually selling the Apple-1's, but everybody was working on the Apple][?

Wendell - Well, that was a little more extreme, and for good reason. The Apple-1 certainly wasn't paying any bills. It wasn't big enough to be a revenue factor. And, as a matter of fact, there was some concern that Woz was answering too many Apple-1 questions on the phone, and they were getting behind on the Apple][. There were things they wanted him to do.

They really had wanted him to do a floating point version of the *BASIC*, but Woz is a kind of funny. He had this ability that if he decided to do something, his focus was as intense as anybody I've ever seen in my life. He was incredibly intense. But, it was very hard to get him turned on to that intensity. So a lot of the motivation was, 'How do we get him turned on, intensely on this project that we want him to work on?' One of the distractions they wanted to eliminate was the Apple-1, so that was when two things were done: they gave generous trade-ins for Apple-1's, and basically they tried to accumulate as many Apple-1's as they could, and destroy them. That was the objective.

Bob - How long after you started did they start selling the Apple][?

Wendell - Well, they were already selling it when I was there. My understanding was the first Apple][was sold in May of '77. I've heard others say June. There's a website called *Applefritter*. Recently one of the guys on there described finding an Apple][in the old case, with a serial number of 101. And he had a receipt, and it looked like on the receipt the unit had been shipped in early July. I don't know about the serial numbers. I seem to remember they didn't necessarily start the serial numbers at 1. I don't know what they started at. Certainly, it must not have been 100, but it might have been like 50, or 20, or 10.

Early July would have been really early in the availability of Apple][s. They shipped a few of them in May. I seem to remember they were only making twenty or twenty-five a month in the first month. By the time they hit August, or September, I estimated that they must have shipped five hundred or more.

I made a comment on *Applefritter*. Somebody was offering to buy it from him, and I said he ought to really do a lot of research before he thinks about selling it. It could be pretty valuable.

You may have heard the story of the problem they had with the Apple][case. They had the old style case with no vent. But they were made by a short-run tool process. Even when I joined the company, their biggest concern about me joining the company was they weren't sure they could get enough cases to stay in business. Because of the difficulty of these things, the quality was terrible, and they just couldn't get that many. They rapidly had Jerry Manock make a hard case, and use a different kind of plastic for sheet cases. They did that as quick as they could, so that, I think by late that year, October or November, they'd cut

225

over to the new cases. Anybody that had an old case and had access to the new cases, replaced the old case. There aren't many of those old cases around. So, having one of those old ones in the original case is amazing.

Bob - At what point did they start putting the engineering team's signatures inside the case?

Wendell - Those of course were pressed-in, not on the Apple-1's, or the Apple][and][+. There were some Apple][e's and stuff with pressings. There may be *signed* ones around, which is more likely of the]['s and][+'s. They never pressed the names in the case, but somewhere in the later generation, they made versions where they put names and stuff in the cases.

Bob - That wasn't at the beginning of the Apple][?

Wendell - If you find a signature in a one at the beginning, somebody *signed* it.

Bob - So, what's the future for your Apple-1?

Wendell - Well, I'll probably leave it to my son. I'm seventy-seven years old.

Bob - I figured you were going to say that. Your son's got a great history regarding Apple, just like yours. The story of him going with you to the Jobs' garage when he was fourteen is neat.

I was just showing my own kids the date codes on my Apple-1 last night. They thought it was neat that I was able to show them "Here's one that says '76, and here's one that says '76, and here's one that says *'74* on it."

Wendell - Yeah, I haven't tried to be terribly faithful with the date codes on the Apple-1. I do have spare parts that are the correct parts. The date codes are too much trouble, though. Man, they're hard. You keep worrying about people making a clone, but you know, to make a real copy and get somebody who really knows what they're looking for, it's virtually impossible to copy a vintage machine.

226

In terms of the differentiation of Apple-1's, there's a couple of series, you have to know what series you're on, the first or the second. Yours must be the same generation as mine.

Bob - Yes, it's the first generation, like yours.

Wendell - On that series, it turns out that there's one resistor on there, in sort of the middle of the board, which must be a metal film resistor, not carbon composition. And it's the strangest color I've ever seen on a resistor. I've never seen a resistor like that in my life.

Bob - What color is it, how would you describe it?

Wendell - It's got a maroon background to it. Okay? There's one resistor on there that's different than all the rest. It's a 330 OHM, I think it is. I have no idea where you get one like that. I know there are some people who are actually making fake parts, and you can do that too, but then the main step is that I look carefully at the boards. You know, I don't know how you'd ever accurately drill patterns on the boards. Because every one of those board clones, if you look really carefully, you'll discover that the drill patterns don't exactly match.

The drill holes, the v-holes, the location, getting those to be exactly the same place on every board, it's an unbelievably difficult job. Think about it. You just can't do it. The Apple-1 board was hand-pinked, it was done by hand. It wasn't done by machine, so trying to get every hole in the right spot is just ludicrous.

Chapter 24

Historic

Brothers Cliff and Dick Huston joined Apple at the same time. Although Apple had stopped selling the Apple-1 and was now on to the Apple][, their story does involve the Apple-1. Not the least that they would have to be considered the very first collectors of the Apple-1. We spoke in October of 2011.

Dick Huston - In 1977, my brother had been working with another guy who had a friend named Rod Holt. Rod Holt was working in a little company called Apple Computer, in Santa Clara Valley. They were looking for engineers. My brother was working as a sort of service technician for nuclear medicine machines. That job had pretty much run its course, and he was looking for something else. He met Rod Holt at the first West Coast Computer Faire and talked to him about Apple.

My brother and I had built a kit computer, an IMSAI. We did it as a hobby. He did the hardware, I wrote some software for it. However, several months later, Rod got ahold of Cliff, my brother, and said they were still looking for engineers and there was a brief conversation then and then that sort of petered out because I guess Apple was having delayed shipping on the Apple][. In October there was yet another call and during that call Rod asked Cliff if he knew of any other engineers, any other people. In particular they were also looking for software engineers. He mentioned that I did software and so we came down together on a Sunday, in the middle of October or maybe the last Sunday in October.

Apple at that time was in what they call *Good Earth*, there's a Good Earth Restaurant and a little strip of office buildings behind it, the kind of office buildings with a medical center and a tax preparation center and little tiny offices off a mall or open strip. When we went in, it's a sort of big open room. Rod Holt had his office in a storage closet. There was barely room for his desk and chair, and junk, and papers so we kind of sat out into the big room on a couple chairs and talked to him through his office door. It was kind of funny.

He told us that Apple was just getting ready to blossom, and they needed to create some peripherals, some cards and things to plug into the Apple][to make it a more complete system so you could connect it to a printer, potentially connect it to a modem, and other things. The Apple][had seven slots for expansion. And his statement at the time was they thought that the Apple][would probably sell about ten thousand units. Rod suggested we come back to meet with everybody. We came back and there were four or five people there, including Wendell Sander, Rod, Woz, I think Steve Jobs, and Mike Scott, who was president at the time.

This panel grilled us on what we knew and what we didn't know. Apparently, we both passed the test. Then at that point they said, yeah, they wanted to offer us a job, but here's the thing. They were just at the stage where they were going to get funded in January or February of 1978, and if that funding didn't come through we would get laid off. So we might work there for six or eight weeks and then be shut down because they wouldn't have the money to go forward.

My brother and I were self-taught. We didn't have any kind of formal education in computer engineering. So they could pay us a lot less than they'd pay *real* engineers. They thought they'd give us a try. At the time we just shared an apartment. I was a printer by trade, my brother had gone to trade school to learn electronic and technical work and had

229

done some designs on his own. He had a little red board, and when we put the IMSAI together, I'd written kind of a little discovery system for it, and put together some tools for it. We did have some experience in doing things and at the time there really weren't any courses on what to do with these little microcontrollers. So, we really weren't that disadvantaged not having a formal education.

But to let you know how small Apple was at the time, I'm employee number twenty-five and my brother Cliff is twenty-seven. There had been a couple people who had come and gone already so there were probably only about twenty-two people when we got there. So anyway, that's how it came to be. I started on the 15th of November 1977, and that's how I got there.

I stayed until 1984. It was after the Mac had been announced and I took a sabbatical in 1984, and then intended to come back a year later. I went off to do video game work for a year and before the birth of my second kid. I came back a year later.

Bob - I know that you said you didn't work on the Apple-1, but that you had one. How did you get it, and did you ever end up selling it?

Dick - Well, what it amounted to is that Apple had decided they needed to support the product and they didn't want to support the Apple-1 on a continual basis. It was taking a lot of time away from in particular from Woz. He would have long conversations on the phone with Apple-1 owners, and at the time there was maybe seventy or eighty people that actually bought Apple-1's. There might have been more than one hundred, but it wasn't a great number of people.

The Apple-1 was a hobbyist platform. At the time we were interested in the technology of it, and hadn't figured out what the hell to use it for. What did you need a computer in your house for? At the time that was a big question. Is there really a market for this? Is there really something to be done with these things? Everybody that was interested in them was interested in developing tools to go further, to make it useful, to make it accessible. A lot of people were enamored with the technology. People had good ideas for applications to do some real work with them. The other thing that really drove the whole personal computer market was games. They thought it was really cool, especially the Apple][, because there you had a whole integrated color computer. And if you could make up some excuse to use it and get your employer to buy you one, you had a pretty cool game machine.

With the evolution of the Apple][, along came *VisiCalc*. *VisiCalc* became a practical thing once a disk drive was available for the Apple][. That became the first application that sold lots and lots of units.

Wozniak had developed his integer *BASIC* on the Apple I (which became the integer *BASIC* programming language for the Apple][), and then there were games, there were all kinds of text-based games, things you could put up on a terminal so these games would be like card games that would print out the names of the cards rather than show you cards. There was also a game called *Star Trek* where you would give it coordinates in the universe that you want to fly to. Then, you would have a mock battle with Klingons and things like that. It would print out a little matrix display of the missiles going back and forth between the Enterprise and the Klingon ship. So, the Apple-1 was a tool for an awful lot of early people. It was a way of self-educating, it certainly was—and I think this is a relevant point—it was Woz's dry run. It was a prototype experience that allowed Woz to do something much better with the Apple][. I don't think the Apple][would have been the success it was without the Apple-1.

That's what I think the story of the Apple-1 is. It was the thing it got Apple started. Woz was motivated to build the Apple-1 because he was too cheap to go buy a kit like the rest of us. It's like the selection of the processer – he chose the 6502 over the 6800. He went to an industrial show where he talked to various vendors, Intel, and Motorola and a smaller company that had a 6502 processor. They were willing to sell him 6502s for like five bucks. Whereas Motorola and Intel wouldn't give him the time of day; they wanted big orders. Just to go and hunt those parts down through second parties and buy one or two of them, I mean we're talking forty, fifty, sixty dollars per processor. And for them, Mostech or Synertech, they had a little booth there and they would sell samples to anybody for five bucks. That's why he picked the 6502. So I'd also like to point out the Apple-1 was designed to run with either a 6502 or a 6800. Although I have to admit I've never seen one run with a 6800, and I don't know that anybody developed any software for the 6800 on it.

Bob - You've said that you and your brother didn't completely understand the point of a personal computer, why people would need them around the house, for example.

Dick - I want to make clear that it wasn't just me and my brother, it was everybody. When we first started, I remember having a conversation with Jean Carter who was head of sales. He said, "Why do people want these? What do you use them for? What's the big idea?" If he'd talked to customers, each person that bought it had some particular reason. Even then there were people trying to figure out how to automate the home, or they thought they could build a controller to run motors, or scientific types were using them as perhaps a means of gathering data. All kinds of people had applications, they had a lot of obscure things they thought they could use them for.

For most of the engineers that came to Apple, and the hobbyists at the time, we were interested in tool development. There's kind of a weird evolutionary synergy that goes back and forth, that each generation of computer has spawned the next. In part because once you have one generation of computer, you can then turn around and immediately use that to figure out how to make it the next one faster to make it more capable. As the computers got better and better, the tools got more and more refined. Making the computers better and better. So it folds back on itself, and from that level of capability comes the introduction of

232

programs like *VisiCalc* or little word processors or various more mainstream kinds of applications. Those were spawned and introduced to a whole bunch of people who weren't interested in computing, per se. They were interested in doing electronic spreadsheets or word processing or some other thing that wasn't not doable before computers—you could do them on paper—but computers supported a way to do them more conveniently. Instead of using erasers you could use backspace.

Bob - What made you and your brother want to get ahold of one of the Apple-1's? What made you have that foresight to know this is going to be something cool to have down the road?

Dick - Well, I think what I was is that from the very get go, going to that first West Coast Computer Faire, we'd invested probably thirty-five hundred, four thousand dollars, in our IMSAI, and it wasn't much of a machine. I don't know if you've gone through the economics of the old kit computers. Let's run through it real quick. In some respects it was a better version of the Altair, it was a more solidly-engineered version of the Altair, and the Altair was the first really good, accessible kit you could get for under a thousand dollars. All you got with that kit was a motherboard and a mess of slots. I don't remember how many, but it was a bunch, maybe a dozen slots, that you could plug design cards into. There was a thing called an S-100. It had one hundred pins. Somebody had gone to the trouble of figuring out a standard, and we're going to put the address on these pins, data on these pins, etcetera. So it was a published, open, everybody had access to it, you could design and build things that could plug into that, including memory. The first thing you had to do was plug in some memory because there wasn't any memory on the motherboard. It was just the processor, and support for the slots and the front panel that just had a bunch of momentary switches and lights. If you ever saw the movie *War Games*, with Matthew Broderick, that'd give you a good shot of the IMSAI. You can look that up and you'll see that it looks like some 1960s or 1970s box with little switches and lights.

233

With the case of the IMSAI, you got that for about six hundred or seven hundred dollars with no memory, no disk drives, just the processor and slots, and the power supply and box. You're probably looking at five hundred dollars for 4-8 kilobytes of memory. When we went to the first West Coast Computer Faire, Apple had what in a lot of trade shows would have been considered one of the worst spots; Apple was were right by an entrance and the normal flow of traffic came through the doors. Apple was at the end of the aisle and the first thing there, and it's crowded. People are coming in and out of the show, so anybody wanting to stop at the booth would be impeding traffic.

Apple had a five foot color projection screen showing what was coming out of the Apple][, in color, and that was awesome. To add color or to have a color-capable card on the IMSAI was more than a thousand dollar proposition at the time. A color monitor was another thousand or twelve hundred dollars. Of course you could always hook it up to a color TV, but even cheap color portable TVs were four or five hundred dollars. The Apple][—even though it was priced in the one thousand five hundred range for kind of the bottom end—you couldn't approach that with any of the other kit computers, and have a processor, and that much memory, and color capabilities. As expensive as it was, it was cheap for the group of things it was capable of. They were just running a little color pattern program, but it was mesmerizing. Apple made quite an impression on both of us, because we really felt like they were a company that was going to go somewhere because of this stunning achievement.

We came over and we wanted to look behind the counter to see if they were hiding stuff from us. Because you look in the box and you say, 'How do you do all that with so little?' We thought you can't buy one of these today, are they really running this thing without there being some more capable box underneath, they haven't really gotten into what they're showing us yet. In fact, it really did work. They did all those things. Once Cliff and I had started there, I realized a lot of things developed for the Apple][software, integer *BASIC*, and some of the other program work, had been done by Wozniak on the Apple-1. There was a little bit of the attitude that the Apple-1 was an awful thing. By comparison, it was already obsolete. It was a piece of junk. And yet, it was the beginning. It was a founding product. I don't know that we really had the foresight to say that someday this would be worth a lot, it was just being enamored of the company and being kind of a true cult believer. Having one to express to our friends, 'Look at the difference between this and the Apple][.'

We knew there would be even greater things coming along. It was just kind of that notion, like, 'Look how fast this is developing, look at the progress from one thing to the next.' Also, at the time, I don't believe Cliff or I had scraped together enough to buy an Apple][yet. We had all our money invested in the IMSAI. By November, we had probably put another five hundred, or thousand, or fifteen hundred dollars into the IMSAI. We'd already put in well over five thousand dollars and still didn't have color capability. The IMSAI came to work with me. I had converted an assembler, this is the name of the program that a programmer uses, you have probably used the term 'compiler,' I don't know if you've heard 'assembler.'

That's just a thing that you're putting together the programs using the language of the processor rather than an artificial language. And there's a one-to-one correspondence between the assembly language and what's called the operational codes or the op-codes of the processor. I'd written an assembler on the IMSAI for the Intel 8080. Or I'd had an assembler, I adapted one we bought on paper tape to run with our IMSAI. Then I had to learn the 6502 because it's different processor architecture. The way I could quickly learn it was to go through and understand each instruction so I could construct assembler logic for it. I converted my assembler into a cross-assembler. Then, when I came to work, I could bring that with me and actually do useful work the first day

235

rather than using a terminal, because Apple didn't have tools to assemble things. They had a terminal and a time share service. I bought the assembler. Of course, it was an Intel at Apple.

There was another fella working at the time, Randy Wigginton. Well, he kind of turned his nose up at the thought of having an 8080 machine anywhere around Apple. He thought that was awful and he was highly suspicious of me coming around there because he was the programmer at the time. He was in high school, and was just there part-time. He was working on *Applesoft* for the Apple][, and he had to do all his work on a teletype machine over at the phone line with an acoustic coupler where you take the phone handset and put it in these little rubber ear and mouthpiece type things to seal it. Then you would dial the number and the modem on another end would announce it. I think the communication speed was something like 110, or maybe as much as 300 bits per second, which is about thirty characters per second. He had to do his work on this Microsoft *BASIC* to turn it into *Applesoft*, and then assemble it. It would take a couple of hours on the timeshare machine. It could take twelve to fourteen hours to print out. It was a laborious, terrible thing. As a result, he didn't get it printed out very often and would only print out very small sections of it. He didn't have a complete listing after a couple of months work into *Applesoft* when the timeshare system crashed, and it lost some work for him.

They had a backup, but when they put the backup on, it also crashed. The tape wasn't reading well and he couldn't recover what was going on. So they went back a month and put that backup tape on. That didn't work, so they went back one more month and put that backup tape on, and *that* didn't work. What they realized is that on the tape machine at the timeshare place, the eraser head was on and it was erasing the tapes. It wasn't even reading them, it just immediately erased them. Wigginton had lost all the work he'd done and stored electronically.

He hadn't lost work in that he had gone through the effort and made a lot of notes, scribblings on the listings he did have, so in a fairly short period of time we managed to get a tape reader working with the IMSAI. We got the source code transferred to a series of floppy disks that we could use with the IMSAI, and then he could do the work at Apple, directly on the terminal, and edit directly on the screen. It only took ten minutes to do the assembly, and we got a printer and he could get a complete print in about an hour, instead of it being fifteen hours over the telephone. After that he thought it was okay to have an Intel-based machine there. He thought I was okay because we had rescued *Applesoft*. So I think that's when Randy accepted that I was potentially somebody that could be an ally and a friend.

When the Huston brothers listed one of their Apple-1 computers for sale on eBay, in the listing J.R. Huston described how they came to acquire the computers:

"The founders of Apple knew that one of the keys to long term success was customer support. In the beginning, that meant Steve Wozniak took customer phone calls to help in any way he could with the Apple-1. With the launch of the Apple][, everyone in engineering (and some of the production line technicians) took calls... but most Apple-1 questions still had to be taken by Woz. It was decided that to best support the Apple-1 owners, the easiest thing to do was convert them to Apple][owners. Apple offered a trade-in deal to Apple-1 owners: trade in the Apple-1 for an Apple][(by late 1978 the offer also included a disk drive!). Most were traded in. This freed Woz from phone duties, rewarded early Apple adopters with a more capable computer, and allowed Apple to fulfill its commitment to great customer service.

Cliff Huston dropped into Steve Jobs' office one day and couldn't help but notice the huge pile of Apple-1 boards - those that had been traded-

in for the Apple][. 'What are you going to do with those?' Cliff asked. Steve told him that they were to be destroyed. 'Mind if I take one? Oh! And one for my brother?' Cliff asked. Steve reached into the pile and pulled out two boards and handed them to Cliff. Many people around Apple were amused and asked, 'Why would you want one of those?' 'It's history,' was Cliff's reply, 'just history.'

Though hundreds of Apple 1 computers were sold, the trade-in deal reduced the population to the few that exist today. This is one of two that that got a last minute reprieve from the band-saw death pile!"

Bob - A while ago, you and your brother offered some unique Apple collectibles, and an Apple-1, to be auctioned. You set a high reserve price so you weren't obligated to sell too low. How much of it sold, and how much do you still have?

Dick - Okay, at the auction the thing you're referring to was actually a set of glasses that Woz gave me, the Apple glasses. That was something I was reluctant to sell. I deliberately asked way too much money and hoped nobody would do it. My brother had a set of Apple relics and I had another set and we kind of pooled them together and sold them together and split the proceeds. Everything sold but that set of glasses, and at more than the asking price.

Another thing I would throw at you is that there were other computers out there like the Apple-1. Just single board, no case, but almost inevitably in the same price range; they were kits and they did less. One thing that was kind of magical about the Apple-1 was, at a standard engineers salary at the time, if you just took an engineer, I believe the price is in that sweet spot where...back then a lot of people got twenty-six paychecks a year. They got a paycheck every two weeks, which means the time of month when you got paid would kind of roll around so every once in a while you got a third paycheck in the same month. You have your beginning of the month bills and your middle of the month

238

bills, and then there would be the end of the month. Every once in a while there would be this extra paycheck that fell out because there's twelve months and if you've just got to pay bills twice a month, these extra two paychecks were like, "*Wow*, I've got this whole paycheck," and the price of the Apple-1 was right in a sweet spot where if you were a nerd, if you were an engineer, a hobbyist, you'd have a paycheck in hand that was more than an Apple-1 cost and not enough for almost anything else. I don't know that that was intentional, but it wouldn't surprise me if they didn't subconsciously plan that. It only came around a couple times a year and it's like found money. Like when you pay too much taxes and you get a tax refund. You've got this extra money and when you're single and nerdy you can't help but think I'm going to blow this on some expensive toy I couldn't get otherwise. We didn't rely on credit cards so much back in those days.

Bob - Yeah, we were smarter back then.

Dick - No, we just weren't considered credit-worthy.

Bob - People we've interviewed have spoken about Apple's role in education, with kids being taught on computers, for example. You'd probably be a good person to ask about that since you were involved in Apple][, which was a more versatile machine, functionally, than the Apple-1. How much of that did you see or experience?

Dick - Well first off I'd like to say that one thing Apple did brilliantly was to infiltrate the schools. There was a lot of engineering activity with the Apple][, and a lot of behind-the-scenes activity where companies that were working on educational software often had direct access to the engineers there. They would call and they say. 'Well, I'm having this problem and can you help me work this out?' or, 'We want to do these little animations are there any tricks that can be done?' They would talk to any one of us. They would talk to Woz, they would talk to Randy Wigginton, and they would have access to us.

They could just call us and often we would spend maybe an hour or two just talking to them and sometimes we would even go off and do little experiments or little projects to try to get them the things they needed. That kind of direct support, it was informal, it was never—in terms of engineering—a group that was just dedicate to support the education marketing. Which meant supporting the developers. That was the first push toward putting together a developer organization. Initially, educational activities involved learning games. It wasn't about teaching students to use computers, it was about teaching them to read and write and do little math problems. One of the first games that I remember was a thing called *Sticky Bear*, which was just a little animated bear where you do math problems, and the thing would pop up. It was cute and it would give you different expressions based on whether you could add two numbers together or not.

I think that was one of the first areas where a computer could be used not just by adults, but could be a teaching tool, like an animated textbook. And to apply what had been learned about games and education, arcade games, where those same techniques could be used to teach different concepts. Steve Wozniak—that was one of the things that really excited him early on—the notion that these were going to be used by little kids. Little toddling around two-year-olds getting their sticky fingers all over the keyboard. I think there was a very rich set of applications that grew up before the introduction of the IBM PC. There were probably hundreds of really cool teaching things. Now there were probably a thousand *more* applications that were fly-by-night crappy garbage that people were trying to sell into the schools just to make a buck. But I think there were, there was easily twenty or thirty extremely high quality games for teaching reading, math, for telling stories.

There's even a game called *Adventure*, a text game, and I can remember seeing a sort of an adaptation of an adventure-like game for teaching history. It wasn't a fantasy world, it was our world that you were

240

walking around in. It wasn't anything like games you're used to seeing these days, but still to go explore, and then you'd come to a place. It would give you a little explanation, and then you'd be at a Mission in California that had just been built, and there would be a Native American standing there and you would talk to the Native American. That would be another paragraph of information, and you might go into the Mission and talk to the Spanish priest there, and he'd give you other information.

If you had a good enough imagination, you could actually put yourself into that place in history and get a feel for what it was like, instead of it being just about dates and wars and leaders. You could get a better feel for what was going on. And I think that game was put together by a teacher, who took the original *BASIC*. There was an adventure game that had been written in *BASIC* and that teacher had studied the program and adapted and changed the paragraphs, and put together little adventures in different places and times. As far as I know, they made it available for free to other schools through that network. It wasn't a commercial thing, it was just a teaching tool.

I think teaching how to use a computer or how to program is something that the people that have a knack for it find on their own; they'll teach themselves. They'll seek it out and find it. And there're tons of books and tons of data sheets and things that somebody who is drawn to them will become great engineers someday. They found it then, they would continue to find it now. It may not be in the area of computers, it may be in some other area that I wish I knew existed because I'm always looking for new stuff, but I don't know that it was all that valuable to have teaching focused on the machine itself. I think there were some kids exposed to that and I don't know if it turned any of them on. It wasn't that exciting for them.

Chapter 25

Christmas Tree Farmer

It was December 2011, and from Washington D.C. I drove five hours south on Route 81 towards Blacksburg, Virginia. The interstate runs parallel to the Blue Ridge Mountains and on that Saturday morning the sun was just coming up and lighting up the valley. Blacksburg is home to Virginia Polytechnical Institute, also known Virginia Tech. Instead of exiting off 81 and going west towards Tech's campus, I turned east towards the tiny town of Floyd. I knew Dave Larsen was the proud owner of four Apple-1 computers, and I looked forward to meeting him and seeing his collection. I pulled into town and parked in front of the courthouse. It was such a picture perfect small town that I started taking photos of the hardware store across the street. The sidewalk in front had wheelbarrows and bicycles lined up on display. Just a block away was a small strip center with Dave's storefront. Inside, it was part technology museum and part Dave's own Floyd County visitor center. The visitor center part made sense, since he has a good reason to be a combination welcome-wagon and Floyd ambassador. He sells raw land for home sites. It's land where Christmas trees used to be grown.

On the top of an old fashioned counter-height display case, Dave had laid out a large soft cloth. Spread out side by side were his four original Apple-1's for me to see. When we were finished, he gingerly lifted each, wearing white cotton gloves, and put them in a box to then return to the local bank vault.

Dave Larsen - Going way back, I've been interested in electronics all my life. I'm seventy-three years old and I started off when I was eight-years-old, back in the '40s, with a crystal radio. That's what got me hooked. It was pretty rudimentary. I had an amateur radio when I was thirteen or fourteen. I was involved in an electronics club in school and I just loved to tinker with electronic gadgets. I guess you'd call me a gadget guru from day one.

I've lived in Floyd since 1968. I grew up on a farm in the late '40s and '50s, so I helped my dad farm. I taught electronics instrumentation and computers at Virginia Tech for thirty-one years. I couldn't do regular farming because of my teaching commitment. So when I came to Virginia Tech, I thought I'll just buy a few acres of Christmas trees.

We bought a few acres, and we bought a few more acres, and it just kept going. It was a way for me to farm. And then I had to hire help, so I hired a forestry graduate to run the farms. We farmed for twenty-five years. We ended up with about five hundred acres of trees, and then retired out of that in the early '90s. It was our desire to farm, but not be feeding cattle. They're just so demanding. Trees don't jump fences, and don't have to be fed exactly at four o'clock. I was very early in the marketing of Christmas trees, and particularly one aspect, mail-order Christmas trees. Our company developed the mail-order Christmas tree concept back in the late '70s and early '80s. We created the whole industry. It's still being done. You put them in a box about six feet long, and so square. The box was wax-lined, so the moisture couldn't get outside. The transit time was three or four days. It was my idea to get the tree from the plantation to the customer directly, eliminate all the middle men. Then we sold the business in 1991.

I got started in the computer field in '59, when I was sent by the Navy to computer school at Remington Van Univac in St. Paul, Minnesota with the ENIAC, when computers were as big as two bedrooms. I'd joined the navy while I was still in high school. Because I had my radio license, I was able to get a little bit of an advancement when I joined and I became an electronic technician. They sent me to school to become a technician for a huge Univac computer that was going to be installed in Virginia. This very advanced computer was going to keep track of naval ships in the Atlantic Ocean, and the Navy did not want civilian technicians working on it. It was so secret, they wanted military technicians.

After the Navy, I went on to college and in my summers I worked for electronics companies. I was a field tourist engineer for Variant Technologies, dealing with large analytical instruments used at hospitals. In 1967 I was offered a job at Virginia Tech out here in Blacksburg, Virginia to teach electronic instrumentation. It was a faculty position, doing what I wanted to do, and I was at Tech for thirty-one years. I taught instrumentation in the Chemistry Department. A good bit of that teaching was automation, especially as you got into the end of the '70s. You were teaching using computers and we actually found that a lot of the material that was available wasn't current when the integrated circuits came along. So we actually created some educational material, me and a group of other fellas. We co-wrote a series of books on computers, called the *Bug Books*. When I started teaching digital electronics, there was no good teaching material. I started teaching with tubes, back in '67, and integrated circuits were just coming along. When we got into integrated circuits, there were no good books. If you look at the integrated circuit, it looks like a little bug with all the legs on it. So one night I thought, 'We'll call them bug books.' Because of the look of the integrated circuit. That's where the word 'bug' came from.

We got involved in microcomputers from day one. We were using minicomputers in the late '60s and early '70s and then when the microcomputers came along, we got involved in them. Today, we call our museum in Floyd the Bug Book Historic Microcomputer Museum.

I've collected computers all my life, and we have a little teeny display right here in Floyd. Elsewhere, I have a warehouse full of all this stuff, and it's huge. I've got about a thousand calculators in my collection. I got a tube collection from an engineer who was going in to a nursing home. He was so proud of it. He'd been an engineer all his life. There are some original Edison lamps of his, a terrific little collection. Some of these are ancient.

This little Intellect here, this was the first development system for Intel in 1972. Well, I had that in my office at Virginia Tech. In 1989 I got a call and this company says, "We're looking for an Intellect 4. We have some litigation, and Intel doesn't have one in their inventory." I said, "What's the litigation?" "We can't talk about that." But I had one on my shelf. "We know you're a computer collector. We've seen your want ads." They said, "Put it in a very good box, insure it for ten thousand dollars, and we'll pay you five hundred dollars for every six months we can use it." The litigation was a case between Texas Instruments and Intel. Who gets credit for having the first microprocessor? The date coding could be used to verify when it was made. The end result of that case was that TI had the microprocessor chip first, but it didn't work. So they don't get credit for it. Intel's worked.

They kept it for eighteen months. They called and said, "We're not done yet. Here's another five hundred bucks." The money was immaterial, but this was really incredible. So, I would make any of my computers available for legitimate things.

I first started running an ad in *Computer Shopper* around 1980. I was looking for historical microcomputers; not necessarily the Apple-1. I started advertising specifically for Apple-1's later. It was just a generic ad. 'Wanted, pre-1980 Computers.' People responded. I got lots of calls, of course, a lot of Radio Shack TRS80s and stuff.

I still run an ad in *QST magazine*. My ad is running right now. I'm looking for a Star, one of those from the Parc Research. I'd love to

245

have an Alto. There was an Alto auctioned off about six months ago. It went for thirty-some thousand. The Star was one of six computers they had at the Parc Research Center, the Xerox Parc Center. I'd love to get one of those. By the way, there was a Star auctioned off actually, about two weeks ago. It went for thirty-six hundred dollars. I kind of regret not buying that one. That was the first GUI computer, graphic user interface computer. And the guy that sold had it running and so forth.

I got a bit of a reputation because of these ads running for so many years. I would say it was probably around 1990 that I put the Apple-1 query in there. And that's when I started to get more Apple-1 offers. They were already, around 1990, selling for ten, twenty, sometimes twenty-five thousand dollars, and it had become pretty significant. I had this collection growing and growing and I said, 'Well, shucks!, I want to see if I can get some Apple-1's.' I got serious, and also started to have a little more money in my pocket about then.

I was offered roughly ten Apple-1's during that period—from 1980 to 2000. Most of them were more than I wanted to pay. And I did pay significant money for *all* of the ones I actually bought, but not in the big dollars, like a fifty thousand dollar kind of thing. I just couldn't do that.

I was able to buy four of them, not all at the same time. I did get two from one owner, Adam Dunston. He called me up one day, and said, "You know, I've got two Apple-1's." He said, "I want to sell them, but not now." I said "Okay." When you get ready to sell them, let me know." He called me up about six months later and said, "My son's starting at school. I need eighteen thousand dollars for tuition." I said I'm not sure I can come up with eighteen grand, but let's make a deal. So we did, and I bought both of these from him. He said he bought those at a Byte Shop as well. There's some wiring on these things. He used them in some control application. I never did quite figure out what he did, but yeah, he had two of them. He was using one for backup.

I bought one of them from Adam Schoolsky, and he gave me long documentation, including letters. He said "Wozniak gave me this computer." And so I emailed Woz, and I said, "Do you remember giving Schoolsky a computer?" He said, "I don't remember it. Well, it's so easy, I could have just said, here's a box of computers, just take one, you know. But, I obviously know him and he's a good guy," and all that. I have no doubt that that's the case. Even the box it came in has 'Woz' written all over it. Schoolsky was working for Intel, and he responded to my ad. Why he wanted to sell it, I'm not sure. He may regret it at this time.

Wozniak talks about Adam in his book iWoz. Zaltair was a prank that Steve Wozniak pulled off at the first West Coast Computer Conference, and he asked Adam to help him with that. Adam was about thirteen or fourteen years old, and that was in 1977. I bought the computer from him in 1995.

The one I got from Adam Schoolsky has never had chips in it. It's never been powered up. It was given to him that way, and he never did put chips in it, and I never did. So, that one has never run. The last time the others were used, they all worked. But we haven't powered them for a long time. I'm a little bit reluctant to power them up now for fear of burning up the circuitry. There are people out there that really want to do that too, have an actual turn-it-on, and run it. I would love to do that, but I'm very busy. I own several businesses here, and so I don't have a lot of time to do it, and it isn't the kind of computer you can just turn over and turn on. I don't intend to do that or have any plans to turn them on, at least not now. They're complete, they should run, but who knows after all this time? There's things that could go wrong with them.

I bought one from John Burch, who was an original purchaser. He said he brought it from the Byte Shop. It's got a wooden box, but I don't know whether that's teak wood or not.

They're all original and in the price range I could justify paying, and at this point I'm glad I did. It took about twenty years to collect these

Apple-1's. I think I got all of these from the original owners. They're in nice shape. And by the way, all of them are in the *Apple-1 Registry*.

They weren't nearly as collectible back then. I've heard some wild stories, I don't know if they were true or not, about people paying an awful lot of money. They're kept at my safe deposit box at the bank. I keep them stored there.

I have people contact me pretty regularly about selling an Apple-1. I've come very close to selling one about two years ago for about twenty-five thousand dollars. I got to thinking about it, and the fellow was rather unhappy when I changed my mind. I really don't blame him, but my thought was that we have four, and I don't think anyone else has four. I doubt anyone else has three, though some owners may have two. We've accumulated them over the years, and if we can display them correctly, that would be pretty unique. Just having one is certainly unique, let alone four. Also, if I could ever find a way to share them safely with other museums for display, I would do that. I wouldn't be selfish in that sense. But it took so many years acquiring them that I'm not anxious to sell them. I just decided, well, I can sell them anytime, never knowing what I could get, because they vary in price. You know the one sold at Christie's for two hundred and fifteen thousand dollars, so that's obviously top of the line. It's more important for the collection to have the four, and share them than it is to have the money for them.

We still, to this day, collect computers. We have a huge collection of artifacts and microcomputers of all kinds, thousands of items, not necessarily all computers but thousands of artifacts from signs, literature, and sales brochures. In fact, I have a warehouse that I just dump this inventory in and we're in the process now of entering the inventory in museum archival software. I'm hoping someday to have a museum. I'm not sure we'll get there, it's a pretty expensive thing. But we have an awful lot of really wonderful items to display.

With my computers, and our little collection here, my goal in Floyd is to have a major historical museum, specializing in microcomputers with the publicity centering on the four Apples. The people that come into this museum, actually, this little display we have, are pretty excited. Often they say, 'Oh, I had that one, I remember this one.'

I've had some of these computers for a long, long time; all of them were bought before 2000. I have a lot of duplicates. In fact, we've donated a good bit of it to the Smithsonian.

Dave and I then travelled across town to visit his warehouse. It's a long metal industrial type building. Inside, there is a second floor loft that runs the length of the building. The bulk of the collection is in row after row of shelving on the loft. As we start up the stairs, on the first floor we pass a grouping of large computers as big as Coke machines.

I've got a 1960 keypunch IBM. I learned the value of long term advertising. Because I advertised for so long, this company called me up and said, "We're retiring this computer and we want you to have it." This is a tube computer, a 1960 computer. Well, I didn't have this building then. And it was a running computer. I said, "I couldn't afford to pay the shipping, and I don't have a place to store it." They called and said, "The president of the company wants you to have this. We will pay to bring it to you." And I turned it down. I wish I had taken the computer. You know, you look back and...

I did take all of the peripheral pieces. I've got a punch-sorter and an interpreter. And manuals that are in beautiful condition. I mean, just gorgeous. It was a working vintage tube computer. It would have filled those two rooms we were in earlier. He knew it was historical, and I didn't have the space at the time.

But I've got this loft up here. This is our inventory area. Everything is packaged clean, packaged up, wrapped. All the inventory has an inventory number and the date we inventoried it. Oh, by the way, this is the Haddock collection. Remember I told you he gave me his collection? This is his little collection; he thought he had a huge collection. He said "I didn't know anyone with a collection bigger than mine." He's got some nice stuff in there, but I have everything he had except for one computer. So that was his collection. I was happy to take his collection for historical purposes.

I have serial #21 of the 8800 Altair. There is one I know of with a lower serial number, I don't know who has it, but I've seen it on the Internet.

And of course the Apple was copied by Franklin Computers, and I've got a whole collection of Franklin Computers. They knocked off, Apple was always suing them... software, etc. And I've got gobs of the early Byte magazines, all of the early publications. I've got most of the significant ones. Multiple copies.

I don't worry about the temperature, but I control humidity. The computer collection is really nice. And it doesn't show that there's so much here, but I've got fifteen hundred plus parcels. But that doesn't tell the whole story, because some parcels include twelve to fifteen computers and so the total would be a big number.

Bob - When we talk about the history of personal computers, this is a time when the people involved in the creation, manufacturing, and design in the '60s to the '70s are still alive.

Dave - They're alive and retiring. Some are passing on, and we need to get that history. That's what my wife and friends say, "You've got to get this stuff down in writing."

250

Chapter 26

Zaltair

In late 2012, Dave Larsen asked if I'd be interested in interviewing the various people whom he'd purchased each of his four Apple-1's from. Well, I thought...you never know who might have a good story, and so we should go ahead and try to contact them. The seller of one was Adam Schoolsky of the state of New Hampshire. His story also went way back to the early days of Apple.

Adam Schoolsky - I left a tech job in May 2012 to do my motorcycle accessory business full-time. Our shop and mail order focus is on sport touring bikes and touring bikes. We handle motorcycle electronics including blue tooth, GPS, radar detectors, lazar jammers, and rider-to-passenger communication. I also do suspension tuning. I've been playing with bikes since I was about fifteen. And cars, too. A bunch of vintage cars. Basically, all kinds of motorized junk.

Bob - You're an old friend of Steve Wozniak's, but also you were slated to be one of the earliest Apple employees.

Adam - When I was seventeen or eighteen, I passed on the opportunity to be Apple's sixth employee, because I didn't think that they would really go anywhere... but I guess I was wrong, huh?

I'm originally from Los Angeles, so I was still living at home, and what they could afford to pay me at the time was four dollars an hour. This was 1977. So, I didn't see how I could move from home, make my hundred thirty dollar a month car payment, and live on a hundred and sixty dollars a week, afford a place to live, and everything else. I just didn't see how it could happen, so there you go.

I was eighteen, just out of high school. I was ready to go to college; I just didn't have any money. I went to a junior college because I was living in California. I think junior college was seven dollars a semester, or something like that. It was dirt cheap. Then I wound up going to work for a company that installed business telephone systems. I'd been playing with phones since I was eleven years old, sort of figuring out ways to defraud the phone company. It seemed like a natural fit, so I wound up working for a company that installed business phone systems, and I did that sort of thing for a long time.

Bob - To back up a bit, what was going on with Wozniak and Apple at the time?

Adam - Yeah, it was like five people, that was it.

Well, the Apple-1 was just out. It launched in the spring of '76. So during that time, while Steve was designing the Apple-1, he still worked at HP in the Advanced Products Division, which was the division that made the hand-held calculators. Steve used to do hardware design for the HP-35 and HP-45 hand-held calculators.

When they were designing the Apple-1, in 1975 I would guess, he used to come down to the LA area. I had a car, so I'd pick him up. There was a place in LA County, Cerritos, maybe, where there was an outfit that had rudimentary CAD (computer-aided design) PC board layout capability. We'd go there on the weekends, because that's when he wasn't working. He'd fly down, plane flights were cheap at the time. A flight on PSA (Pacific Southwest Airlines)—which used to be this regional airline—from the Bay Area to LA was twelve bucks or something. It was really cheap.

We'd go to Cerritos, and Steve would work with the guy there to lay out the board. That was pretty advanced stuff at the time; people were laying out PC boards by hand, so to be able to do it on the computer was kind of unusual. I guess that was one of the few places that did it. I wasn't really involved in the process, I was just kind of the chauffeur and I'd just go there and sit around and watch.

Bob - You were based in Los Angeles, so how did you come to meet Steve?

Adam - Well, that's sort of-telephone-related. In 1972 or maybe 1973, I was still in junior high, I'm guessing I must have been in seventh grade. The phone company, every exchange in the country, had these transmission test numbers, called 'loop around numbers.' They'd use them for transmission testing. You'd dial in to the one number, and you'd dial in to the second number, and the two would connect. And a lot of these numbers that you'd dial into, there was no charge. They were really intended for phone company test use. So you'd dial into one of these numbers and they were sort of widely known in the phone hacking, phreaking community. You'd just dial in; there were sort of popular ones. You'd dial in and just sit around and wait, and eventually someone else would call in. And so, I'd called into one and was waiting, and the two Steves (Jobs and Wozniak) basically called in from a phone booth.

Bob - You're kidding.

Adam - Nope, I'm quite serious. They'd called in from a phone booth at Homestead High School, in Sunnyvale, where they'd both gone to school. So that's how we met. We met on the phone. And we became very close friends for a very long time, years and years.

Bob - You and Wozniak?

Adam - Oh, yeah.

Bob - About this phone exchange, you'd get on just to see who else would randomly get on?

Adam - Yeah, that's it. It would always be somebody calling to talk about something related to the phone company, or making free phone calls, whatever. Basically, it was a way to talk to other people.

253

Bob - You could conceivably have dialed and waited two hours and nobody would've come on?

Adam - Absolutely. But there were some of these numbers that were more popular than others.

Bob - So the probability was high that somebody else would come on. And then there would be a "Where are you?" "Where are you?" conversation. "What is it that you'd been able to figure out?" And you'd trade back and forth ideas.

Adam - Exactly. I don't remember whether it was on this day, or a different day, but one of the things that happened around that time was they both were at Homestead High School, and Steve had designed his first Blue Box. They were at this phone booth, and a Sunnyvale police officer approached them as to what they were doing. He asks what this thing was that they had, and they showed it to him, and said it was a device for playing music. And the police officer said, "Well, that's a great idea, but a guy named Moog beat you to it." Pretty crazy.

Bob - What transpired in that initial conversation that ultimately led to a friendship?

Adam - God, you know, I don't remember. You'd meet people this way, and I can't remember. It's so long ago, I honestly don't remember. We traded phone numbers. At some point not long after that, Steve came down to LA, or I might have flown up to the Bay Area. Times were a little different then. My folks were pretty liberal with where they let me go without supervision. As a twelve-year-old kid, I'd go with two or three friends, and we'd get on the bus and ride thirty miles to Disneyland. And go to Disneyland all day long, and then we'd come home, and my father would pick us up at the bus station in downtown LA. At the time, you didn't even think about it. This is a couple of fourth, fifth graders, right? Taking off for the day, going thirty miles away to Disneyland. Now, if your parents allowed that, they'd probably wind up in jail. You'd never even consider it today. So, things were a little different. Steve would come down to LA fairly often. He'd drive down or I went up. Anyway, we became very good friends for many years.

Bob - Was it a number of years later that you had that opportunity to join Apple?

Adam - Yeah, that was after about five years, right? But, in the interim, I'd see Steve fairly regularly. I'd either fly or drive to the Bay Area. I'd just go up to hang out. We used to go and eat, and play pinball. There was this company that had very early consumer VCRs. He would buy these surplus VCRs and I'd go up there and help him work on them, and fix them up. We'd get them working, it was just sort of electronic geekdom, you know?

Bob - Did you then resell those VCRs?

Adam - No, no. He used to buy this stuff. These were pre-Beta VCRs. Having a video recorder at the time, that was unheard of, right? No one had even seen anything like it.

Bob - He must have been older than you, right?

Adam - Yeah. When I met him, Steve was going to Berkeley. I'm going to say that Steve now is probably sixty – I think he was born in 1950. So how old would he be? Sixty-two?

Bob - When you and he first met, the age difference would have been another thing we'd look at now like, *what?* We didn't think about that the way we do today. Did you have similar interests?

Adam - I had a number of friends that were older. The stuff that I was interested in, only a couple of other kids that were my age really had any interest in it. I was interested in ham radio, CB radio, and electronics. I'd say I had maybe two or three friends that were my own age. Everybody else was older. I had a number of friends that were local that were older. All these kids were sixteen, seventeen, eighteen; they were all older than I was. It was not unusual. You just didn't think of it. Wozniak's a big kid anyway, really, still is. While he's an incredibly smart guy, he's still a twelve-year-old.

255

Bob - It's hard to characterize it, but he has that fun way about him. What was it that appealed to you about him? Did he have a magnetic personality?

Adam - Oh, absolutely. I mean Steve's a character, really, totally. He just liked to do stuff, whatever it was. He wasn't a guy that sat around watching TV. That was fun, really.

I know I met him when I was about twelve. My mother threw this big surprise party for my thirteenth birthday. Anyway, she threw this terrific birthday party for me at an ice-cream place in the LA area. And Steve came down for that. And my mother had this cake made for me at this deluxe cake place and the whole thing looked like a Blue Box. Yeah, it was pretty wild.

Bob - So you guys had considerable history prior to your involvement with Apple, such as it was.

Adam - The Apple-1 was around for about a year. They sold them mostly as just bare boards. And then there were only two places in Southern California that sold them. One was Computer Land, or Computer 'Someplace,' (Actually, it's the Byte Shop; this comes out later,) and another place that was in Santa Monica.

But that was the first computer store that sold computers for the public. And they were selling the Apple-1. There was another place, in Orange County somewhere, in Westminster, and they had things set up there where you could come in and rent time on a computer and play games, elementary as they were. *Pong*, or whatever the hell it was. And they had Apple-1's. I'm going to guess they bought maybe half a dozen, or eight, Apple-1's. And they might have had other computers, too. I follow along with the Apple-1 for a time; I went to the West Coast Computer Faire, which was April of '77. I remember that weekend, because that Monday I bought my first brand new car. That was a bad experience.

It was a '77 Volkswagen Rabbit. It was the biggest piece of crap that ever rolled out of a factory on four wheels. The thing was well

256

beyond lemon status, it was just an absolute disaster. It soured me on ever buying anything made in Germany for well over thirty years.

But anyway, I'd gone to the first West Coast Computer Faire, in San Francisco. I worked in the Apple booth when they announced the Apple][. Apple, at the time, was both Steves, Bill Fernandez, and Rod Holt—who was an engineer, I can't remember whether he came from Atari or HP—he was a hardware guy. Mike Scott, who was going to be the president; I don't know if he had an official title. Mike Markkula was there; I don't think he was officially with the company, but I remember we all went to dinner afterwards. It was then, you know, when it sounded like Markkula felt like they really had something. And I think that was pretty much everybody. That was the whole deal.

They announced the Apple][, and I remember going around the show, seeing what all of the other companies had to offer, and they all seemed like they were more well-established. They all had a computer that was already in a case with a keyboard, and a disk drive. Apple offered me a job as a shipping clerk, for four bucks an hour. The situation for me, just for a variety of reasons, didn't really line up to where I thought I could work there for them.

I finished high school in '77, so that was a couple of months after. Maybe they'd just put the Apple][into production, because they launched it in April, and this is June, a couple of months later. It just didn't go anywhere for me. What can I say?

At the Faire, I couldn't really see that Apple had something that was really different. And the other thing too, at the time, this was a market that was totally for hobbyists. There was no practical use in anything but somebody that just wanted something to play with.

These were toys. It was a toy.

You have to keep in mind, when I went to high school, I was working as a file clerk after school for fifty bucks a week. Gas might have been fifty cents a gallon, or not quite. And I could go buy a great dinner

257

somewhere with my friends for five dollars. Here are computers from MITs, and whatever; if you bought a computer and a memory board, you're talking three or four thousand dollars, right? I just looked at this stuff and thought, who'd ever buy any of this stuff?

The Faire was the introduction of the Apple][, and In the booth, they had a projection TV. The screen was the focus of the booth. You know, the Apple][was in color; I don't think anyone else had color. But, anyway, yeah, that was the focus. This whole show was the introduction of the Apple][.

Bob - Can I go back to when you talked about those two stores in southern California, in Orange County and Santa Monica? Was Steve keeping you abreast of what was happening at Apple, and that the Apple-1's were available in a couple of the stores?

Adam - I don't know if I ever went to the computer store that sold the stuff, but I do remember going to this time-sharing place. Because I think Steve had gone there a few times to sort of help them install the stuff and get it working. I'd gone there a couple of times.

Bob - Was one of those a Byte Shop? That's the name we always hear.

Adam - There we go. The Byte Shop.

Bob - In terms of the fair, did they need some help manning the booth? How did you come about participating in that?

Adam - Steve and I had done those Zaltair brochures for that thing. I did help out in the booth. I think I was there mostly to check things out, and to distribute Zaltair brochures.

Bob - Was the Zaltair prank something that you and Steve had planned out much in advance?

Adam - What we did was, I'd gone to his apartment a few weeks in advance, and we basically hashed the thing out. So that it would be untraceable. I went to a printing place in LA, and I had them typeset it and print it. They printed several huge boxes of them. We had them printed in four really bright colors. And I printed thousands of these.

258

Then I went to another place, and I had *them* print envelopes, because we were going to mail them out. Steve paid for it, and I just shipped this stuff up to him on PSA. You know, you used to be able to air freight. I'd go to PSA and ship all of them, twenty dollars or whatever to ship all of them up there by air freight.

Bob - What was the thinking behind doing this? It was just a goof or something?

Adam - The Altair was the popular computer at the time. So what we did was to screw with them. The Apple][was coming out, and it had capabilities that nothing else had. One of the things on the Zaltair flier was a chart—it was pretty funny—and it had these totally meaningless benchmarks. It had all of the current competitors of Altair; Apple, Processor Technology, and Sphere, and whoever else we put on there. And it had benchmarks features like speed, numbers that were totally meaningless. Of course, everything for the Zaltair was like, 1.0 or whatever, and then all the others are like 0.5. But they didn't relate to anything. Anyway, that was pretty funny. One of the ones we did, we just put 'Apple.' It didn't say 'Apple-1' or 'Apple][' it was just 'Apple.' And, of course, for Apple, which was the Apple-1, we just put really low numbers. Because we knew the Apple][was coming out, which was going to be way better than the Apple-1.

Anyway, we'd take stacks of these things and dump them on the literature table. All these companies had tables, and they'd put literature out. So we'd put stacks of these brochures out, and go by, see that the stack was gone, and we'd go and put out another pile. There were like fifteen thousand of these things. They had one or two of them up—It was a riot!— in the MITs booth, on the wall, and they'd written on them in black magic marker 'FRAUD!' It was pretty funny. Yeah, it was good.

Bob - Do you recall where you guys went to dinner? A nice restaurant?

Adam - Yeah, it was a restaurant, and I don't remember which one. All I remember is that I stayed in a really nice hotel. I think PSA owned the hotel at the time. The St. Francis at the time. It was a really nice hotel which was a big deal for me at the time.

Bob - And Apple was springing for that?

Adam - Apple, or Steve, paid for it. Keep in mind, a really nice hotel at the time was probably forty dollars or something, right? There were no three hundred dollar hotel rooms unless you were staying at the Park Plaza, or something, in the Presidential Suite.

Bob – You indicated seven Apple people went to dinner.

Adam - It might have been. Half a dozen people, maybe.

Bob - And you described that Markkula was probably not quite part of it, but he was espousing the vision.

Adam - If he had joined on, it's possible that he'd just joined on. I think they were looking for somebody to invest some money, and it was at that show, or about that time when he decided that he was going to put some money in.

Bob - When you were offered a position and you opted not to, did you continue to stay friends with Steve for a long time after that?

Adam - I was the best man at his first wedding, and I was one of the groomsman at his second wedding, and so, yeah, we were good friends for a very long time. In fact, in the early '80s, maybe 1981, he'd recently got his pilot's license, and he went out and bought a really hot airplane, which was probably beyond his capabilities as a pilot. Not a plane he really should be flying. And so, he had this brand-new plane he'd only flown one or two times, and he was going with his fiancée to Las Vegas to buy a wedding ring. At the airport in Santa Cruz, Steve crashed the plane on takeoff.

I was living with my mother, and had a job working for a business telephone system company. I got a phone call from either a friend of Steve's, or it might have been Steve's mother. And I took off, went up there, and wound up staying. I quit my job and stayed there for

260

the whole time he was in the hospital. I took care of him for quite a long time, months and months, until he was able to get back on his feet.

Bob - I think we heard the other side of that from whoever you ended up talking to. I remember Dan Sokol telling us that he made a call. I didn't realize that that person was you. It sounds like it was. I also didn't know that you were that far away.

Adam - I came up, and I'm going to guess that was around, it was in the early spring, so that was around February or March of 1981, it was around in there. I was staying at his house. He had a small house in Scotts Valley at the time. So, I was basically staying at that house, and I wound up going back to school at a JC there, for a while. And then suffice to say that I wasn't thrilled with his new fiancée, and I don't think anybody else was either, really. That was Candy, Candice Clark. And so I wound up moving when the semester was over. I have a friend from LA, and his grandmother, since deceased, had a little house in Santa Cruz. I wound up taking all of my possessions and moving them out of Steve's, which, of course, I didn't have very much at the time. I took it all, and moved it into the garage at my friend's grandmother's place in Santa Cruz, and I took off on a cross-country motorcycle trip for three months. When I came home, I moved in with a friend of mine in Sunnyvale, and basically wound up going back to work.

Bob - Did you stay with the phone business?

Adam - I did. I did that for a long time. I did that phone crap for... fifteen years probably, or so.

Bob - That was your thing, I mean that's what you do, right?

Adam - Yeah, that's what I did. I shared a birthday with Alexander Graham Bell, so I guess I was destined.

Bob - So, when did you get your Apple-1?

Adam - It was right in there somewhere. I had more than one. I had an Apple-1 that was fully functioning for a long time. I had an Apple-1 hand-wired prototype, which honestly, I don't remember what the hell happened to it. I think I may have given that one back to Steve when he gave me a regular Apple-1 board. I had a hand-wired Apple-1 prototype which was done on a board that Steve used to snag from HP. In fact, all his parts and all that crap, he used to get from the parts bin at HP. Parts, circuit boards, wire, everything. He used to just snarf that stuff from HP.

But the one that I sold to Dave Larsen was essentially just an Apple-1 board. I think I also had a hand-wired prototype of an Apple][. This is some years ago. I just used the power supply off that board. I just wired a little harness and connector to the power supply to power this Apple][prototype. That's all I used it for. All for power.

Bob - And at some point, you put the thing on the shelf...

Adam - Put it on the shelf, you know, what was I going to do with it? I just used the Apple-1 as a power supply.

Bob - At some point way down the road you would have seen Dave Larsen's ad, that he wanted Apple-1's.

Adam - I don't remember how I learned about Dave, or how he found me. It was while we were living in Oregon, I was working for Intel at the time. We were living in Portland. I don't remember.

Bob - Larsen ran a little ad in a trade publication for many years. Through that ad, he's been offered a lot of stuff over the years.

Adam - This was sort of early public Internet time (the mid-'90s).

Bob - Your selling him the Apple-1 would have been a really early sale at that time. How did you decide its value, what you would let it go for?

Adam - Well, I was a schmuck. My wife was starting a business, and she needed some money to fund that business. So, we kind of figured out about what she needed to get started. And I sold the Apple-1 to cover that.

Bob - And you guys just did a transaction where you sent it to Virginia. You didn't actually go there, right?

Adam - No, I just sent it.

Chapter 27

Scrapped

Craig Solomonson first became involved with Apple in the early 1980's due to his work in the field of education software. This led to him seeking out Apple-1's to purchase. We spoke in December, 2012.

Craig Solomonson - I taught computer literacy courses back in the '70s, and I got all excited about computers in education. Then I was with MECC (Minnesota Education Computing Consortium, later Corporation), a software company in Minnesota, in the early 80's. We developed most of the early software for Apple. I mean, our company is what made Apple what it was. We put out the software that all the schools in the country were using.

I also tried to get a computer museum going here in Minnesota. It didn't work out because the funding got shifted to a museum in Boston.

Bob - I remember reading about the vintage computer collection housed in your garage.

Craig - Oh gosh, I had a two-and-a-half car garage, and it was stacked to the ceiling with mainframes and stuff like that.

Bob - There was one particular machine in your collection that stood out to me. The entire housing was dark red acrylic.

Craig - Oh, I still have that one.

Bob - That computer sounded like a work of art.

Craig - It is, and absolutely nobody out there can figure out who did it and why.

Bob - Do you assume it was a prototype?

Craig - Well, in terms of the work that got put into the case, it is elaborate. So it was not done by a hobbyist, I'm convinced. And I think it was done at Honeywell or maybe Sperry Rand Univac, in Minnesota here. The guy I bought it from also had Altair # 5, which I have, and some other early micros. He worked for a computer company, but I was so enamored of the computers, I wasn't paying attention to his name. I just wanted these before somebody else got them.

Bob - I wonder if it was custom built for a computer show. It reminds of when an auto company builds a dream car for the big annual auto shows.

Craig - You know it very well could have been, and the thing that's amazing about it is the chip dates are late '71 and early '72. It's got to be one of the first eight bit computers off anybody's line.

Bob - Are the components Honeywell?

Craig - No, the board was made by Intel. It's an Intel development system that they sold to developers to hopefully produce programs and applications for their hardware, in particular that was for the 8008 chip.

Bob - In terms of Apple-1's, I believe you've owned three?

Craig - I've had three of them.

Bob - And they're all sold now?

Craig - Yep.

Bob - I know Boglione bought his from a Christie's auction in London. Were you the consignor?

Craig - No, no. Here's the history of that computer from day one: it was bought by electronics dealer Frank Anderson in Great Falls, Montana. Frank bought it in December of 1976. Something like that is on the invoice. Well, let's see if I can find the invoice. December 7th, 1976. And he bought it thinking he could run his business with it. So obviously, he

264

couldn't. He wrote, he called Apple and he said, you don't even have a keyboard and monitor. Jobs wrote him a letter to tell him how to hook up a keyboard to it. That's the typed letter on three ring binder paper that is still with the computer today. Anyhow, he was advertising this thing for sale in the *Computer Shopper*, back in the early '80s.

So, Steve Jobs had come and spoken at our annual MECC banquet in 1982. And of course, he told the Apple-1 story, and I'm sitting there thinking, 'God, I've got to have one of those.' After the banquet, we had a reception for him at our suite. So I asked him, how can I get a hold of one of these? And Jobs said, "Ahh, don't even worry about it, you'll never find one." He was a brash guy. And so he kind of just blew me off. But the guy with him, his name was Mike Murray, and I think Mike had a position at Apple for years. Mike said, "Here's my card, give me a call. I'll put you in touch with someone that's got one." So, I called him the next week and he sent me the information.

Turns out it was a guy in Indiana, Joe Torzewski. Well, Joe had two Apple-1's. He was looking to trade one for an Apple][with a whole bunch of software, and printer. I had an Apple][and I said, "Okay, we'll trade." So we drove out to Indiana. That was my first Apple-1. And that was probably, in my mind, one of the neater ones because it was a Byte Shop model. It had the 01-0005 serial number on it. It had the white 6502, and as I recall, it had the dull board. You know, I didn't realize there were all kinds of variations, so I actually called Wozniak, and he picked up the phone and he said, "Send me some pictures and I'll let you know." So I sent this detailed letter with all kinds of questions. And he wrote back, answered all my questions. And he said, "Yeah, this was a first run computer that was sold by the Byte Shop." And he said Apple didn't put the serial numbers on, but that the Byte Shop did. And so that was my first one.

And when I was there picking it up, Torzewski told me about another Apple-1 in Montana that was being advertised by Frank

265

Anderson. I figured, what the heck? Let's go for that one too. It turns out that the company I worked for, they also wanted one. So, fine. They flew me out there, I bought it, brought it back, and we made a display case at MECC where it was on display for a couple of years. And then it got stuck away in a drawer, and stayed there until the company closed in 1999.

In the meantime, I had found a third one. Again, advertised in the *Computer Shopper*. And this one came out of Indiana also, from Jim Alinsky. Jim had four of them. Jim's board was framed (like a painting), and it was mounted on a piece of gray Formica board. It was restored and supposedly running, but I never tried it. So anyhow, I had three of them now. Well, they all got sold.

The first one, the Torzewski machine from the Byte Shop—serial number 5, is the one Apple's Jean Louis Gassée got (Gassée was head of Apple Advanced Product Development and Worldwide Marketing).

One of the guys I worked with was at a meeting with Jean Louis Gassée at Apple, and he told Jean Louis about my Apple-1, and Gassée said he wanted it. He wanted to trade me a Macintosh for it. I said, "I don't need a Macintosh, I've already got one." Then he was going to throw in a laser printer, and I said, "I don't need one, we've got one hooked up to this one already." "Well, what do you need?" And I said, "Well, we want to buy a new van. So, I need enough money to buy a new van," and he said, "How much?" And I told him, and he said, "Okay, it's done."

So, Jobs sold a VW microbus to finance the Apple-1.... and I sold my Apple-1 to finance a van!

So the machine from Joe Torzewski went to Gassée, and hasn't been heard from since.

Then I thought to myself, "Okay, we've got this really nice boxed one at MECC, collecting dust. I wonder if they would trade me for the framed one?" So lo and behold, my boss said, "Yeah, I can hang that one on my wall, and this other one's just in a box." So, we traded. And so now I had that one.

I had it for a while. I'm one of those collectors that some things I'll never sell, but some things I'll let go of. Jesse Sackman, who's a collector in California, found out about it. He contacted me many times, made many offers, and eventually the offer was enough. So Jesse bought the boxed one, the Anderson machine. And that was probably—in my mind—that's probably the most pristine and complete Apple-1 in existence, it's in the original shipping box, with the original invoice, the letter from Jobs, all the manuals, the cassette interface, and the original *BASIC* cassette tape. It was all packed in foam, and it was pristine. Frank Anderson had only hooked it up one time and got it running, and then said, 'This ain't gonna do what I want it to do,' and put it on the shelf. So Jesse, after a number of years, decided to sell it on *eBay*. He sold it for fifty thousand dollars. And whoever bought it on *eBay*, they ultimately consigned it to Christie's where it was purchased by Boglione.

Bob - That seller is a mystery person.

Craig - I guess Jesse Sackman is the one who'd have that information.

Bob - Must be someone smart, because they made a lot of money.

Craig - If I'd kept all three of mine, I could have been having some fun. And then, let's see... *Oh!* And then the one from Alinsky, on the gray Formica board, a few years ago my old boss contacted me and said, "Are you interested?" and I said, "Yeah." We kind of went together and I sealed the deal on that one. And Rudi Brandstöetter got that one. That one was running, and Rudi's got it working.

Bob - How did Rudi find you? Did you advertise it?

Craig - I did. I put on the *Vintage Computer Forum* that I had some early micros, and that ad had been on there for months; I hardly ever checked it. One day I checked my email on there, and Rudi said, "Get ahold of me."

Bob - There was one mounted on a board which was possibly stolen from Steve Jobs' office.

Craig - Oh, yeah, Jim said that was the case.

Bob - Who would even consider stealing from Jobs office?

Craig - Jobs told me about his mounted Apple-1 getting stolen in 1982. But the one on the gray board that came from Alinsky, that was all done in the early '90s. And he did four. I got one, and Yoakum I think is the guy that got one, Dell Yoakum.

Bob - Alinsky thought it would be neat to display the computers on a board, so he was the guy who mounted them all?

Craig - Yeah, he scouted around and he found four Apple-1's, most of which had been bastardized and converted from 8k to 20k. And he redid the whole board to put them back to the original 8k, and mounted them for display. He's still got one. Well, at least he did a year ago.

Bob - I'm curious why you didn't keep one.

Craig - Um, none of them had that much sentimental value. My interests shift. I collect old cars. You wouldn't believe all the stuff I collect.

Bob - Do you still have a garage full of computers, or have you pared that down?

Craig - I probably got a hundred-plus micros left.

Bob - But that's a lot less then you had at one time for the museum?

Craig - For the museum, I had mainframes. I had a Bendix G-15, and a Burroughs 3300. And, most of a Univac III system.

Bob - So, what did you do with those?

Craig - Scrapped most of it. I wished I hadn't thrown a lot of it in the dump, because it was a lot of gold I threw away.

Bob - When you said that the funding for the museum went to Boston, what did you mean?

Craig - Originally, I worked through the governor's office in Minnesota, trying to get one started, and their suggestion was that we get together with the Science Museum of Minnesota. Then there was some controversy internally. Well, let's say funding is limited, but Control Data was willing to get behind this thing. But we were kind of shuffling our feet and not getting anything done, and Boston came through with their proposal, and that's where a lot of this money went. Other people were after the same kind of funding we were after. And they got their act together before we did.

Bob - You referenced the Byte Shop numbers. We've talked to everybody about the numbers. When we talked to Paul Terrell who started the Byte Shop, he said they didn't put the numbers on.

Craig - According to Woz, he and Jobs didn't put the numbers on them.

Bob - Right, everybody's told us that they didn't. Early employees, friends, and all.

Craig - I've seen three with the numbers on them. They're all in the same place on the boards and they're all identically written.

Bob - It does seem that the numbers would relate to the Byte Shop.

Craig - That's where they came from.

Bob - It could be that the ones with the numbers came from the Byte Shop, and the ones without the numbers didn't come from the Byte Shop. Mine's not a Byte Shop machine. I think we've identified seven or eight that have numbers on them.

Craig - What's the highest number you've found?

Bob - I think it's 01-0070.

Craig - Oh, no, hold it, Torzewsky, I just found his letter. His is 01-0057.

Bob - The one you had?

Craig - No, I had 01-0005. Torzewski had number 57. And I don't know, he's probably still got that one.

Bob - So, you had number 5, he has 57.

Craig - He had them both at one time. Yes, I got 5, and he kept 57.

Bob - More recently Woz said that area was something that Steve Jobs handled. And that he wasn't really involved with that, so he doesn't really know.

Craig - This one was $666. I found this kind of neat, on the box the shipping label says "Crist Drive." And that was different than the Apple Computer address, which was "Welch Road."

Bob - Oh, Crist Drive is the Jobs home.

Craig - Yep, that's what he said. That's the house, and Welch Road was nothing more than an answering service. Well, I sent Woz a copy of the invoice that was in the one I got from Montana, the one in the box. And it had the shipping label on the box, and so anyhow I just sent him a copy of all that. Woz said, "I never knew about any of this stuff. Jobs must have sold it without me knowing." *Whoa!*

Bob - That's not an isolated story. My Apple-1 was sold directly from the garage and bought by a guy who lived four miles from Jobs. I have the cancelled checks for mine, made out to Apple, so we know it didn't go through the Byte Shop. I think one of my questions to Wozniak was about mine being sold for six hundred dollars even, which is different than what you usually hear about the pricing. Woz suggested that the price must have been what Jobs decided he'd take for it that day. No one else necessarily knew.

Since you were involved in the beginning, did it seem that both Woz and Jobs were interested in the education application?

Craig - Woz went back to teaching after the whole thing. I don't think Jobs cared who used their computers, or why they used them as long as they bought them. And that was the big thing about us in Minnesota, is we were generating the software that was selling *thousands* of Apple][s. There were states out there that would put contracts out for computers and their schools couldn't buy the computers unless it would run our software. And California was one of those states. We had a forward-thinking CEO way back then that said, 'We've got to choose a microcomputer.' The company spent time looking at Texas Instruments, at Radio Shack, Commodore, all the different brands. It was like, 'Which one are we going to develop for?' And a deal got struck with Apple.

270

We were out there courting different companies. We were mainframe computer producers. Our software was running on a timeshare system. And we knew micros were the thing of the future. It was just a matter of which one? Are we going to do it for all of them, or get out and go for it? And for a while we did a lot with Commodore and Texas Instrument, but it just didn't work out. And the sales of their machines weren't even close to what Apple ended up doing.

Bob - What caused the relationship with Apple to end?

Craig - It never ended. We had that relationship until our company went away in 1999.

Bob - What was the reason MECC went away?

Craig - To begin with, we were a state agency. We were part of the Department of Education. And of course, that raised the ire of other software companies. Like, we'd get tax breaks and they didn't. Other companies would say 'What's going on?' So, we became a public corporation and eventually the state sold us off. But for years and years we were a state agency.

Bob - So it was an initiative for educational purposes and it turned into a business?

Craig - Well, we would produce thirty or thirty-five packages for the Apple every year. And we gave them free to all the Minnesota schools, and we sold them to the other forty- nine states. That's what financed us, and then some. So, I think at one time we had a hundred and seventy-nine employees.

Bob - When you described that Jobs came out to speak to you all, I know that you described what it was like to talk to him, but what was his talk like?

Craig - Well, I actually have a copy of it. It's kind of garbled a little bit, but I mean parts of it are pretty audible.

Bob - You recorded it?

Craig - Well, a buddy of mine recorded it, and when we shut the company down, he's cleaning out his office and he threw it on my desk and said, "Here." He says, "I don't want to throw this thing away." I said, "No, we'll hang on to that." So, Jobs told the Apple-1 story, and he talked about different projects, and initiatives around the country in communication.

Bob - Have you ever published that?

Craig - I haven't, I've actually had the cassette converted to CD. The quality isn't that great. I was hoping that the company that did it could have enhanced it. At one point I was thinking about seeing if there's any interest in it on *eBay*, but I haven't.

This is kind of neat because I guess it's fairly early: November of '82. Apple had only been up and running for probably four years. Yeah, there's nothing earth shattering, I think the one part that sticks in my mind is he literally described the iPad there, back then. As he said, this is what we envision in the future, but we don't have the technology to do it yet. And it was to a tee. So, I think he had that in his mind way back then.

Here is an excerpt from the 1982 speech by Steve Jobs, recorded by Craig Solomonson. The recording is not high quality, so there is some paraphrasing:

"I had one or two really incredible teachers and the mark that they were able to leave, as I look back, was enormous. My mother taught me to read when I was five, so I hit school. I was bored, and I just got into all sorts of mischief. I had a friend, Rick Barentino. He and I would cut out endlessly. Second grade was terrible. My third grade teacher had a nervous twitch that we gave her. Rick and I were scheduled to be in the same fourth grade class, and at the last moment, the psycho principle of the school noticed this and said, "No." It turns out that one of the saints in my life was a woman named Mrs. Philip. She said, "Well, I'll take one of them." I was the one. What she did was she said, "Steven, I'll tell you what. I'll give you five dollars if you complete this workbook." I had never encountered the free market before. She was wonderful. She got this little box of camera kits to build, got me interested in geology and things like that. One of the things she did was she got me an Abacus, and she taught me all the bases of numbers, and actually got me reading about computers. That was actually my first exposure into the whole thing, old Mrs. Philip, and I learned a lot.

"Made a lot of money too. Woz and I grew up in Silicon Valley. We're sort of products of this entrepreneurial risk culture that is there. Our heroes were sort of Hewlett-Packard. We saw a lot of people try to do things, some succeeded and some failed. We noticed, with people who failed, it was almost like you could leave a company and experience failure. Then, you could go back and be worth more to that company, because you had an interdisciplinary experience. So the penalty for failure was very, very low. There is a culture there that sort of breeds a lot of this innovation.

"What happened was Woz was working for Hewlett-Packard designing these calculators, HP calculators in the early '70s, and I was working for Atari designing video games. I was employee number 40 at Atari. There were these really crude computer kits on the market that you could buy for three, four, five hundred dollars, and Woz and I didn't really have the money, so we designed one and sort of liberated the parts from Hewlett-Packard. It took fifty hours to wire one of these things together, because it was very intricate. All of our friends, the minute they saw it, wanted one. It hooked up to a television, and it was basically an Apple-1 which we made two hundred of subsequently. All of our friends wanted one, so we were spending all of our spare weekends helping our friends to wire their little computers up as they would raid their parts, and this had to stop.

"Woz sold his HP65 calculator, and I sold my VW Microbus, and we got thirteen hundred bucks together. We paid a friend of mine to

273

make what was called printed circuit board, which is a piece of fiberglass with copper on both sides and it's photographically etched, so that you can cut the assembly time from sixty hours to maybe six hours. These were going to cost us twenty-five dollars apiece to make, and so we thought that if we make up a hundred of them, we figured we could buy them for twenty-five dollars and sell them for fifty dollars, and then we would make two thousand five hundred dollars profit, which we could then spend on our transportation and calculation bills. That was the plan. But we didn't have the two thousand five hundred dollars to make these things, so we were going to go out and take orders before we had made them. We walked into a one of the first computer stores called The Byte Shop. The guy said he wanted fifty of them. We saw the dollar signs in front of our eyes, but he said he wanted them totally assembled and ready to go. This was a whole new twist. We took our little prototype down to the local electronic parts distributor and we showed it to him, and they gave us about twenty-five thousand dollars' worth of electronic parts net thirty days on thin air. We had no collateral. They took a gamble on us, and we didn't even know what that thirty days was. We took the parts home and we built one hundred computers and we delivered fifty to The Byte Shop, and they paid us in cash. We paid for the parts in twenty-nine days, which started our attention to cash flows. Then we're sitting there with fifty computers on the floor, which represent our microbus and calculator, so we had to learn about marketing and distribution and stuff like that."

In the talk, Jobs also shared a quote he'd heard from a CEO:

"The first person to get to a marketplace is akin to the first contestant in an archery contest that can pull the bow back, fire the arrow and hit the wall, and then paint the bulls-eye around where their arrow hit." Jobs then added his thoughts, "I think that in any fast moving marketplace, there appears to be truth to that, so we really want to be very aggressive in going ahead and trying..."

Chapter 28

Registry

The *Apple-1 Registry* is an online listing of all known surviving Apple-1 computers. Mike Willegal started the Registry a few years ago, and it appears to be just one of his many hobbies. His personal website has sections for photography, model railroads, tropical fish, and war gaming, as well as vintage computers. The Registry has become the *go-to* resource for anyone with an interest in the Apple-1 computer.

In the Registry, Mike breaks down the survivors into two series. The earliest are the "First PCB Run," of which his count is twenty-five survivors. The newer series is the "Second PCB Run," of which seventeen are known to survive. A handful of others are listed, including Steve Wozniak's prototype, and so the current grand total list of survivors is at forty-eight. These are the computers Mike lists as "Positively identified to date!" There are questions about certain machines, such as whether they're listed in the correct series category, because of a lack of known details on some models. And there are machines whose whereabouts are unknown. The eleventh machine listed is known to have sold at a Vintage Computer Festival in 2003, but there's no indication of who might own it today. The twenty-fourth on the list, and the last of the first series listed, was "seen at De Anza College Vintage Computer Display, December 29, 2007" and that's the most current information available on it.

From the top, the first unit listed is Woz's hand-wired prototype. At one time, it was in an Apple Computer historic display, but Woz indicates its current location is unknown. Next up is freelance teacher Liza Loop's machine, given to her by Woz (but only after Jobs made Woz pay for it out of his pocket). After Apple veteran Jef Raskin mentioned in an interview that he owned the first Apple-1, Woz proclaimed that he'd given the first one to a school teacher. Woz's statement came over twenty years after Liza had gotten it from Woz, and its special status came as a surprise to her. Original owner Wendell Sander's machine is listed third. Purchased by Wendell from a Byte Shop in 1976, today it has a top-notch Plexiglas housing built by Wendell. Next on the list is one of four that was framed years ago by Jim Alinsky. In terms of appearance, that means that the original circuit board is mounted on a gray surface, and bordered with a metal picture frame. Next is the Joey Copson machine, currently in the collection of the author, and purchased directly from the Copson family. Joey originally installed his Apple-1 in a housing that looks very much like the IBM Selectric typewriters sold in the 1960s. The housing, still with it today, is kind of a clamshell design.

The Registry notes instances when the machines are numbered; some are and some aren't. Also, there are units with a little label or stamping on the backside of the board. The stamping might be a 7, an 8, or an L. No one seems to know for sure what these markings mean. The next two machines listed are the former Apple employees, the Huston brothers' Apple-1's, both of which were sold on *eBay*.

Next up is an Apple-1, which was donated to a now-defunct historic computer association by a former chief scientist at Apple. That machine is now in private hands. Two down from it is a machine believed to have always been installed in a briefcase, and now in a museum in Maine. The thirteenth listed is the Ricketts machine, also owned by this author, and described as having been sold at the La Salle Gallery to Captain O'Mahoney in 1999. Two down from there is a machine now housed in a museum in Bern, Switzerland.

The order of the machines in the series one or series two groups is probably no indication of which came first. Without actual serial numbers, sales records, or (in most cases) original purchase papers, it's difficult to try and put them in proper order. And questions abound, such as in reference to the last machine in the first series, "Could this be the missing mate to Glen Hoags machine?"

In the list of the second series, or "Second PCB Run", first up is Jef Raskin's machine. The Second PCB Run machines can be identified by the NTI logo in the copper, under the *Apple Computer 1* label. Next is Rick Crandall's, listed as having been first purchased in June, 1977. After that is the first Apple-1 sold at a Vintage Computer Festival, originally purchased by Indiana computer-chain store owner Ray Borrill in late 1976. It's now in an Asian collection. The next unit listed still has the original box it was shipped in, from Apple. There's also a letter with it, signed by Steve Jobs in January of 1978. The letter was an offer to the owner. He could trade in his Apple-1 along with a check for four hundred dollars, and receive a new Apple][4k board. This is an example of the company's desire to get those old Apple-1's to 'go away' (be traded-in so they could be destroyed). That unit has a sticker with the number 37 on it, as does the next one on the list. After that is a machine owned by the Computer History Museum in Mountain View, California. Two down is a unit said to have been traded for a Cray-1 Supercomputer, and the Apple is slated to be part of a computer museum in Korea.

Two down from there on the list is the "cursed" Apple-1, presently in a museum collection in France. The 'curse' attached to it is due to the deaths of two subsequent owners. The next unit was found and purchased in a garage sale by Monroe Postman. It has a sticker with 49 on it, and is in a museum collection. Next is one of the four owned by

Dave Larsen, of Floyd, Virginia. This is the one purchased from Wozniak's friend Adam Schoolsky. After that is the unit sold by Christie's to Marco Boglione in Italy. Three down is a machine in the Science Museum of London.

At the end of the lists of both series are five units about which there's very little information. One is the Apple-1 in the Smithsonian, which is currently not on display. Many of the computers in the Registry text feature details as to which memory chips they have, and originals are identifiable partially because they're all white and gold. Many of the small components are date-coded: the system uses the specific months number in the year, and the last two digits of the year. So, the date-stamp 7620 would indicate the 20th month of 1976.

The biggest question has to do with the meaning or relevance of a series of numbers that are hand-written on the back of some boards. They're commonly referred to as the 'Byte Shop numbers.' The problem is that the founder of the Byte Shop, Paul Terrell, says the Byte Shop didn't apply the numbers. Mike Willegal relates that Steve Jobs said that Apple didn't apply the numbers. I've also asked the same thing of many of the early employees, all of whom are unaware of the numberings actual origin.

We spoke with Mike in October of 2011.

Bob - Could you tell me how you got so interested in the Apple-1?

Mike Willegal - I bought an Apple][back in 1978. I kept it in the attic, and then a few years ago I had a little electronics project where I thought it might be useful, so I pulled it down and got it running again. I eventually built a reproduction of the original circuit board, because at one time it had been repaired. I had fun with that, and then, of course, the Apple-1 is the model more interesting to a lot of collectors. So I ended up doing the same thing with the Apple-1, primarily because I had so much fun doing it on the Apple][.

Bob - What got you interested in building *The Registry*, and figuring out where all the existing ones were?

Mike - I was gathering a lot of data when I built my reproduction of the original Apple-1; what parts they were using for instance, and I gathered a snapshot of different Apple-1's. And I thought, 'Well, I've got a lot of interesting data here about Apple-1's, why not put it up and share it with people?' Because, as you know, there's a lot of interest in the Apple-1. And I had a lot of data, so I figured I'd share it. And then, once I put that registry up I actually started getting more data. People noticed the Registry and started sending me more information, and it kind of snowballed a little bit.

Bob - So a lot of it has been people helping you out with details?

Mike - Reproducing the Apple-1 involved a lot of research, and as I did the research and gathered data, I learned a lot. I was looking for differences between boards. I don't actually own an original board or even have access to one; I was doing research on the Internet. I contacted a couple of owners that actually had Apple-1's, and they sent me information.

Anytime anybody sends me new data, I update the Registry. There's a guy in Virginia named Dave Larsen that's got four computers. He's sending me information on them and I'll probably be updating in the next month or so, adding another four systems on there.

Bob - How did he get four?

Mike - Well, in the old days, there used to be a magazine called *Computer Shopper*. He used to advertise for old machines in there. So that's what happens. People come out of the blue. Some people don't want to get in the registry, because they're so afraid of these things getting stolen.

Bob - Are computers just kind of a hobby for you, or do you work with computers regularly?

Mike - I bought that Apple][in 1978. I learned to program and within a year after that, I got my first job. I've been in the industry—either in minicomputers or networking—since then.

Bob - Have you used or had an original Apple-1?

Mike - No, not an original. Like I said, my Apple][was early. I think the serial number was 2600 or something like that. But I got into computers just after the Apple-1.

Bob - Do you work with any other brands of older computers, or are you an Apple person?

Mike - I have interest in other brands. In school, I used some early stuff. I've used Amiga's at work in years past. I have a compact portable that I had to buy for a company I work for, because we were using them for development. That was the first true PC-compatible, but as far as personal machines, I've mostly been into Apple.

Bob - What do you think of some of the ones that have sold recently? Like the one in London that sold for like over two hundred thousand dollars, did that surprise you?

Mike - I think that surprised everybody. Every once in a while someone will send me an email, and say 'Can you find me an original Apple-1?' and the way I answer them now is, 'How serious are you, are you willing to pay Christie's type prices?' I don't think you'll see many people put them on the market until they figure out whether that's a real price or not, and whether it can be repeated.

Bob - Earlier, you said the Apple-1 is more interesting than the Apple][. Is it due to the machine itself, or because it's the original?

Mike - I'm just speaking in terms of collectors. For collectors, it's more interesting because there's so few. In terms of the architecture, the Apple-1 video system is very clever, but the processor system is extremely simple.

Bob - How long have you had the Registry up, and when did you start getting involved in the replicas and all that stuff?

Mike - I think the Apple][thing was three years ago. And then I started on an Apple-1 replica and I really didn't have any good data. So I put it aside, because I just didn't have the information I needed. And then, I'd say a year and a half ago, some guy put one up on *eBay*. So I sent him an email to see if he could send me good scans of the board. And he did, so I said, 'Oh, this is good.' That got me restarted, so about a year and a half ago I started again on the Apple-1.

Bob - Have you come across especially interesting stories?

Mike - Well, most of them I've put up on the website. That one in France that supposedly is jinxed, you know? It seems like very quickly they became collectors' items.

I don't know if you talked to Howard Cantor – the guy that laid out the PCB. Well this guy, I don't think he gets any credit for laying out the print circuit boards. Back in the old days, they basically laid it out on a drafting table, laid tape on a clear or a white piece of paper, and took a photograph of it. So, this guy laid out the Apple-1. He did an unbelievable job, because there are no mistakes in the PCB. And this thing has 1700 holes in it, and wires running all over the place. He just did an incredible job; I don't think he gets enough credit.

The other thing is when they laid it out, it's clear (I haven't had this confirmed by anybody.) they weren't sure if they could afford to put a silkscreen on it, which is how the white lettering is done on the green board. That's an extra step in a process. So they laid it out to be made just as a copper board, with or without a silkscreen. I actually contacted him at one point, to find out his view of what happened. And it's kind of funny, his response. He said, "Oh yeah, I laid out a hobby board for the two Steve's. But I didn't do anything with their production stuff." But I know he did it because he says, 'Oh yeah, they had one of my boards in the display of old computers at Fry's.' Fry's is a computer store in Silicon Valley. Their display of old computers included an Apple-1. Wendell Sander told me there was one in there at one time. And Howard says,

281

'They had one of my boards in the display case at Fry's Computer at one time, but it wasn't a production machine. It was just done for hobbyists.' So he thinks he just laid out a board for some hobby guys, and doesn't realize he laid out the first board for Apple Computer. At least that's the impression he gave.

Maybe he just doesn't want any notoriety.

Bob - As for Steve Wozniak, how and why did you go about contacting him? Was it for *The Registry*, or was it so you could build a replica?

Mike - We eventually figured out his email address. He's very approachable, and I was curious about some things. For instance, there's a common misconception about how they built the boards in their garage or whether they really had a contract house build the boards. So, I sent him a question like, 'Did you guys really build the boards? They look like they were flow-soldered, which is an automated process that the contract houses will use to make and assemble boards.' And Woz said, "Oh, yeah, we had this contract house down in Santa Clara build the boards; I couldn't believe how cheap it was so, we just had them go do it." What they did in the garage was to take the assembled boards and test them.

It took some money to build those boards. But both Steves worked in the industry. Steve Wozniak worked at HP in the engineering group. He was in the industry, and they knew how people in the industry did things. It wasn't like a bunch of guys decided to build a car, whom had never built a car before. But I think the real reason they were successful is probably Steve Jobs. Without marketing and business being able to sell these things, they would have gone nowhere.

Bob - What is the lasting appeal of the Apple-1 for you? Why is it so interesting, above other old computers from a similar period?

Mike - For me, it's kind of simple. It was a simple machine. It was built with off the shelf chips, so it's actually feasible to try to reproduce it. I don't have to spend hundreds of thousands of dollars getting some custom chips made to do a reproduction. So it's an era. The Apple][, a year later, had *custom* chips in it. Later models are virtually impossible to reproduce for someone just doing it for fun. That early microcomputer era is a lot of fun because they're repairable. You can still get parts, which is kind of incredible. Some parts are very hard to find, but you can still get them. If you look at an earlier era computer, like HP had a computer that Wozniak was familiar with (he talks about it in his book). They had a desktop computer, but there's no way I could reproduce that. It was way too complex. So there's just this little period in time where these microcomputers were out there, and you can repair them, work with them, and understand them. You go into the early '70s, and it's not true. And once you get into the '80s, it's no longer true. So it's kind of a funny window in time.

Bob - That makes sense.

Mike - Maybe! We're a little nutty.

Chapter 29

Snake Byte

When I first spoke with Lonnie Mimms in October 2011, he was thinking about plans for the growth of his computer collection museum in the Atlanta area.

Bob - Tell me about your background, your museum, and how you came to have these interests.

Lonnie Mimms - I started in computers in the mid '70s. It was as a student and I was introduced to the IBM 360 on a timeshare system. At that point, the first language I learned was *APL* (A Programming Language), which is a rather bizarre language. *APL* is one of the fairly early languages that IBM developed, and it uses a lot of special symbols and characters that you don't have on your keyboard. It's very powerful; with one little symbol you can do an incredible amount of things. But it makes it hard to understand somebody else's work, or even your own work after just a few days.

From there forward I was absolutely hooked, and computers basically became a hobby for me. I was about twelve years old. Toward the end of the '70s, I started using computers in Atlanta. A friend's father was a professor at Georgia Tech, the Georgia Institute of Technology, in downtown Atlanta. He and I would go down to their computer center. They had a Cyber74, which was a Control Data Corporation computer. It was one of the early super-computers. They didn't really call them that back then, but we would use that timeshare system. We'd go in—these little kids going in with the college students. Just to keep people from getting totally pissed-off at us, we'd help students with their *FORTRAN*

284

programs and get them working. We tried to endear ourselves, rather than have them look at us like we were just taking up space. It seemed to work pretty well.

In '77 or '78, I got a hold of my first mini-computer. It was a Sol-20 from Processor Technology. Back then, they weren't called *personal computers*. I look at the beginning as being two different paths. You had the Apple path, which gradually got created. And then, you had the PC path. Apple and Dell, for example, was the way things evolved. I never really had much to do with Apple in the early days. I always viewed an Apple computer as a toy, for games. They just seemed more limited. The Apple-1, of course, was extremely limited. It wasn't one of the first ones out at that time. The S-100 bus machines like the Altair, IMSAI, and the Sol-20 were of that lineage. There was a lot of stuff available for them. You'd buy a disk drive for your computer, and it would come with software. There wasn't any great standardization on the software side. I picked out a disk drive that had what appeared to be the best *BASIC* language version and the most capacity. That was my Micropolis disk drive.

I guess my first real Apple experience was when I was in college in 1980. One of my roommates, Chuck Sommerville, had an Apple][and he was writing games. He wrote a game called *Snake Byte*, where you have a little snake and worm that goes around the screen directed by the arrow keys.

Bob - Like they had on original cell phones?

Lonnie - Yeah. It would go up and bite an apple, and you'd try to aim it and hit the apple. Then, different levels would add mazes and things that were very hard to manipulate. I was basically the test person for his game. As Chuck created new levels, I would advance through them and tell him if they were hard or not. He ended up selling it, and working as a freelance author for one of the early game companies in California, Epyx. He was pretty successful at the gaming thing, and I think he made a decent amount of money. Back then it wasn't a whole lot, though, by today's standards.

He went on to write a program called *Gruds in Space*, which was one of the early graphics-oriented adventure games. Another friend of ours at college did all of the artwork. He had these neat screen shots; nothing was really animated, but very cool screen shots that he would come up with based upon Chuck's description of what he was looking for. I was the test rabbit for that as well. You know, I would try to solve the puzzles and make sure that there was continuity and logic to it.

So that was my first real exposure to the whole Apple thing. But I never really took to it. I just stuck with the PC line. As for the museum, I just kept going with this collection. I now have two to three thousand machines that include a few bits and pieces, mainframe computers, big tape drives, one of the more modern Cray Computers, and things like that. I had a goal of getting one machine of each type, representing the early days of the computer industry, because they're disappearing.

Bob - Two to three thousand machines?

Lonnie - At this point, I've pretty much lost track. I've got so many duplicates of some of the more common ones that I don't really have an exact count. But it is quite a few machines.

I asked about his purchase of an Apple-1 from Dick Huston.

One of the neat things about buying the Apple-1 from Dick Huston was that I arranged to go out to the Valley after the purchase, and sat down and talked to Woz for a while. Then, we went over to Wendell Sander's house and met with several of the other early engineers. It was very cool. One of them actually took us into the computer museum out there. Unfortunately it was under renovation, so they only had the lobby display. I've got about ten times more than that, so it really wasn't a big deal, but just being with the people was absolutely incredible.

If you can picture going back and meeting Gutenberg, or being at the beginning of the industrial revolution—picking out a handful of the key players—I mean it's phenomenal. This is a moment in time that's changed the entire direction of mankind. I don't think even the automobile, a thousand years from now looking back, will have the impact as the beginning of the computer industry. I've essentially witnessed the creation of an entire new world. You know, you think about those little cusps in history that really make a difference. And to be able to accumulate all this stuff and then try to put a storyline with it, something that has meaning.

You had the first kit computers that were from Albuquerque, New Mexico. So it was very much a national thing, it wasn't just focused in Northern California, or in one little area. A guy named Ed Roberts, with the MITS Altair, he's the guy that got Paul Allen and Bill Gates started. They wrote *BASIC* for the Altair, and went out to Albuquerque. Now everything has gravitated to Silicon Valley. Everything from the transitives to the integrated circuits being invented, those were in Texas and New Jersey. Apple, at least in the beginning, was more the exception than the rule. They all point to HP and Apple as being the famous garage businesses, but most of the microcomputer industry was not in California at all.

Since the auction in Europe, Apple-1 prices have soared. I purchased three Apple-1's and it was all before that auction. I thought I was paying a pretty hefty number. What I paid for each one of them is more than I've paid for anything else. And some of the other machines, frankly, could be viewed as historically much more significant. You know, an Alto from Xerox is technically a much more important machine than an Apple. That's actually where most of the Macintosh and the Lisa stuff came from. So as far as originality, Xerox created so much of the look, feel, and design of what we use today. The Apple-1, because it was the first machine from a company that's now the biggest technology company

287

in the world, is significant. But it could've disappeared, like two hundred other machines that you've never heard of, and nobody would care. I've got two versions of a machine considered by the Boston Computer Museum as being the first, quote, *personal computer*, electronic, affordable, and already assembled. It was the Kenbak-1, and they only made forty of them. Whereas, with the Apple-1, two hundred were made. From a rarity standpoint, it's actually a much more common machine.

Bob - When did you get your first Apple collectible? Was Dick's the first one or did you have others before his?

Lonnie - I had a lot of Apple stuff, mainly Apple]['s, long before this. I'd seen other Apple-1's come up for auction before, and at that point I guess I just didn't have the feel for the pricing because there were so few prior examples. I wasn't comfortable with the price people were paying. I remember the one before Dick's actually was the exact one that sold at auction for fifty thousand dollars. I thought that was an absolutely outrageous number. A year later, Dick's came up, and at that point it was a void in my collection. There're only a couple of machines I'm missing that have real significance, and that was one of them. So you pay a stupid price to make the collection complete from the average person's perspective, in order to include all the recognizable machines. I talked to Dick before the auction came up, and said, "Well, would there be any chance I could meet Woz? You're one of the original engineers, maybe you could introduce us." And he said, "Oh, no problem, Woz is an incredibly friendly guy." Huston said, "You know, I can probably introduce you to some of the other early engineers I'm friends with." And I said, "Well, that would be absolutely amazing." So I was looking as much to the value of the ongoing relationship with Dick and his associates as I was to that of the machine itself.

Bob - Can you tell me about your museum?

Lonnie - Right now, it's really for tours by arrangement only. I built a couple buildings just to house some of the collection, but they're not big.

One of them is about three thousand five hundred square feet, the other one is two thousand five hundred square feet. And there's a farmhouse and other more barn-like, raw spaces where I have the less important computer stuff stored. Overall, it's about eight thousand square feet of computers and related paraphernalia. Unfortunately, most of it is stacked floor to ceiling, with little walkways that you can hardly get through. But I do have one building where I have a pretty good chronological display of machines, starting with some old analog machines in the '50s, and the Heathkit Analog Computer from about 1960. And then on through the mid-'90s. At some point, I need to level off. When everything became a Dell or an HP clone, they just became less meaningful. I have Steve Jobs' NeXT computer, which was an invention from after he got kicked out of Apple. I also have a BBOX, which is another cool recent machine.

Bob - Do you have a vision for the museum in the future?

Lonnie - I think eventually I'll have a nicer building, to have a much more public facility. And of course, to develop the educational component of it, and have some hands-on activities. You really don't see anything like that on this side of the country. The museum in California is by far the number one in the world; as far as the number of computers, the depth of the collection, and the amount of people working there. They completely take it for granted that they have access to all these people. I went in there with one of the early Apple guys and the minute he walks in the door, they're harassing him about some program they want and how they'll send people to his house to go through his hundreds of floppy drives and find it. I'm like, 'My God, you should be kissing his feet just for walking in here, you know, this is pitiful.'

They're too close to it; I really don't think they appreciate what they have. I want to spread the love around a little bit, and to not have one place in the whole world where everything is accumulated, or focused in one spot. If the museum burns down, what's left? I'm a firm believer in distributing things around. I think the fact that the Ancient Egyptian

289

antiquities are in the British Museum in London, and at the Neues Museum in Berlin, is fantastic. To repatriate that treasure, and bring it all back to Egypt, would be a huge mistake. I think you can see with the Arab Spring how much we don't even know about what's been destroyed. Having everything centralized, no matter how stable the country is, or how great everything looks, is a mistake if you want to keep cultural artifacts for true posterity. So, I'd like to be the computer museum on the East Coast, outside of the Smithsonian, that really focuses on computer history and has examples (hopefully *working ones*) of a lot of early machines. Stuff that's actually come from other parts of the world, besides California. A good example of that is the Hayes Modem, which early was a very big player in the whole networking thing.

Bob - Do you work with computers for a living?

Lonnie - It's a big hobby. If I worked with them, I would probably hate them! It's bad enough having one on my desk that I have to be chained to for emails.

I'm in real estate, a family business that's been going on for four generations. I'm in the third generation, so we've been lucky to be in a very good part of the country.

Bob - Have you ever sold duplicates of anything you have in your computer collection?

Lonnie - Believe it or not, to date I have not sold a single thing. If you've ever seen shows like *American Pickers* or the *Hoarders* show, as collections go I've literally seen houses and condos that look worse than anything on those shows. The worst-case was where there was only one room in the house you could get into, only enough room to walk sidewalks in the hallways and up the steps. Well, I'm probably in that category. But, I've been able to give some of the old computer guys around Atlanta a way to get rid of all of their clutter. It's going to a good home, not to the dump.

290

Bob - How do you find out about things like that? Are they advertising they want to get rid of their stuff?

Lonnie - No, not at all. It's like this massive self-feeding network; just word of mouth. I actually had Cameron Cooper come and visit just like Dick did, and bring his Apple-1 that I bought from him. And we sat at my work bench and hooked up the other Apple-1's to see if they were going to work. And even though Cameron's much younger, he knows more about the Apple-1 now than anybody that originally built it can remember. He's hands-on and he wants to know how everything works. So it's just been this huge network that's grown tremendously.

There's some clubs of old computer guys. I met one guy that started out working on Sage Computers in the Air Force back in the '50s, and I got a whole bunch of stuff from him. Part of the engineer mentality is you don't let things go because you always feel like something can be used later. It would be a waste to throw it away. That's really helped quite a bit to accumulate a lot of these machines and fill in the bits and pieces, and also get the stories to go with them, to tie it all together.

Bob - Do you ever plan on selling anything in the future, or will you be a hoarder?

Lonnie - Oh, I think I'm there. But the weird thing about collectors is that you're always looking to upgrade for something that's in better shape. You keep the extras because you figure you're not going to be able to get the parts to keep that one pristine machine working. And at some point, it does become absurd. So there will probably be a time when I'll move into a bigger facility that will be planned and organized from the get go. It won't be cluttered up, it will be set up in nice displays, and my existing facility will be the prep facility and storage. And if there's twenty-five IBM XTs', we'd have a board of directors say, "Okay, we only need eight to maintain for this amount of time, so let's go ahead and sell the other ones, or trade them with other museums. I definitely think there will be a process to the whole thing.

Bob - How many Apple-1's do you currently have?

Lonnie - I have three. You can get them off the *Apple-1 Registry*. Mike Willegal just refers to me as 'the same guy who has Dick Huston's machine has this one.'

And if you mention anything at all about me, try to do it under the 'passionate' category rather than the nutcase!

Chapter 30

Jesus Jeans

In November of 2010, an Apple-1 was auctioned in London by Christie's. It achieved a world record price of $212,267. Steve Wozniak traveled from California to attend the auction. The winning bidder made his bids by phone, but his brother was said to be onsite at the auction. The buyer was 54 year old Italian sportswear magnate Marco Boglione, who founded BasicNet in 1983. This particular Apple-1 came with its original shipping box, and a period signed letter from Steve Jobs. The original purchaser was Frank Anderson of the Electric City Radio Supply in Great Falls, Montana. I spoke with Marco in June 2011.

Bob - Congratulations on your purchase of the Apple.

Marco Boglione - Thank you very much, I know you are an Apple-1 owner too. There should be a club or something.

Bob - It would be a small club.

Marco - A small club, very exclusive. We should do it.

Bob - I want to ask you, how did you get into business? How did you become an entrepreneur?

Marco - I wanted to be an entrepreneur when I was a kid. I started my university, but I was feeling wasting time and then I quit and I started working as an employee. I did it very successfully for basically ten years. Then my boss got sick and was passing away, so I decided to quit and to start my own business, and I did it. And then I stayed, I'm what you in the States call a garage entrepreneur. So, I somehow survived the garage stage and it grew and in Europe in the mid-'80s and jackets and stuff with soccer and football teams, Italian football teams. I grew and developed in my mind a business model for producing and selling my products, which is still today the core of our business. And then, after ten years later, in the early '90s, the company I was working for–which had good fashion brands in Italy, very well-known in Italy—after my boss passed away went broke. The company went broke, and I bought it. I bought it with my small company. And we're still here. We got quite a good business worldwide. Our sales of products are more than a billion dollars per year worldwide and we're still here.

Bob - One of your businesses is Jesus Jeans?

Marco - Jesus Jeans is a very old brand and we are re-launching in December. Then we have Kappa which is a sport brand like Adidas or Nike. It's quite known in Europe. Then we have Superga. We call it People's Shoes of Italy. It's really very famous. We have a very famous brand in other parts of the world that is K-Way. It's a rain jacket and windbreaker, which folds in this pocket and you can wear. You can carry it by having on your wrist.

Bob - Will Jesus Jeans be sold in the U.S.?

Marco - No, not yet.

Bob - So do you start in Europe, and if it's successful, go to the U.S.?

Marco - Possibly. The aim is to go global with our brands, for sure. So, the U.S. is still forty percent of the global market. But it's not something that's close to do.

Bob - When did you first become interested in Apple?

Marco - I became interested in Apple, in fact, when I was in my twenties. When I started, you know, playing and dreaming with these things. I was watching from Italy what was going on and there was no Internet at that time. I was an owner of an Apple][and then I made my life and became entrepreneur. I started my business, thanks to Apple, because I started printing catalogues for mail order in the mid-'80s by using Macintosh and laser printers and reducing master costs of printing the catalogues. So, I was able to be an entrepreneur thanks to these new technologies. Then my life went on and the company grew. At a certain point, in fact in the early '90s, we very sadly had to say 'bye-bye' to Apple because they weren't following the developments of service, and they were very late in integrating new technologies with the web at that time. So my company became a Microsoft addicted company for more than a decade, and that's it. And then, Steve came back to Apple and restarted the new life and the new era of Apple with those new devices – *fantastic*. And at that time, I started reconsidering my life, but independently from the iPhone. There was *eBay*, and I was going on *eBay* at night looking for memories of my life. Then I started buying; and that was three or four years ago. I considered what I enjoyed in my life, what the technology meant to me. I said *'Wow*, that really was a revolution,' so I started putting together the costume revolution. We are a jeans company, in fact we come from that business.

So I started thinking to that revolution, the information technology revolution, which started in garages and really changed the world, you know? More than any other important revolution of those years, the musical, political, social, and that of costume, the freedom of being dressed like you want, and being able to express yourself with your

294

clothes. But more than all these others '60s and '70s revolutions, the information technology revolution really changed the world more than any other ones, because in fact, it gave access to knowledge to common people. According to me, the world is a freer world, mainly because of it.

So I started thinking to buy the computers that created the revolution, to have a memory. And then I started thinking maybe one day, if I want to waste some money, maybe I would promote a museum in Turin, the place where I live, dedicated to the freedom of information and the so-called information technology revolution. So I started buying vintage machines, and I enjoyed setting up a little structure within the company, buying them and looking for the numbers—the specific numbers for the Apple][—and then cleaning them and testing them.

So I entered a little bit the community of vintage computer collectors in Italy. My friends started following and listening to help me with leads and one day last October a guy said, 'Wait,' and sent me an email saying there's an Apple-1 at Christie's. And I said, 'That's okay, that is like cheese on macaronis.' Like we say in Italian, the cherry on the cake. I said, 'This must be mine.' So, this I have to try. I'm rich enough not to destroy myself. I don't know whether it's the right price, or not the right price. Who cares at the end? The piece was good. It was sold at the very high-profile place, Christie's. And was complete with its box, with the letter of Steve Jobs, with paper of *BASIC*, and so, I said I'm reaching out. It's at the right time, and I'm crazy enough and I'm passionate enough of these things. Maybe to some extent, I have to do it because it's part of my life. So I went and I did it. And that's it.

Bob - Well, you acquired an excellent example. It has the provenance and the documentation.

Marco - Yes, it's complete. And then we receive it. We involved the Polytechnical University of Torino, which is a very big and important Italian university with forty thousand students. They were very passionate, too. We cleaned it and we tested it, with few specialized professors. Then we prepared to restart it publicly at the Aula Magna, the big theater at the university, and there were four hundred students and we did it.

Bob - And you turned it on?

Marco - Oh yes, it works perfectly.

Bob - Some people say they wouldn't want to turn one on, because they're afraid of the worst thing that could happen. It might melt or something.

Marco - We restarted it with a procedure similar to change a heart to a man. There were fourteen professors, all equipped. They checked all the components. They did everything perfectly, and they restarted it. There is the video of that.

Bob - That sounds like fun. Did your collection begin with your own original Apple computers?

Marco - Absolutely. Actually, no. The first one, no. But the second one, because the first one was a used one I bought from a friend of mine. It was an Apple][Plus, but it was a little complicated. Fifteen days after I bought that, in a window of a store I saw a magnificent Apple][c, white, and I bought it and that one is still there.

Bob - Did you ever try to purchase an Apple-1 before this one?

Marco - No and actually not even, I didn't think of doing it. But this guy, when he said there was an Apple-1 at Christie's...

Bob - Am I correct in recalling, was your brother at the auction?

Marco - Yeah, my brother was at the auction. I was over the telephone.

Bob - And was that exciting?

Marco - Yeah, quite exciting, yes. Because it started at sixty thousand pounds, plus all the fifteen percent stuff. And then it was very short in the room, they went from sixty, seventy, eighty, ninety, one hundred. And so, I was there actually, between you and me, I was ready to go for something more than that. Not much, but something more.

Bob - When I have bought collectibles over the years, the prices often seem high at the time. Later, I look back and am happy, and I don't think I paid too much.

Marco - And for me, it's basically the same. I've bought maybe three hundred pieces or more on the *eBay*, and I don't regret to have bought one.

Bob - Are you buying Apple only, or other computers too?

Marco - No, even other computers. The old computers go with the logic of telling the story of the information technology revolution. So, I have the first Altairs, and everything we have, it works. And then, we have some Commodores, we have some IBM's, we have some Sinclairs, all the historical machines. And also, some advertisements of the machines, some documentation, some books and software. Basically, up to 1995. It's '75 to '95, where '75 to '85 is stronger because it's where everything started, according to me.

Bob - Is your collection in a private museum?

Marco - Not yet, we expose for tourists these days. The Apple-1 is exposed in Apple store in Milan, and next week it's going to Florence, but it's not a permanent exhibition. And you know, I have this kind of collection '75 to '95, but within this collection I have all Apples between '76 and '85. So all models of Apple, I have. And I have other brands, and other models, but not complete collection. Apple Liza 1, and 2, Apple][plus, e, c, and Mac up to the Plus.

Bob - When they put it in the Apple store, did they put it in some kind of secure display, like in a Plexiglas box?

Marco - Yes, we have made a Plexiglas holder for each piece of the pie. So, there is one for the motherboard, one for the cassette, one for the manuals, it's safe.

Bob - It's interesting, I've been in Apple stores before and I'll occasionally mention to employees about the Apple-1, and they usually don't know what it is.

Marco - Yeah, it looks very different.

Bob - Two of the people I've talked to have more than one Apple-1. One of the fellows lives in Atlanta, Georgia, and I believe he has three. His story is similar to yours. There's another fellow in Southern Virginia, and he owns four.

Marco - Yeah, I wouldn't be surprised if someone tries to buy ten now. It's like buying ten Picassos. I wouldn't be surprise if a Russian or a Chinese guy goes and buys ten.

And do you know, Steve Wozniak was at the auction. He wrote me a letter and we spoke later.

Bob - He's a great enthusiast for the brand.

Marco - You know there is another guy in Italy with an Apple-1? For sure, you know.

Bob - I think that's on the registry as being in some sort of museum.

Marco - No, actually this is a Sicilian guy, he's a friend of mine. He's a young guy, he's younger than us. He's thirty-five or thirty-six years old, and he's a very large collector. He has a huge number of machines and he specializes in prototypes. This guy has a good story because he's a young guy, he's not a fifty-something guy, so he wasn't around when all this started. But he was passionate.

Chapter 31

Music Machines

Catching up with Rick Crandall of Colorado in December 2012, he told me about his Apple-1 and the case he had made for it.

Bob - You said you made the case for your Apple-1. Some boards are known to be hand-numbered on the back side, with a sequence like 01-0050. Does yours have a number like that?

Rick Crandall - We'll take a look.

Bob - They look like they were done with a black marker.

Rick - Do you think it's handwritten?

Bob - Handwritten, yes. Most people say it's from the Byte Shop, but it's a mystery, because the fellow who started the Byte Shops says they didn't.

Rick - Well, let me put the phone down a second, and pull it out.

Bob - Terrific.

Rick - Okay, are you there?

Bob - Yes, sure.

Rick - So, take a look here... Where would it be?

Bob - If you're looking at the upper right, there's a space where there's kind of a blank area, which must be why they chose that area. The pictures of the ones I've seen, all look like a black fine tip magic marker. If yours has a number, you'd notice it right away.

Rick - Oh, on the bottom? Underneath? Well, that's hard for me to look at.

Bob - Because you have yours actually screwed into your box?

Rick - It's actually mounted, yeah.

Bob - Okay, well...

Rick - You know, I've got cables connected to it.

Bob - By any chance, would you have taken any pictures of it before you put it in the box?

Rick - No, I took pictures of the top of it, and I've got them on my website.

Bob - Okay, well, it's a question that'll remain open. With mine, I don't have quite enough clearance to get at it with any kind of a mirror. If there was a little more clearance, you could stick one of those dental mirrors under mine. I've tried to look through the board, from the front, with a strong flashlight. That didn't work, either.

Rick - Well, you know, it's only five screws. I mean, if it's important to your work, I could probably get it out.

Bob - That's only one of the mysteries of the machines. To elaborate a little bit on that, in the registry there's about 48 Apple-1's accounted for. Out of those, maybe seven or eight have this numbering on the bottom. I think the lowest number is 01-0005 and the highest is 01-070. If you decide at some point to take a look, it would be great to add to the knowledge on what survives. Every little bit helps. Mine wasn't bought through the Byte Shop and yours was, right?

Rick - Yeah.

Bob - So, right now we think that every machine that has a number on it came through the Byte Shop. Of course, that's one of the things that makes it really seem that the numbering was done by the Byte Shop. I still need to pull mine out of the case sometime, and look at it. I know mine came directly from Apple, and didn't go through the Byte Shop, so if I find a number on mine, it would be significant. Just curious, I guess you are a collector. Is there a story of how you found your machine and the purchase of it?

Rick - I collect a number of different mechanical things. I had an extensive collection of the very earliest cash registers, and wrote a two-volume book set about them, and their history. And I sold off most of the registers, but kept a few. I also collect some of the rare antique automatic music machines. The Hupfeld Phonoliszt- Violina, the Connorized Music Company Banjorchestra, and The Gabel Automatic Entertainer, all three of which are rare, great machines. The Phonoliszt-Violina is a German-made machine. It's the only other violin-playing machine besides the Violin Virtuoso. Phenomenally realistic, very complicated, more-so than the Virtuoso, but the Virtuoso's a very fun machine. And there are quite a number of them around. It was very popular in its original day.

Bob - How long have you been interested in those?

Rick - Oh, probably fifteen, twenty years. I've been writing about them as well.

I'm pulling this board out now... I've got all the screws out. Just gotta concentrate a bit here, so I don't... *Here* we go. Okay, so there's actually a tag on it, but it looks new, it says 82. I don't think that means...

Bob - It has what? It says what?

Rick - A little white tag, but I can't swear that it was on it originally.

Bob - Did you say it says 82?

Rick - Number 82.

Bob - Yes, that's on several. At least two other machines have that tag and number.

Rick - Okay.

Bob - I would consider that original. Yup. We don't know why. It's another mystery.

Rick - And I'm looking for any... The only other thing that I see looks like a stamp. The number 8 or 3 in a circle.

Bob - Yup. Some have a stamp with a number and a circle. And there's only a few that also have that. Two, possibly, other than yours.

Rick - It may be a two-digit number.

Bob - And, I think, there's at least one other than yours that has both the number and the circle. I think one of the early Apple employees has one that has both.

Rick - So, I'm scanning for anything handwritten, and I don't see...

Bob - If you're looking at it closely enough to see what you just saw, then you would have seen it. It's really obvious.

Rick - No, then it doesn't have it.

Bob - And another thing about yours, I think, is that it came from a Byte Shop in Indiana. It's also possible that, you know, the numbers could have to do with California Byte Shops.

Rick - You know, that is true. That's where it came from.

Bob - So, how did you find yours when you purchased it?

Rick - When I get interested in a particular area of collectible, I'm a crazy bird-dog. And it's hard to describe how I go about finding something. I generally only go for very rare things, and I network like crazy. I eventually find enough people that have been there, and I hear little whispers of leads or whatever, and I chase those. I've got actually quite a few stories about how I found this and that. I've had this computer now about eight or ten years. So, in this particular case, I know that I put a few feelers out.

Bob - I think it's written in our notes that you've had it since 2002.

Rick - Yeah, and I got a response, I think his name was Larry Nelson. He was the original owner, and it was fun getting it from him because he had some recollections, and, as well, some literature that went along with it: materials and documentation. And, all the additional components, so you could put the whole thing back together again. And he had an original keyboard, although there was a short in it, which is what caused him to stop using the machine.

Bob - And you ended up making a box yourself with a keyboard.

Rick - Yes, I wanted to do that first of all to protect it, and to gather all the bits and pieces in one place. But also to have some fun looking at other cases, some of which I'm guessing were made by the hobbyists at the time of, when it was contemporaneous. So, I designed a case that was pretty much in that style. I had a friend who is a great craftsman, so he made quite the beautiful case.

Bob - I have a picture and it is beautiful. I don't know whether you'd call it 'dovetailed.'

Rick - That hinge itself is all wood.

Bob - That part is incredible. I can't figure out how the hinge is done. It's not that good of an image.

Rick - Well, this guy is a genius with woodworking, so that was his extra little touch. The top and the keyboard flip open.

Bob - I can see that.

Rick - So, I've not attempted to actually completely wire it up and make it work, because I just don't want to risk that.

Bob - Me neither. There're actually a lot of people who will say, "Does it work?" I think it may have come up because there's a couple that have been offered for sale in the last couple of years, which were represented as being in working condition.

Rick - You mean the ones that got the big prices?

Bob - Yes. I think one was characterized as *running* in one article, and then it carried to other articles. It suggested that if one was operational, it was more valuable. I don't look at it that way.

Rick - I don't necessarily either, with an antique. In music machines, it's quite important. It's more important that they're original, because you always get them restored. Although it does cost a fortune to do it. The most important thing is originality.

Bob - You're retired, I guess.

Rick - Not really. I'm retired from a full-time job, but I serve on a bunch of boards, I've been in the tech industry for a long time, and I run a roundtable of software industry CEOs, and a whole bunch of things still related to tech. But it's not a nine-to-five job.

Bob - Do you have long range plans about what will happen to your collection, or to the Apple-1 in particular?

Rick - I don't really... I have had a few collections of other things; one of the major ones was the cash register collection. I did wind up selling it, because I'd done my research and writing, and it was all done. I like writing about this stuff in specialized publications. Also, I was moving and I didn't have the room for it. So, they went to another major cash register collector.

I do have a number of other early microcomputers; I've never really set them up as a display. So I don't really have a game-plan. My focus went off to music machines, and then gambling machines. Since computing is my field, I suspect these will be with me for a while.

Bob - You're a bit of a rare breed in that you got to the point where you sold one of your collections. I think the majority of collectors can never do that.

Rick - I agree. Believe me, I know it. I've studied the psyche of collectors.

I again, I don't normally have a lot of pieces in a given collection, but they're usually very rare and very desirable. Most often, I kind of know that if I did want to sell, I know three or four guys that would want them.

Bob - Right. You're buying the best.

Rick - Yeah, just because I have limited space. I mean, some friends of mine have built whole houses to hold collections. Especially music machines, which are big. I've integrated them in our house, and so I'm limited to relatively few pieces. So, for me, the chase needs to be hard, the machine needs to be rare and cool, and it also needs to be something I can do a bit of research on, and do some writing on.

Chapter 32

Pirate Flag

David Waldack, Bruce Waldack's brother, welcomed me into his Virginia office in July 2012. We were in the building Bruce had once owned, and Dave still works there for one of the companies Bruce had started. Our talk was bittersweet, as David has a wide spectrum of memories of his brother. Some wonderful, some not.

Bob - Do you know the date DigitalNation sold?

David Waldack - I've got the actual date here, July 13th, 1999.

Bob - (showing David an old newspaper article) Here's where he was bidding on the Cray computer on *eBay*. I kept the article about him bidding on the Cray computer, because in it he said he'd bought an Apple-1 the previous year for around fifty thousand dollars. It says he had other vintage computers.

David - I still have some vintage computers in my house.

Bob - Those would have been his?

David - Also mine. I think I've got three Lisa's. I've got four or five of the five-megabyte hard-drives, and all the documentation and books.

Bob - You describe your family as 'Mac-heads' since day one.

David - Since day one.

Bob - How many years between you and your brother Bruce?

David - Bruce was six years older.

Bob - Was the origin of the Mac-heads Bruce or your dad?

David - I think it was my parents that started that with all of us. I remember—this was some time in the mid-'70s—my dad coming home from Radio Shack with one of the first game consoles you could buy. What you could do was play *Pong* and *Bullet*. That's when we were living in Washington State.

Bob - Was your dad in the Foreign Service?

David - My dad was Army. To the best of my knowledge, he was artillery. We lived in Tacoma and Ft. Lewis. While we lived there, Mt. Saint Helens erupted for the first time. After leaving Washington, we moved to Indonesia for three years. And that was where I was first introduced to the Apple][.

My brother and I both went to the International School at JIS there, one of the largest schools in Southeast Asia at the time. They added an entire computer department, which was really unusual for the location where we were. You had Apple][['s everywhere, I remember learning *BASIC* there. I don't think Bruce was ever the best student. School was more about partying.

I'll share an anecdote to show you the kind of person Bruce was early on. In Indonesia, we were in a nice house provided by the embassy. My dad had to go on a business trip, with my mom. No sooner than the door closed and they got in the car to leave, my brother was already up talking to me, saying "Okay, I want you to start gathering stuff around the house, we're going to have a yard sale." I was in fifth or sixth grade. And my brother had already graduated from high school, but was working at the school. So we were literally selling all of our parent's stuff. Stuff that, you know, we would be going through the closets, 'You see mom wear this dress? No? Okay, *sold*.' We were selling furniture that the embassy provided us with. And, up until 1993, mom and dad never knew about it.

Bob - When they returned from their trip, they didn't realize you'd had a yard sale?

David - They didn't realize.

Bob - Because you sold stuff they wouldn't miss?

David - Right. Years later we actually came clean on that.

Bob - Going back to the yard sale, was there something he wanted to spend the money on?

David - He wanted to throw a party. He threw a lavish party while my parents were away. He was going to fund a good party. They were having caviar and champagne. And, you know when you're in a foreign country and you've got the black passport, which is the diplomatic passport? There's almost no trouble you can get into. I mean, I remember stories of them going to one of the tallest hotels in Jakarta, and they started throwing kegs off the top.

Bob - Your brother and his friends?

David - 'Cause all his friends were also diplomats from other countries.

Bob - Even at that age, when he had just graduated high school, he liked to party?

David - Oh, yeah. Without question.

Bob - So I guess, even at that point, he was on track to be someone who worked hard, but also played hard.

David - Definitely his motto.

That's the entrepreneurial spirit that I knew my brother had. We moved to the Maryland, the Washington D.C. suburbs. We had a local ice cream parlor, Giffords. When they shut down the business, he drove a pickup truck over there. They had one of the big ice cream tanks in the back. Bruce threw it into the back of the pickup truck, drove up to Maine, and filled it with lobsters. He drove it back down here, and we sat on the side of the road and sold live lobsters. We're doing this in high school, by the way. I'm there selling lobsters, a police car pulls up, and the officer comes over and starts questioning me. As I look up, my brother's walking away, down the sidewalk.

Bob - You and Bruce had a close relationship?

David - We did. I worked with my brother ever since high-school. He literally started his first company in a small room in the back of a

307

pharmacy off Route 50 in Maryland. At the time, he was doing nothing but building PCs for people. Sending them out. It then kind of snowballed from there. My brother and his partner started a company called Desktop Publishing Center. We really focused on selling Macs. Then, that partnership dissolved. My brother and father then started DigitalNation. My dad was actually the founder. It was his money; he was actually the sole owner.

Bob - Was it really Bruce's idea?

David - Without question. My brother had a great business mind and was a serial entrepreneur.

Bob - But your dad was the investor? It was in his name because he put the money in?

David - Bruce knew that web hosting was going to be the key moving forward for our business. We started doing web hosting in 1992, so we were there very early on. And by the time we sold to Verio, we had approaching four thousand servers online.

We ran into a problem really early, which I think had forced our shift into the hosting industry. There were two companies that we resold for, Apple and Silicon Graphics. Both of them didn't like their VARs (Value Added Reseller). Both of them would constantly undercut the prices resellers could offer.

Bob - Including you?

David - Including us. We were going to sell NIH (National Institute of Health) a large Silicon Graphics system. Priced it as best we could. Silicon Graphics came in and undercut us, and my brother on purpose undercut them, just to get the deal to piss them off.

Here's the astonishing thing. He did DigitalNation for a five thousand dollar investment. It sold for a hundred million in cash. That's not a bad return.

It was shortly thereafter where my brother—this is where it gets a little touchy—fled the country. Which is ultimately why the sheriff's auction came about.

My brother did pass away about five years ago. This was a lifestyle thing. You know, you get that kind of money, and it can lead you down the wrong path in life. And that's exactly what happened.

I still work at the company that he started, called Adjuggler, and it's about advertising space. We're still primarily focused on the technology part of it, providing sales solutions. Managing the advertising that people put on their websites, this was a concept my brother came up with in 1995. It was nothing more than a program that rotated banners on a lot of websites.

Almost everything I learned in business I got from my brother. I inherited his entrepreneurial spirit.

When it came to family, my brother didn't care as much as he did care about impressing other people. I'm much more of a family-oriented man than he was.

Bob - You chose your priorities.

David - I love my brother for who he was.

Question about Bruce's real estate activity.

David - That's a little vague. There's a lot I didn't know about and a lot I did know about. There was extensive property. Where that has gone, I don't know, because a lot of it was international. He did own a house in Malibu, right on the beach. Yeah, it's what he had overseas that was kept pretty private. For all I know, there's bank accounts sitting around the world with millions of dollars in them. Who knows?

Bob - Can you tell me about the SteveJobs.com domain name?

David - My brother, early on, if he heard somebody say a phrase, he would get the domain name. If he heard something funny, he would get it. I still have a number of domain names, mostly I got from my brother. I've still got Albuquerque.org. The domain SteveJobs.com was available, so he registered it. And, yeah, he actually did sell it to Jobs for a dollar. He didn't cash the check, it was for the sole purpose of framing it and putting it up on display.

In a way, I want to say my brother compared himself to Steve Jobs. And you know, even with the purchase of that original Apple-1, it was more about the competition against the guy. Well, I think my brother idolized him. I had the pleasure of meeting Jobs once. Kinda cool. I'm still, as you can tell, still a Mac guy. As I mentioned, we were a big Apple Value Added Reseller, on the East Coast. We sold one of the first digital editing systems to Virginia Tech, at the time. All Mac-based.

I can tell you, Bruce and Steve Jobs would never have gotten along... *never*. Steve was, I think, a self-proclaimed hippie. And you don't get more Republican than my brother was. One of my brother's mottos was on one of the cars, 'More Me Now.' At one point, we had about twenty-five cars in the back garage here.

My brother was just a weird individual. I don't know of anything he bought which he really, truly appreciated. And it was just more the fact of buying, because he could. Along with the Apple-1, a lot of stuff my brother bought was unique for a certain reason. He had a Lamborghini which was money-green. There was a plague on the dashboard that said "Custom Built for Malcolm Forbes." So that's one example. You know, he built the shark limousine specifically just to go to local Jimmy Buffet shows. He had the first edition of *Playboy* signed by Hefner, which I still own.

Bob - Tell me about Bruce bidding on a Cray supercomputer.

David - You know, my brother loved to buy things that he thought were interesting, or he thought had some historical value. I don't know if he ever bought the Cray. I know there was talk that he had, but I never saw it at the office. One of my brother's intentions was, whether it was this building or one of the DigitalNation buildings that we had wanted to build, that he was going to put in a museum of technology. Which is why

310

he wanted that Cray. Certainly it wasn't because he wanted to use it. Do you remember a computer called the Franklin? It was an Apple][clone. The first one that got shut down quickly. We had one of those as well.

There were a ton of things like that. I mean he had a collection of guitars that was probably eighty deep, the most expensive one being in the sixty thousand dollar range. There was no rhyme or reason to what he would collect. He was eccentric in his collections. He had a large Tiffany glass collection. In fact, sitting on his desk for the longest time, he had a Drop Head Dragonfly. That was an original Tiffany lamp, appraised for half a million dollars.

Bob - What happened to that stuff?

David - Sold it off.

Bob - He sold it off?

David - It was most likely his assistants that took care of stuff like that. He knew he wasn't coming back to this country.

My brother also never paid a penny in taxes on the hundred million.

Bob - Is that part of the reason why he left?

David - I would assume.

Bob - You said he developed a tax liability.

David - Yeah.

He left everything behind. Then he had his assistants ship him the things he needed. And one of the items that got shipped down was the Segway.

Bob - Is that when the sheriff took over?

David - Within weeks. It was described to me that he was going on a trip. Which was normal. My brother loved to travel. But he knew he wasn't coming back. Here's the most poignant thing I can tell you. After he left, I was going through his personal books. And I ran across a book titled, *How to Run Away and Hide as an Adult*. For the record, too, I'm

311

still not one hundred percent convinced he's dead. And I've got his ashes sitting in my house.

Could be anybody's. When I got the call and I called my sister, the first thing out of her mouth was, "I don't believe it." Not because, my brother and sister, oil on water. Never got along as far as I can remember. You ask anybody that knew him, they'll probably tell you the same thing (that is: 'I don't believe it').

Bob - How could he leave, or why did he leave like that?

David - Didn't want to pay, didn't want to give his wife money. Didn't want to give the IRS money. Didn't want to give his creditors money 'cause he had a plane that was in jeopardy, with G.E. Capital.

Bob - Giving up everything else was worth it to be able to accomplish those things?

David - You know, quite frankly, I think my brother went out how he wanted to go out. I don't think he wanted to live a long life.

Bob - The thing that I think about is that besides everything else, he had kids.

David - Which I can't fathom. And that was when I lost every bit of respect I had for him. Because I don't know how you just leave your kids. And then, on top of that, leave them with nothing.

Bob - How was it that he left them with nothing?

David - They have whatever the mother has. And she didn't get anything from my brother. She got the building, but again after all her legal fees, she didn't get a lot. My brother structured things in a way where it was going to screw her. Not somebody you wanted to be on the wrong side of. And, like I said, my brother has made me who I am today. By knowing what I don't want to be. Again, I love my brother.

Bob - Tremendous influence on your life.

David - Yep.

Bob - Did your dad end up doing okay?

David - My dad passed away before. He died in '94.

312

Bob - My original interest in Bruce is that he was such a character...

David - He was a cross—and this is probably a good way to describe him—between John Belushi and Gordon Gekko.

My brother was always fascinated with music, too. I think at some point, after the sale of the company, he wanted to get into the music industry. He quickly befriended Kid Rock, and then started... I think this is where the downward spiral started in terms of substance abuse. Being around that crowd and thinking you can party that way. And if you've ever seen my brother, he wasn't the picture of fitness.

He wanted to start a record label. I know he'd vacationed a couple of times with the founder of Atlantic Records, Ahmet Ertigan. I've got this entire photo album of my brother, Ahmet, Pam Anderson and Kid Rock on a retreat somewhere.

Bob - Was Jimmy Buffet far and away his favorite entertainer?

David - No. His favorite entertainer of all time was the band Queen.

Bob - But he didn't build a Queen limousine.

David - No. But Queen wasn't touring at the time. But he did throw the after-party when Queen was inducted into the Rock & Roll Hall of Fame. He threw the party for them in New York. That was, in fact, with Pam Anderson. I think that there's a few pictures of the party. (from a book Bruce had had made up.) Yeah, these are all at the party. Joe Perry, Kid Rock... He (Bruce) was eccentric.

Bob - I guess the limousine was used to go to other concerts?

David - No, just Jimmy Buffett.

Bob - So how many times would it have been used?

David - Two or three times.

Bob - And after it was used to go to those concerts?

David - It sat in that garage there. Like I said, my brother was extravagant. I'm a serious golfer. We flew with some friends on a private plane to the Dominican Republic for ten holes, rented a villa, and came back the same day. We went and had one of the biggest feasts I've ever had in my life, drinking bottles of Dom in the pool, slept on the way back.

The crown jewel of his car collection, in my opinion, was a '69 Shelby GT 500 Convertible. My brother and Kid Rock actually decided to swap cars for the summer. Kid Rock got the GT 500, my brother got a Lincoln Continental in return. The Shelby burnt to the ground in Kid Rock's garage. Broke my heart.

Bob - You said you sold recently the Pamela Anderson car?

David - Well, again, because my brother was friends with Kid Rock. Kid Rock started dating Pam Anderson, Pam Anderson then wanted to sell her Escalade, and of course my brother had a chance to buy something that was from a celebrity, so he jumped on it. He's helping her out. He's getting what he wants, then used that as his daily (vehicle), being driven in that car. As he was getting ready to, call it, 'flee the country,' he sold it to me. And I finally just got rid of it.

I have very few things left from my brother. I have one of his guitars from his collection. It was an impressive guitar collection.

My brother and his business drive; I've never seen anything like it. As I mentioned, he started a magazine purely out of spite for an employee. Now, when print is starting to die? Not the best move.

Bob - When you said you've never seen someone that business-oriented, what did you mean?

David - When it came to business, it was pure business. Now there were some offshoots there, but as an example, we start work at nine a.m. This was true here, this was true at DigitalNation. My brother was in front of the building with a cigar in his mouth, and if you were one minute late, he would let you know about it.

Bob - You couldn't come in twenty minutes late?

David - Oh, no. That would never have happened. Even with myself.

Bob - Was he intense?

David - I very rarely saw my brother angry. But I would definitely call him intense. That's maybe not the right word for it. My brother was a good visionary. He was a good entrepreneur. I think some of his shortcomings were in true business process, which I don't think mattered to him. He had built a culture. I don't know if this is manipulation, but he would purposely go out and hire younger people that were impressionable. So, they come into the company and they quickly become part of the culture. My brother was always the first one there, and was always the last to leave. Whatever we were doing, he had the most knowledge about it. He was a constant reader.

Bob - Was he a micromanager?

David - No, not a micromanager at all. He would give people free reign, but he knew the details.

Bob - I saw in a magazine that he hung a pirate flag out front.

David - That one right there? (He points to the flag, displayed in an adjacent office.)

Bob - Funny thing is Steve Jobs did that too. Is that where he got the idea?

David - Absolutely, absolutely.

Bob - What happened to the special Segway? And did it have special trim?

David - The original Segway was never seized by the sheriffs. I still have the keys for it. There're different colored keys. The red ones make it go faster. So that's something that only the early ones had, or the special ones had, I'm guessing. My brother clearly overpaid for that Segway he bought. 'Cause it was over a hundred thousand dollars. It *was* a charity sale. That Segway made its way down to Argentina. And I was slated to bring it back. They were supposed to ship it back to me, and to say that my brother's crowd there, in Argentina, weren't the best group of people. My brother had a bodyguard down there. I went down there two days after he passed away, met the guy, and wanted to leave the country

315

immediately. After I came back to the states, I actually got a death threat. I did nothing. The guy expected me to pay thirty-five thousand dollars.

Bob - Like he was owed that? The Segway disappeared, I guess.

David - It was actually listed on *eBay*. They tried to sell it on *eBay*. Citing all my brother's information. Citing the bill of sale, the charity, and I don't think it ever sold.

Bob - Did other items disappear?

David - You know there was very little down there. And of course by the time I got down there, I will stop short of calling Argentina a lawless country. But, first the police, they sift through everything they want to take. Then friends come in, they take everything they want to take. I did bring that first edition of *Playboy* back.

Bob - There's a reference that he died after he'd had a fall earlier in the year?

David - Not as a result of that fall. But he actually had a fall off of the Segway in a shopping corridor. Split his head open pretty bad. Had his twelve thousand dollar Rolex taken off his wrist, while he was down on the ground.

Bob - What do you consider cause of death, 'cause it didn't have anything to do with the fall?

David - Lifestyle. The one thing I can tell you from going down there, right after it happened, walking into his bedroom, to me it appeared to be a violent death. Like he was hemorrhaging.

The interview with journalist Federico Ini (from Chapter 7) continues:

Federico – Bruce passed away in 2007.

Bob - David told me when Bruce went to Argentina, he just told David that he was going on a trip. They thought he was going on vacation, and of course he never came back.

Federico - Actually Bruce, he flew away from here a few times, too. He went to Mexico. He must have gone to the Bahamas, because he was in this place which has the two towers with the thing that connects them.

The thing you had with Bruce, I really cared about him. That's part of my life. He was very supportive, and I don't mean financially, because there was no business besides the sponsorship of the show which was for two months. Bruce was a guy that you could look up to because he was a self-made man. Most of the time when you were chatting with him and he didn't have that much vodka tonics, the guy was really interesting to talk to. You wanted to know more about him. He was kind of an enigma.

I got angry many times, because he disappeared. And I'm a guy that takes... I like to think that I take good care of my friends, and I want to know how they are. And Bruce sometimes stopped answering the phone. Stopped answering emails, and he was, I guess, on two or three occasions where he disappeared for a month or month and a half. I was so pissed with that. So, Okay, dude, we can go out and have a few drinks and go to your beautiful house, whatever, but if you disappear and I don't know if you're having some problem, or you're dead. That's not friendship for me, that's another thing.

Bob - You expected at least the consideration of him letting you know he was going to be gone for a while.

Federico - Yeah. Yeah, yeah. And another time when we were supposed to meet to go out, he disappeared for a week. And we were there waiting and he says "Hey, I'm sorry, I went into the cab, I lost my phone, I freaked out, and I came back home, and I was scared," or something, "I didn't want to talk to anyone." I said, "Dude, are you kidding me? Just send me a message. 'I have a problem. I won't be able to go,' whatever. I'm concerned. We're scared that something might happen to you."

Bob - And when that happened would it sometimes be that he had left town, but sometimes it would be that he was just in town too?

Federico - I really, really cared about the person behind the millionaire and the entrepreneur and the character that was Bruce. And it was really complicated. When he died, I couldn't even get ahold of most of the pictures he had of us, doing stuff. There was some times that Bruce didn't want pictures taken for security reasons. There was something that was a big blank that you didn't know what it was about.

Bob - How did you find out that he died?

Federico - It was a really sad story, too. There were some computers he wanted to lend me, or for me to have. I guess we talked over the week; the previous days we had just some texting going back and forth. I was near his place. He'd been really depressed. He wasn't being very cheerful lately. So I was next to his house, and I say, "Dude, I'm downstairs. Do you want to hang out? And he said, "No, I don't feel really well. I don't want to see anyone." "Okay, but are you okay? I can go to your house." "No, no, no, I'd rather not. Let's talk some other time."

I sent him a message and he didn't answer. And then I learned that he had died. I called his bodyguard and he had told me what had happened. They found him dead in the house. But it was a really, really horrible moment, because I was texting him while he was dead, you know?

I know he went out with a few people that night, and they went out to have a drink or something, and they left Bruce at his house.

At some point, I got the information that David was coming here, and he wanted to meet us, and talk to us. I wanted to talk to him too, to tell him that I was sorry for what had happened, and to tell him he can count on me, and to support him here. So, that was how I met David.

Bruce didn't like to be woken up. This was the phrase he used, he said to the housekeeper, or the maid, 'I don't care if Baby Jesus himself lands on Earth, do not knock on the door.' So his room was a private thing for him.

Bruce said that his kids were going to be taken care of, that there was a trust fund and he left the money for them that they could collect when they were of age. He said that at some point when I was talking about it with him. He didn't like to talk about his kids or the divorce. But when that came up, it was really clear, that his children were not going to have any financial problems, ever. They were going to be well taken care of.

Bruce was the first friend I've lost. So, you know, you lose a friend, and you don't understand what's going on. But it wasn't a surprise. Bruce really drank a lot, he had health issues, he complained of landing in the hospital a few times, and he didn't give too much explanation of what was going on.

I really enjoyed the person, when he had all the lights on. You know, without alcohol, or without whatever. He was a very powerful force. And I didn't understand why he disappeared. What was going on, why he left you hanging at some point or the other. It wasn't all the time, because if it would have been all the time, I couldn't be friends with someone like that. I got angry with him, you say, 'Dude, understand that this is not friendship for me, if you do this, you know. I have to know your whereabouts, or what is going on. If you tell me I'm going to eat with you, and two hours pass and I'm still waiting there.' That's incompatible with my view of friendship.

And whatever happened, he was in very poor health. He ate a lot. He was a huge guy. He was fat, and he walked with problems, and he landed in the hospital. He drank a lot. Some of his friends were really not taking very good care of him.

I really don't know what happened. Why is this guy away from home besides this legal issue? Why is he drinking this much? Why is he disappearing sometimes? He wasn't the type of person that really let you help him if he didn't really want to. Well, yeah, that's why I told you, you could write a whole book about Bruce.

319

Chapter 33

Tiger Moth

As much as I've tried, I couldn't find any sign that the mysterious Apple-1 purchaser at the La Salle auction, 'Captain Owen O'Mahoney,' ever really existed. I wondered if this retired RAF pilot was just a made-up character and name. Somewhere along the way, I tried the name in a search with a little different spelling. It may have been an accident on my part, but typing in "Owen O'Mahony," (less an *e)* helped me find him.

The keywords I used were "Captain Owen O'Mahony," and "Royal Air Force Pilot." I stumbled upon a story (in *The Independent*, a British newspaper) about a race car driver, in fact one of the finest racers in history: Ayrton Senna, who was considered one of the greatest Formula One drivers of all time, having won three world championships. Senna was Brazilian, and the newspaper described the fabulous Brazilian resort community in which Senna lived, his lovely girlfriend, and the trip he and his pilot took from Brazil to Italy for the 1994 San Marino Grand Prix. Then, it detailed the build-up to the race, and its heartbreaking outcome; a fatal crash. Senna had had a close relationship with his pilot. And the pilot was Captain O'Mahony.

In June 2012, I found O'Mahony's UK phone number in an online classified advertisement for a vintage Tiger Moth aircraft. I phoned him and told him that based on my best information, I believed he'd purchased a 1976 Apple-1 computer in 1999 from the LaSalle Gallery in San Francisco. Since he was a pilot, I asked if he might have once piloted Bruce Waldack's private jet. This was my guess as to where he might fit in. Was there some reason that he'd acted as a straw man for Bruce in the auction? The problem with that theory was that I knew Bruce relished publicity, so why would he have camouflaged his identity as the auction purchaser of the Apple-1?

O'Mahony started by talking about the man he'd been engaged to fly, a Mr. Jack Sacks. O'Mahony was off and running in the instant he answered the phone, and I failed to start my tape recorder soon enough, so I didn't capture his initial comments. To help create the right atmosphere to read this passage, let me say that he came off as an irascible character. The term 'swashbuckler' comes to mind.

Owen O'Mahony - I do know that he (Jack Sacks) returned to Israel. He was without a doubt an Israeli agent in South Africa. The thick plottens.

When asked permission to record his comments, he replied:
Owen - I have to be very careful then, I'll have to use the word 'allegedly' all the time.
Bob - The extent of your involvement was just through this partner?
Owen - He wasn't a partner, I was actually...he had his private jet. He owned the jet which was on the British register when he was in South Africa. Now I am an ex-RAF pilot, and I used to fly this private jet for him as an employee.

Now the thing was that it was a British registered aircraft. This was during apartheid in South Africa. Okay, well I think it was about 1988, I can't actually confirm the date. I was flying this British registered aircraft in and around South Africa or Southern Africa during apartheid when South African aircraft were not allowed to fly in that area. Because of the apartheid business; the white men persecuting the Blacks and what have you. Well, what happened is all the African states all ganged up and said you can't fly South African registered aircraft around here. I had a British-registered aircraft intentionally, which I believe he was lent the money to buy by the South African government. I had all British crew, all British passports, with a British- registered aircraft, and I was flying around Africa. It was picking up Dr. Savimbi, the UNITA terrorist leader in Angola. He's dead actually, now. And I used to get reconnaissance photographs from the frickin' airforce. I'm not making this up. If you land on this road between that point and that point, and it was *roads* (as opposed to *a runway*), alright?, you'll be all right. You don't normally do that with a jet. And I'd land there and pick up Savimbi and fly him in to Waterkloof, in Pretoria, for his meetings with the South African government, because they were financing him at the time against the Angolans.

Then I was also picking up Mugabe. Robert Mugabe. And he got up at the United Nations thumping the table saying, 'We'll have nothing to do with these filthy South Africans,' or words to that effect. Within seventy-two hours I was picking him up in Harare, Zimbabwe at one-thirty in the morning to fly him down to Pretoria for his monthly meetings with the South African government. Very two-faced.

Why then, then of course there was a change of government, and the jet went... in fact the jet was sabotaged. And I flew from Johannesburg back to the UK, to bring it here for maintenance. When I landed, I noticed there was a fuel leak in one of the tanks. There was five pounds of salt in the tank. *Salt*, as in sodium chloride. And it rotted the wings. It rested on the bottom of the aluminum tanks. What you could do, when they eventually got into the tanks, you could shine a torch on the inside of the tank and you could see the light shining through the paint, 'cause it had eaten the metal away. It was horrendous. I was very, very lucky to have got back in one piece. Anyway the aircraft was written off because the wings were all totally corroded. Then Sacks went out to the United States, and he was on the East Coast, and San Francisco way. He was always one for dabbling in a bit of this and a bit of that. Often with Israeli... He was a very Jewish guy, okay? And very, very pro-Israeli. And he did some partnership deal out there on an auction house. And that's when this first Apple was coming up for sale, and he phoned me and said, "Is it alright if I say that you are selling it?" It wasn't me. I can't even spell 'Apple.'

Bob - We assumed that you might have been the private pilot for a dot-com mogul named Bruce Waldack, who ended up in possession of the same machine.

Owen - No. Never heard the name. Does he know where it came from?

Bob - Well, he's deceased.

Owen - No, I don't know the guy.

Bob - The coverage we have is that you're the one that *bought* the Apple, right? It sounded like you just said that you were licensed to *sell* it.

Owen - I thought I was supposed to have *sold* it. I can't remember now.

Bob - If you sold it, you wouldn't have picked it up and transported it, because it was the opposite...

Owen - I never touched it. Never seen it. No, no, no, no. The thick is plottening, isn't it?

Bob - Is there anything you can tell me about Ayrton Senna?

Owen - I can tell you, Ayrton Senna, as you know I used to fly him. Yes, I worked for the family for twelve years; I only worked with him for five. He died after five. Absolutely first class guy. My compliment to him. He was a total gentleman. He was big enough to be little. Senna was great, and the first phone call I had after him was Schumacher the race car driver. Eventually I flew for Schumacher, I flew nine months. I couldn't take any more.

You can't make up those stories as you go along. There are several things that I couldn't say, or else I'll end up face down in a ditch somewhere.

Chapter 34

Archive

Below is an email to Sarah, my intern. I think this email will tell the story of an important discovery in regards to my Apple-1.

From: bob luther
To: sarah hutton
Sent: Sat, Jun 18, 2011 7:37 am
Subject: apple

Sarah

When you left the office last night, I was planning a call back to Dan Kottke. I figured, because it was a Friday afternoon, that I might catch him and schedule another interview for next week. But if he happened to be available to talk on the spot, I needed to review your previous interviews with him. As I was going through your interview transcript, I was reminded of the interesting comparison between Dan's and Randy Wigginton's recollections, in regards to the question of whether they knew who Charles Ricketts was. Dan had simply indicated that he did not recognize that name, but he did say:

"But as another side note, in my memory the most promising customer for the Apple-1, out of all the people (there was lots of people that came by the garage to look at it, it was clearly a start-up opportunity), the most promising application was some guy who had a big car dealership where they did car repair. What he wanted to do was put a monitor in a waiting room and instead of announcing it over the public address system when your car was ready, someone would just type on the screen. You know, 'car number 57, your car is ready for pickup.' And at the time, there was no way to put text on a screen. Or that is to say, the Apple-1 was the cheapest way to put text on a screen. Which is not even a program. That's just typing text and having it go on a screen. But you could almost do that just with the TV Typewriter. I didn't know that at the time, but the TV Typewriter let you type and put text on a screen. So I wasn't sure, maybe the guy didn't know that."

Dan gave no indication that he could recall the customer's name. Whereas, when asked if he remembered Charles Ricketts, Randy said, "Umm... yeah...you know who would know a lot about that is Steve Jobs. I remember that name being said, so yes, there is something there, but no one let me near the money. You don't let sixteen-year-olds near the money."

And Randy said in a later interview, "As I recall, he (Ricketts) was owner of a computer store, or something like that. And he was definitely a real hustler. He wanted to make a business out of these things. He kept coming up with ideas on how it could be used. I remember Steve Jobs discussing him a whole bunch of times. Steve would probably be the only one who really remembers him. Oh, have you talked to Dan Kottke?"

And when I described that my Apple-1 had come back for "programming" in August of 1976, Randy continued with, "Right, you

325

know I could be mistaken, but I'm pretty sure that's a program I did for them, which actually I think he wanted to put it into Sears Automotive Centers, so when people had their number, yeah that's one of the programs I wrote back then. I think that's who he is."

And when I mentioned Jef Raskin (at that point, I was following the line of thinking that Ricketts and Raskin might have known each other, since they had evidently both consigned Apple-1 computers to auction at the LaSalle Gallery), he continued to seem to have specific recall, "Rickets was well before Raskin, so I don't know that they would have known each other."

So, sitting at my desk late on a Friday evening, I was comparing in my mind the 'clues' surrounding Ricketts. I just couldn't help but do some searches for Charles Ricketts, *again*, on Google. If I have searched for him once, I have searched for him a hundred times, using various phrases. This time I plugged into Google the words "computer," "Charles Ricketts," and the year "1976." Just like other searches, I skimmed over the page of results.

Towards the bottom of the page, I caught a glance of "Apple Computer, Inc. Records," and kept on scanning, getting ready to click to the second page of Google results.

Wait, I thought. Why is that coming up? My eyes went back to that result and I saw wording "in the 1970s with the Apple." It was kind of strange, because I was half aware that I had not even included the word "Apple" in my search. So, why in the world would a search for Charles Ricketts bring up Apple Computer, Inc. history?

Of course, I had seen the Google results many, many times for the old *Wired Magazine* article about the San Francisco auction, which had included the words "Apple" and "Charles Ricketts." I had seen that Google result and a similar one from the *Macgeek* website, and also results bringing up the *Apple-1 Registry* countless times. So I would recognize right away if I was finding those results. This was bringing up

326

the hairs on the back of my neck. I looked at the URL for the Google result, and it started with "cdn" and "calisphere."

Okay, that didn't register, but it was some kind of an organization or institution. I clicked through on the result. There was a logo which I didn't recognize, and a company or organization name "OAC". That didn't register, either. Then I saw "Guide to the Apple Computer, Inc. Records, 1977-1998." *Wow*, Ricketts' name is going to be in *here*? And below that, "The Board of Trustees of Stanford University." That made some sense. The University could have ended up with archival material from Apple. But where did Ricketts fit into this?

It clicked on the link and it opened up as a PDF. In the top left corner, it said "1 of 237 pages." This is exciting, but I may have to look through a lot of pages to find something... I started to glance thru the first few pages to get a feel for what it was, and then ... *Bang!*

There's the name, *Charles Ricketts*. In something like the first four pages. I was really excited. I'm thinking, in a moment I may get up from my desk chair and do some jumping up and down with excitement. I may have a private moment of real cheer here...

Starting at the first page, almost the entire page was blank. All it really said was "OAC, Online Archive of California, Guide to the Apple Computer, Inc. Records, 1977-1998," and "The Board of Trustees of Stanford University." The rest of that page was blank.

The second page said "Department of Special Collections and University Archives, Stanford University Libraries," and said it was processed in August 1999. It gave a descriptive summary, including the creator as "Apple Computer, Inc." The "extent" was described as six hundred linear feet. So I wasn't exactly sure what that meant, but it sounded like this 'collection' was taking up a lot of shelf space. The abstract described that it contained "organizational charts, annual reports, company directories, internal communications, engineering reports, design materials, press releases, corporate memorabilia,

327

etcetera." And information regarding the "Board of Directors and their decisions."

'Access' was described as "closed until it can be fully arranged and described." It was a gift of Apple Computer, Inc. in 1997. There was a brief description of the company. There was a brief timeline of the company, starting in 1976 and running to 1998.

On the fourth page, it was titled "Timelines & Corporate History." Then, it started to list the contents by box number and folder number. Each box was described as holding folders, so it was Box 1 and Folder 1, Box 1 and Folder 2, and so on. Box 1 had 17 folders. And then it jumped to Box 9, which contained 14 folders. And then Box 10. Scanning all the way down in the pages, the highest number box was Box 92. It seemed to be generally chronological, oldest to newest. Also, it was broken down into categories. Internal communications, R&D, corporate library, corporate culture, sales and marketing, etc.

Back to Box 1. Box 1 and Folder 2 was listed as including "Photocopies of checks written to purchase an Apple-1, 1976, July." Next it said "Subjects and Indexing Terms and Ricketts, Charles." And that was it. After that were listed subsequent folders with corporate timelines, Apple products, etcetera.

Geez! Right there in the beginning. On page 4 of 237 pages? What did this mean? I had to think about this. Why was this check copy here? Of course a business makes a copy of checks received, or at least some do. Would they have done so in 1976? I was trying to think if the small business I worked at in the late '70s even had a copier. I remembered we had a very rudimentary fax machine. And why did it only mention this item? It said the word "checks" as plural. Were there other checks in that folder? If so, why just mention this one? If I were able to look into that folder, might the check have some notes with it? Might it say something like, "Our first sale directly to a user?" Who knows? I knew the first big sale had been to the Byte computer store, which was well documented as the transaction that really turned Apple Computer into a business. Could they have kept this check like is often done in a convenience store, when they frame and display the first dollar they receive when the business first opens?

So that was my email, to Sarah, in June of 2011.

Chapter 35

Aquarius

Based on the 1999 Wired Magazine *article about the San Francisco auction, I believed it was Ricketts family members who had consigned my Apple-1 to the LaSalle Auction Gallery. Subsequent research indicated maybe it hadn't been consigned by the family, but possibly by someone who had sold or brokered Apple-1 computers more than once. I recalled collector Dave Larsen telling me about someone known to have been involved in a number of those sales, so I contacted Dave to see if he could lead me to the broker. Dave, the owner of four Apple-1 computers, had earlier mentioned that he'd almost sold one of his through this broker. I called Dave, and he said it was Sellam Ismail, the organizer of the annual Vintage Computer Festival from 1997 to 2007.*

I reached Sellam by phone in July 2012, to ask if he had at one time sold the Apple-1 that I now owned. I described it as being in a blue metal box, and having been originally purchased new by Charles Ricketts, and subsequently having been offered at auction in San Francisco in 1999. Sellam said that he was not the consignor.

Sellam Ismail - I don't know who the actual owner and seller was. A guy I knew had a store in Santa Cruz called Computer Jones, and it was basically just a computer sales store. He was kind of a—how would I describe it?—not shady so much, but it was just hard dealing with this guy. His name was Brian. I forget his last name. He came across old Apple stuff because Apple employees or former employees came to his store. He got to know these people. And he was kind of crass about selling this stuff, whereas I was more interested in the historical aspect of it. He was always interested in squeezing every last penny out of what he had, he clashed with my style of doing business. But he was a vendor at my Vintage Computer Festival event a few times.

I could spend some time digging into my past emails, and try to pull up more information on him. I heard he's a musician these days; he's promoting his albums and stuff. You'll be able to find him. I'm positive he was the guy shopping this Apple around. I have a friend who knew him better than I did. I recall my friend Jordan telling me something that made it easier to deal with him, or what his angle was. I just want to confirm that I have the details of the story right so that I can make sure it's what you're looking for, that this is the same guy and everything. He'd be the one for you to talk to, if he's willing to talk. He might be a little weird. He's a strange guy. He's just had a sort of, I don't want to say angry, I don't want to say malicious, but somewhere in between. He's kinda been a jerk, is what I'm trying to say. He might be under a non-disclosure, anyway. I think he may have been selling it on behalf of someone else. I'm positive that he didn't own it.

He most likely approached La Salle Auction house on behalf of the owner. There were rumors that it sold for fifty thousand dollars. I was aware of it at the time. It was really early, that's when people were still speculating about the value of Apple-1's. It's the first sale that I'm cognizant of, for an Apple-1, other than one that was written about in the history books. That one was a charity auction, I believe in 1984, at which time Woz paid fifteen thousand dollars for one. Up to that time, that was the only written record of the sale of an Apple-1.

So yes, nobody had any good information about the La Salle auction. My friend Jordan kind of cleared up some stuff. Because, apparently, he knew the real story with this guy Brian; he talked to him all the time. He didn't much like him either, but liked talking to him so he could see the cool Apple stuff that he'd come across.

The next known recorded sale of an Apple-1 was in September or October of 2000, whenever the date for the Vintage Computer Festival was. The opportunity came up to auction Ray Borrill's Apple-1. He's passed now, but he was a really nice guy. He was retiring and was actually sort of an unknown.

So with the first auction, this guy, Ray Borrill was a guy who had one of the first computer stores in the Midwest back in the '70s, so he had an Apple-1. He'd ordered a bunch directly from Steve Jobs back in the day, and there was one that had never sold. It was on display in his store window for the longest time, and then he held onto it after the store closed down and he was getting on in years. He used to work for William Higinbotham, the scientist at Brookhaven National Laboratory, in New York, where they did a lot of nuclear research. He was Higinbotham's lab chief, and then he went on with his own career. He wanted to sell the Apple so he could expand one of his children's houses and move in with them. His health wasn't that great.

So I said, "Okay, let me start putting something together." We came up with an idea of how much he wanted, so I started doing press releases. The auctions I did were well organized, and publicized in advance of the event. Actually at one point, there was a blurb for one of my Apple-1 auctions on CNN headline news. It was like for fifteen seconds. They said, "In California, they're selling an Apple-1 computer, and the Apple-1 was Apple's first computer," and they'd move on to the next story. I generated some good publicity.

I set up an auction system on the VCF website and had people register in advance to be able to phone-in bids using the touch tones of the phone. You could also submit bids online. The bidding was open, and we watched it climb. It ended up at around seventeen thousand dollars, I believe, and that was not enough for Ray. He had his mind set on twenty-five thousand dollars. After we announced that the reserve was not met, I was contacted by one of the bidders. He was from Japan, and asked if we could work out a private sale. I said, "Yeah. What do you have in mind?" I think Ray agreed to take twenty-five thousand dollars, and I'd take one thousand five hundred dollars of that as my commission.

And so, that's how that one ended up. Then the next guy who had an Apple-1 to sell had seen all the hoopla around that first auction. He approached me and asked if I could auction his machine off, and I said, "Yeah, sure." I think that one that sold for sixteen thousand dollars. Then, a third guy came along. He had an Apple-1, and saw that they were selling, and he needed money. This was the 2002-2003 timeframe. We got his machine working, but that one actually ended up getting less than the one before it. That was the fifteen thousand dollar transaction, I think. After that, the pricing escalated to the twenty thousand dollar area, and then twenty-two thousand five hundred dollars. The last sale I arranged was between a guy in Denmark who had an Apple-1, and a guy in Italy who wanted it. All of these Apple-1's were of varying condition, quality, accessories, documentation and things like that.

So I'd become sort of the go-to-guy on Apple-1 sales, and I'm still interviewed nowadays when auctions make the news. I've been interviewed by the *San Jose Mercury News, Newsweek,* and *The Wall Street Journal.*

Personally, the reason I started collecting computers was because of nostalgia. My first computer was this little dinky thing made by Mattel and called Aquarius. It was actually made by a company called Radofin of Hong Kong, but it was marketed by Mattel in the United States. At that time, in 1983, everybody was trying to come out with a computer. Every company was trying to cash in on the home computer craze that was taking the country by storm. By the end of that year, the whole market had crashed and these came out right around that time. So they were just dumping them wherever they could.

At the time my parents and I lived in the San Fernando Valley, in Los Angeles. This timeshare campground in Southern California was giving away a free computer if you came in to take their two-hour tour. You had to listen to their marketing pitch. I convinced my parents to take us out there and we went through the whole tour. At the end they got the hard pitch and had to say, 'Oh, it's nice, but we'll have to think about it,' and all that stuff. So we got our free computer. That was my first computer, and I was so excited.

It had 4K of memory. I wrote games on it, and I learned how to program on it. I taught myself programming when I was ten or eleven years old. I wrote a database system that I put all my comic books into. Then I decided, after I had it for a little bit over a year, that it was time to get an Apple][. I wanted something that I could do more with, and so I decided to sell my Aquarius. By that time, I'd accumulated all these peripherals for it. I had a printer. I had an expansion memory thing. I mean, it was a cool system. By any measure though, against any other computer of the day, it was a piece of junk. But I loved it because it was my friend, and I spent hours and hours of the day on it. So, I sold it and my Atari 2600 System to get my first Apple][, and I immediately regretted it. I missed the Aquarius. I was like, 'Man, I wish I didn't sell it.' It was just such a cool computer. So after that, I vowed I would never sell my computer ever again after I'm done using it. I'll keep it and use it, or

I'll put it away somewhere where I can always go back and check it out. It's that nostalgia, that's what suckered me in.

I had twenty-five computers when I found the mailing list. You see, the way I discovered other collectors was that I was on the *Usenet*. This was the old Internet version of a listserve. On one of the groups I was reading, somebody had posted a message about a vintage computer collector mailing list. I was like 'Oh, my God, there's a mailing list?' So, I contacted the guy and he put me on the list. Lo and behold, there're all of a sudden a couple of other guys to talk to around the world who were also into collecting vintage computers. I thought, 'Wow, this is great.' So we just started introducing ourselves and talking about our collections. It just got me really interested and excited to go look for more. I didn't have any hobbies, at the time. I don't even remember what I did back then for fun. I was pretty boring and I thought, 'Hey, this is cool.' I was making a lot of money in my day job and these old computers were all cheap anyway. I just started going to all the Silicon Valley swap meets, the thrift stores and the surplus shops.

We had many surplus shops back then. We had a bunch of different swap meets you could go to. It was fun finding them, it was like an Easter egg hunt. The hunt is on. And all of a sudden one day I bumped into another guy who was looking at the same stuff I was, and I was like, "Oh, you collect computers?" And he's like, "Yeah, you do too?"

So this guy and I started to meet up with other collectors as we all bumped into each other, out there in the wilds collecting this stuff. Pretty soon a little community developed. Then the computer collecting mailing list got bigger and bigger. Now, I think it must have five thousand subscribers worldwide.

I often wondered, 'How can I exploit this collection?' I've long been an enterprising kinda guy and am always thinking in terms of social get-togethers, because that's really the way to expand knowledge and to advance learning, right? And so, in this case, it would be really cool to have a convention, a classic computer convention. I proposed this to the mailing list, and it received uniformly positive responses. So I said, "Okay, I'm gonna start planning something out". That was in 1997, and the first Vintage Computer Festival event was in the fall of that year.

I had started collecting computers in earnest in early 1997, when I met up with other collectors on the Internet. Up until that point, I didn't even really think of it as a formal endeavor. I thought of it as a *tic* of my own, or something. I was self-conscious about the fact that I was collecting old computers. I didn't have a good reason for it. It just seemed the right thing to do, because they were all being thrown out, and I loved them too much as technology to allow that to happen. So, my idea was to at least preserve the culture in a small way.

It never even occurred to me that there'd be anybody else who collected, because in computers everything's about progress; newer, better, faster. And here I was, revering the older ones. People develop an attachment to a computer that they do a lot of work on, and you especially see that with Macs.

One thing I do today is run an electronics recycling warehouse where people come and drop off their old computers and other things. Every now and then somebody will bring in their old Mac from the early 1990s, and they'll say, 'Oh, I was holding on to this for so long and it's time to get rid of it, but I did so much work on it and I feel bad about it.' Usually they're older models that I'll keep, even though I already have some. I like to have backups in my collection. So I say, 'Don't worry. I'll actually add this to my collection,' and they're so pleased and happy. They say, 'I'm so glad because I hated to think that it was going to be torn apart.' This is a real common thing I hear from people, and so that's where my collecting really started. It was a nostalgic thing, but I didn't think anybody else felt that way. It's like the happy ending of *Toy Story 3* when the toys don't get thrown away after all.

335

When I first got into doing the Vintage Computer Festival events, I was like a groupie. I thought of these guys as living gods. I had the opportunity to meet Lee Felsenstein—an industry legend and creator of the Sol-20 and Osborne 1—he graciously agreed to be the keynote speaker at my first Festival. When I first met him, I must have had this crazed look in my eyes. The way he looked at me was like 'What's this guy talking about?' I was like, "Oh, it is such a pleasure and honor to meet you, sir. And thank you so much for being here..." I was clearly kind of revering him, and he was like "Yeah, okay. Where do you want me to speak?" But that's also his nature. We've since become friends, and he's actually just a very humble guy. He doesn't take himself seriously at all, even though he's definitely got a solid position in the pantheon of computer history.

Then, later on, I got the opportunity to meet Gordon Bell, who designed all of the computers for Digital Equipment back in the 1960s. He was this amazing engineer who'd written all these books, and was fairly well-known and well-respected throughout the computer industry. When I first met him, I thought 'Wow, here's another god,' and I introduced myself. He sticks out his hand and goes "Oh, hi," in a nasally, nerdy voice. He's just like a total dork. I was like 'Oh, my God.' And it struck me that these are just regular guys. They're the same kind of guys that I grew up with, because I'd been in computers all my life. They're nerds themselves, just like the guys in school, awkward, in some cases socially inept, even.

I was collecting old computers, and meeting people and hearing their stories as they handed their prized possessions over to me, their first computer or the first computer they'd built. They had all these amazing stories about the history of computers or Silicon Valley. A lot of times, at the festival, I'd invite people that nobody had ever heard of before. They all had something significant to contribute, but nobody knew their names. They weren't Steve Jobs or Steve Wozniak or Bill

Gates. I really strove to highlight these guys at the festival... the stories that people ordinarily didn't hear.

When I had people who were famous, like Woz or Felsenstein, I'd have them talk about stuff that people didn't know about. Why rehash what everyone knows? We wanted all the interesting little details about 'How did you build that circuit?' or 'Why did you choose that component rather than this component?' and all the dumb little technical questions that you'd love to ask people. I learned that these guys are just human and regular folks, even though they're gods in terms of what they've accomplished and contributed.

Over the years, through the notoriety that I attained from articles and reviews related to the Festival, I started to get approached by people for different things like, 'Hey, I have these old tapes. Do you have computers that can read them?' I always thought I could rent vintage computers out as props to Hollywood for movies, and other uses. Then, in 2000, this guy contacted me, an engineer working for a law firm. The firm had hired him to look for a computer design that had a particular door that was in dispute for a patent. I was like, 'Oh, okay.' I'd never even thought about something like that. So I found three computers that fit the bill, and rented them to him. After learning a little more, I realized there was this whole world of patent litigation and consulting that I could get into.

By this time I literally had a warehouse full of computers going back twenty years, with all kinds of different examples of technology. I think I had about five hundred computers in the collection. So I started to think about all the ways that I could exploit the collection. There was the patent litigation and the props for Hollywood. People had been approaching me about appraising and auctioning computers. They were asking how much I thought they were worth, because I was in the market almost every day buying and selling and trading. I was on *eBay* a lot, watching the auctions there. I was in the thick of it, driving a lot of this activity. So I got into sales, brokering, and appraisals, and then later I was approached for prop building. So, in 2000, when I started Vintage Tech, it was basically going to be the parent company that produced the Vintage Computer Festival. I also had my consulting day job.

I was a professional computer programmer and software engineer for a few years. I still enjoy programming, but I don't like doing it for money anymore. But, on that note, it was one of the reasons that I developed such a strong bond with my computer.

Programming allowed me to express myself. It was the expression of the logic, thinking of a concept, and then converting it into the form, language and syntax the computer requires. Doing it nicely, neatly, succinctly, perfectly, and beautifully. The whole thing, to me, was always more along the lines of writing poetry rather than performing a mechanical process. It wasn't something I was conscious of, it was subconscious. Over time, I started to understand my relationship with computers. For me, it was a natural way to express myself in the way other people express themselves through something like dancing.

Working as a programmer is what funded my computer acquisitions. Making good money in the consulting business didn't really take off until 2003, and it kind of matured in 2006.

In the meantime, when I put programming behind me—it was sort of a leap of faith—but I put all of my time into developing the recycling business. That came about because I needed to find a place to store my collection. I was losing my warehouse. I had a sweetheart deal through my then father-in-law; his friend was the manager of this building in Oakland that was being renovated. He let me store my stuff in this part of the warehouse that wasn't being used, but then he needed me to move out, because the owners were going to redevelop it. I was in a bind because I didn't know where I was going to put my collection. This was the middle of the recession, and I wasn't making very good money.

When I was out looking for computers, I'd seen a sign for computer recycling. I thought, 'Oh, I'll stop in there and see what it is.' I found that James, who owned it, and I shared some interests. He had a computer collection himself, and so we talked about maybe doing a museum together. Also, he'd say, "Hey, if you ever need any space, just let me know." So I called him up and explained what was going on. The first thing out of his mouth was, "How much space do you need, and when do you need it?" So, he gave me this space in his warehouse that I could use for free until I could figure out what I was going to do. I put all my stuff in there, and then I started to learn about the computer recycling business through his operation. I used his space for about three years. We had this symbiotic relationship until he had to move his operations to Berkeley, and there was gonna be no room for me. We had this falling out over something stupid, so I had to find my own place. Anyway, so—long story short—I started to think about where I might find space for my collection.

I was out looking in the Central Valley of California, where I was trying to find cheaper rent. Nothing was cheap enough, and so I was thinking, 'What can I do to make money at the building itself?' And I thought, 'Oh well, maybe I can do electronics recycling, and I could be a feeder for James' operation.' So, that's what ended up happening. I worked out a little deal with him. I would be a collections center for his non-profit, located in my hometown of Livermore. So it got me the warehouse I needed for my collection, and it gave me a business to bring in some regular revenue while I built the consulting business. It was tough because I was kind of torn between two completely different businesses at the same time. The stream of incoming stuff ultimately feeds into the consulting and the hobby operations. Instead of having to go out looking for stuff, now it would come to me. I would pick off the good stuff and recycle everything else.

As time went on, I started to do more and more consulting for law firms. I was doing a lot of patent litigation support and research. I started to get an eye for the kinds of things attorneys looked for. Now, something might come in that's kind of modern; it's certainly not classic. Nonetheless, it had some interesting or unique feature that makes me think, 'Hmm, I betcha someday there's gonna be a patent dispute over that.' So I held onto to those types of items. In the meantime, I got really successful working some big cases like the huge patent case between Microsoft and Lucent. I provided most of the exhibits for the law firm that was representing Microsoft. There was a good stretch of almost two years when I was renting them a big pile of computers, software, and manuals for five thousand dollars a month. Every month I'd basically just bill them for five thousand bucks, and here would come a check. It was really nice.

They spent literally... *millions!* Tens of millions, I think, on that case. It was ridiculous. They didn't flinch when it was month after month, year after year. I knew it was a big deal, and I didn't try to exploit it or anything, but it was definitely very nice. And that was on top of all the consulting hours that I billed them for putting systems together. But, I mean, I gave them some key stuff; I got them a working Xerox Star. It's officially the 8010 model, and Star was the operating system, but that was the first GUI ('gooey' or Graphical User Interface) computer, the first commercial GUI computer. This predates the Mac, it predates the Apple Lisa. It was 1981, and it uses a really finicky hard drive, a very touchy old 8" behemoth that tends to crash if you look at it wrong. So, to have one working was a real coup for them because that was one of the key pieces of evidence for their defense, and so they were more than happy to pay for it because it saved them literally billions of dollars, I'm sure, in the end.

My collection is, as far as I know, literally the largest privately-held collection in the world. So that's kind of my strength. When I started collecting, I always emphasized the whole machine and everything with it, as opposed to just the CPU. A lot of people in the past would just collect the CPU, like a trophy. It went from collecting them to just admiring them as static pieces, to ultimately, 'Hey, I can get this working again.' The whole hobby just exploded.

I was always about collecting the machine, documentation, and all of the software, and all of the magazines and the culture around it. The intent is keeping them running to whatever extent possible, to be able to show people how these computers actually worked. My ultimate goal was to one day have a museum, a living museum where you could actually come in and use the machines and stuff. But I have a ten thousand five hundred square foot warehouse, and it's pretty much covered in pallets right now, stacked five or six feet high. I have over three thousand computers, from large mainframes all the way down to handheld models.

I estimate there's probably fifty thousand individual magazine issues. I have complete runs of almost every computer publication. I've got technical and electronic journals going back into the '20s, '30s and '40s, just an immense technical library. I love to have the information. The big push these days is to digitize everything, and that's great, but I'm convinced that in the long run the hard-copies are gonna outlast even the digital representations of the software.

I'd built a reputation of being an all-around vintage computer consultant. I was working at the Computer History Museum as their first software curator. Any time the museum would get a loan inquiry for an exhibit, they'd always refer people to me. They'd say, 'Well, Sellam has one,' or, 'Sellam can build a replica for you.'

So, I got a lot of referrals through them. Microsoft co-founder Paul Allen had a team touring around the world looking for artifacts, and visiting different museums. He was working on opening a computer museum Albuquerque. He wanted to use the building that Microsoft's

341

first offices were in. The building is in a really rundown part of town now and it just wasn't going to be feasible because he would have had to do a multi-million dollar renovation project to renovate that part of town. It was just gonna be a huge project that wasn't going to be practical. In the end, he decided to donate a bunch of money to the Natural History Museum in Albuquerque, and they added a huge computer history exhibit that was funded by him.

They hired me to locate a bunch of chips, and an Apple-1, and to build some replicas for the museum. So, I built some small-scale replicas for them. They wanted a 4004, Intel's first microprocessor. I was able to find an Apple-1 owner, and agreed on a sale price, and brokered the sale.

When you think about the history of the Apple-1, it came out and it was very fleeting. It was only around for about a year, if that, before the Apple][came out, which was much more capable. Then everyone who had an Apple-1 was, 'Oh, I want to get an Apple][; that's a much better computer.' Their subsequent success was so rapid that people who had Apple-1's were like, 'Oh, I'm gonna hang on to this, because this is the computer that really started it all.'

Now I had to try and find a musician.

Chapter 36

Computer Jones

Larry and I searched the web, using the few clues we had. "Musician." "Used computer store." "Brian" or "Neil." That was about it. We came across a fellow who had run an unsuccessful campaign trying to unseat well-known U.S. Senator Barbara Boxster in 2010. The state, California, was right... but our guy wasn't a politician. But then we found the same guy strumming a guitar, onstage in a club, on a *YouTube* video. *Hmmm.* 'Musician'. Maybe he'd run for office. This was worth a shot, but in the variety of places we could find him online, there was not much in the way of contact info. Finally we found an email address and sent a note. Within a day, we got a reply:

"Yes, I had an Apple -1 with rare documentation.
It sold for more than any mentioned.
The story, from how it was acquired,
how I hid it from thieves who heard about it and tried to steal it;
until it finally sold in an amazing way.
...and then, there was the historic phone call from Steve Jobs about that particular machine and the offer he made.
The saga of the Apple-1 prototype,
documented to have been built and sold from Job's parent's garage in Los Altos;
could easily become an entire chapter in your book, and one of the most fascinating and entertaining...
but that would be a business matter."

I thought... 'This guy has a story, and he thinks it's such a good story that he can sell it. Well, I can play that game.' So, I got in touch.

It turns out that Neil Brian Goldberg was lead singer of a band that played on the Steel Pier in Atlantic City, in the 1950s. Professionally, he dropped his last name because a Jewish-sounding name might hurt his pop music career. Over the years, he wrote almost a hundred songs that were recorded and ended up on radio or television. In 1970, he landed the job of songwriter for the popular children's Saturday TV cartoon *Archie's Funhouse*. Neil had always been interested in the environment, and passionate about issues of the day. He decided to include some educational content in songs for the show. The animators picked up on Neil's messages and joined in, integrating content not usually found in children's cartoons. His most famous *Archie* segment was Mister Factory, and showed children wearing gas masks, because of what factories had done to the air.

Neil begins his story in 1989, with he and his wife and living in a van in Santa Cruz, California. Santa Cruz is a popular beach town, sitting on cliffs overlooking the Pacific. East of town are the Santa Cruz Mountains, and on the other side of the mountains is the South Bay region of San Francisco, also known as Silicon Valley.

Neil Brian Goldberg - I was homeless. Then suddenly, a baby was on the way. We had to do something, we were living 'freegan,' my wife and I. We were completely broke. I came up through the music industry, and I had some serious royalties stolen from me and I wound up going down. My wife and I were living kind of free in a remodeled van. A big van. You've seen them; that was cool. We had a wood-burner. We were living a pretty good life, simple and austere. Then suddenly I had a baby on the way, so I had to do something. I remembered a big double dumpster that always had good stuff in it. I never bothered with it because I was sort of like a free hippie. So I immediately thought, '*Dumpster*... there's a raging

344

flea market in Santa Cruz every weekend.' I started looting that dumpster, taking the pickings to the flea market, making two or three hundred a week. So then we got a little tiny place to live, and it was cool. One thing led to another, and I ended up having a whole dumpster route up there in the Scotts Valley area. And I was getting good stuff.

Next thing I knew, I came across this one dumpster that was always overflowing with books. No matter how deep down in the dumpster I reached, I couldn't get past these weird books. They looked brand new, and the covers were strange, and they had odd symbols and stuff inside. I didn't know what they were. I didn't take any. They had these little black plastic things inside.

Then one night I had a dream, and a strange, mystical thing happened. A sage kind of guy, like a holy wise man, asked me about that dumpster. It kind of gave me a clue. It turned out that it was the Borland International dumpster, overflowing with all their best products.

Borland Software Corporation was first headquartered in Scotts Valley, California, six miles from Santa Cruz. In the 1980s, Borland successfully launched a series of blockbuster software programs. The books in the dumpster were software manuals and the black plastic objects were floppy disks.

So I took some of those books down to the flea market, and they were selling like crazy. Two, three, four, five bucks apiece. So I got boxes and boxes of them and stashed them anywhere I could find: old cars, old sheds.

One thing led to another. I had a lot of amazing stories of this magical business. I'd really started making money at computer trade shows, and no one else had the Borland manuals. They were red hot. There they were selling for fifteen bucks a book, like hotcakes. I started making really good money. There were other vendors who'd found their

345

own dumpsters with thrown out software. And they had tons of inventory. They had Adobe and Microsoft. They were raiding other places on the other side of the hill (the other side of the Santa Cruz Mountains, facing Silicon Valley). They wanted the Borland dumpster, so they could get the Borland books and software. They just didn't even know where that dumpster was. It was just by God's grace that I came across it. So I would trade them a box of Borland books and they gave me just a whole bunch of stuff that was more than they could sell. I had eight tables at every trade show with all the best packages and manuals. I became one of the biggest guys there.

From there, I realized I should have a store. I got a little store I rented in Santa Cruz. My business was going to be called Computer Jones. Now, when I started that business, I knew nothing about computers. I didn't even know how to turn one on. Back in 1989 it was all just beginning. *eBay* was there, but I didn't even know what *eBay* was. My wife came up with the name Computer Jones. Had I known what I know now, I would never even have even tried to open a store with that junk and old Borland manuals and stuff.

It was the day before the store was to open. We'd set up the store using all recycled wood and little hand built shelves. I was on the phone with my wife, and she said, "I'm worried, what's going to happen?" I was already making good money, without the expense of a store. I said, "Don't worry, honey, I've got a feeling God's going to do something wonderful." Right then, while I was on the phone with her, the whole place started to shake. It was the earthquake of '89. The big quake. Every electronics and computer store in the whole area was wiped out. Except mine.

The Quake of '89, also known as the World Series Earthquake, struck the San Francisco Bay area on October 17, 1989, at 5:04 pm. Caused by a slip along the San Andreas Fault, it lasted ten to fifteen seconds and

346

measured 6.9 on the Richter Scale. The quake killed sixty-three people throughout northern California, injured 3,757, and left thousands homeless. It occurred during the warm-up practice for the third game of the 1989 World Series, and was the first major earthquake in the United States to have its initial jolt broadcast live on television. The epicenter was ten miles northeast of Santa Cruz. It caused severe damage in the San Francisco Bay area. Some twelve thousand homes and two thousand six hundred businesses were damaged. In Santa Cruz, forty buildings collapsed, killing six. It was the largest earthquake to occur on the San Andreas Fault since the great 1906 San Francisco earthquake.

With my store left standing, I became the number one store in Santa Cruz, in the wink of an eye. The only guy open.

Chapter 37

Taxi Driver

Neil Brian Goldberg - One day I'm in my warehouse, doing business. I look up, there's a guy with dark hair. Young man. Mid-to-late twenties, I'd say. And he's standing there and he says to me, "How much would you pay for an Apple-1?"

Well, at that time I had tons of stock. Everything was beginning to move into PC; 286's, 386's, 486's. And the old Apples became worthless. So, I had stacks like ten computers high, standing out in my lot outside the warehouse. It would rain, I'd just leave them out there. I would have *dollar sales*. I just wanted to get rid of them. I had so much junk coming in. I would just say like, take anything for a dollar. I had these machines out for a dollar, before they were rained on. Nobody would even take them.

"An Apple-1? – Nothing!" I said, thinking of the piles of Apple][-e's – Apple Plus' – and Apple-III's I had stacked up all over the place, and which I could not get rid of – even at my one dollar sales. I do wish I had them now, because they have become fairly valuable. So he said to me, "How much would you pay for an Apple-1?" and immediately I actually saw a picture in my mind of all these old Apple computers, 2Es, IIs stacked out on the lot and I said—I paused for a second and I said, "Nothing!" just like that, I said, "Nothing," and he was jolted, and almost thrown back a step, and he said "Nothing?" And because of his reaction, it made me just give it a little double think, and I realized he had said "Apple-1." And I said, "*Oh*, an Apple-1."

"Nothing!?" He said. I had to stop a minute and think, because of his amazed reaction, and then I realized, 'An Apple-1 – a collector's dream.'

"Oh, an Apple-1" I said, "How much do you want for it?" I had heard a few reliable stories about Apple-1's selling for good money; ten thousand, twenty thousand, thirty thousand. So we got to talking. He told me his dad had died, and it was in his dad's storeroom with a bunch of stuff. And his dad left it for him; wanted him to have it. He said his father, Charles Ricketts, bought it directly from Steve Jobs.

And he said he'd been driving a cab, and he wanted to get his own cab. And to get a taxi cab license would cost him three thousand dollars. So I thought about it. Usually the way I bought stuff was that I used to say "I don't buy anything unless it's for free." You know, I'd make a trade or something. And I bought very low, for the stuff coming in off the street. Because a lot of times you'd find out it had a problem. But here, this was a very valuable thing, if it was what it was supposed to be. And the story about his dad. And so I wanted to be fair with this guy.

He wanted three thousand dollars for the Apple-1. So I asked him to bring it by, and I would see what I could do. He came by with the computer, and it turned out that he not only had the Apple-1, but he also had what might have been the first two checks ever written to Apple Computer, and labels mounted under plastic, with each check.

The first check was for about $600. It was made out to Apple Computer, July 1976, and the label above it said, "SOLD BY STEVE JOBS, FROM HIS PARENT'S GARAGE, IN LOS ALTOS CA. July 1976". The second check was also made out to Apple Computers, and the label said: "PROGRAMMED BY STEVE JOBS August 1976." He also had the original Apple-1 manual. The Apple-1 was encased in a metal box, and with a cover of hard see-through plastic. Everything seemed to be in good shape.

When it comes to collectibles, one never knows if there is some little nuance, or bad model, that renders the great find almost worthless. One has to be very careful, especially, when they don't know the ropes. So I called up my friend Jordan, who is an avid Apple collector. He is a fanatic, an aficionado. I said, "Come look at this thing," before I would buy it. He came and looked at the machine, and told me it was the real thing. What made it really valuable was that it had the documentation, the original manual, and most of all the two cancelled checks that are with it and the little labels saying "sold by Steve Jobs from his parent's garage."

He said it looked like it might have been modified. He said that could be a problem. So I wasn't sure what to think about it, but I still knew it had to be worth something.

Usually, when I would buy something that came in off the street, I would be very tough. In an industry where a great buy could become obsolete junk in two weeks, or was even before you bought it, where a fine collectable could turn bad with one new piece of information, or one missing part, you had to buy as low as you could. And still, many deals only broke even or turned for a loss.

But this deal was different. He told me his father had left it to him, and I always believed that there are some lines you don't cross. There are times when you don't take advantage, or drive a guy down. Like if you know he's in trouble, and desperate – you don't smile to yourself and make him crawl. You don't use his misfortune to cheat him. In this case, this man's father tried to leave him something. It was something that would give him a boost. I could have said that all I could do was one thousand five hundred, 'because.' Or I could have said I wasn't sure what I might get for it, and gotten it for two thousand dollars. Or, for two thousand five hundred. Instead, I got him his three thousand dollars, so he could get his cab. 'Cause I knew it was what his father would have wanted, and I believed it would bring me good luck with the Apple-1.

So, I gave the guy his three thousand. Any other situation, I would have got it for fifteen hundred, or two thousand, or certainly twenty five. But I had a feeling because his father left it to him. It was this boy's chance to get something going in the world from what his father left him. So I gave him his three thousand.

I *did* pay him cash. I remember. We rode in his cab. He had the Apple-1 in the front seat, and we were going to the bank so I could get him his money. I gave him his cash, and there was something I forgot or some reason I had to go back into the bank. So I got out and I left the door open. And there he was with money and the Apple-1. I could almost read his mind, he was wondering if he should just drive off. I can't say that for sure. The thought may have never crossed his mind. But I was wondering, is he going to disappear? That was an error there, on my part. That was a definite error. Anyway, I came out, he was still there. He'd have thought better of it, or just never thought of it at all. I got the Apple-1. I took it and put it right in the trunk of my car. Secretly, because I knew that's the one place that my workers couldn't get to. I had a big problem at Computer Jones with stuff disappearing.

Chapter 38

Toy Story

Neil Brian Goldberg - The first problem to overcome was to keep the Apple-1 from disappearing.

At that particular time, there were some characters hanging around the warehouse, helping out part-time, and pretending to be friends. Every week, expensive software packages were turning up without the diskettes inside. Other valuable things, like memory chips and hard drives, were also missing. I knew I had to clean house, but for now, I secretly kept the Apple-1 in the trunk of my car. I knew that's the one place that my workers couldn't get to.

One new guy had come in out of the blue, and offered to work for spare parts and a little cash. He knew all about the computer recycling business, and had great abilities. One night, while I was working late in my office, he said he was going to test a load of stuff. It seemed that he never needed to sleep or rest. At the time, I didn't know he was a speed or crack addict. I was so naive about that drug world.

So from inside my office, I heard him methodically going through all of the pallet racks and the deep storage over the office. He was searching hard for something. My theory is that one of the thieves already there, who had heard about the Apple-1, and knew it was worth big money, had brought in a pro to find it, and then disappear.

First of all, this guy was an out-and-out criminal. I didn't know it at the time. Later, there was someone who was giving me trouble, and this guy actually said to me, "Want me to kill him for you? I'll kill him out there by the dumpsters across the street, and they'll blame it on the homeless people." He was ready to murder somebody, you know? And I said, "No, I don't think we'll do that." And I'm trying to think about how to peacefully get him out of there without having him come after me.

So this guy was a definite criminal with no scruples, no boundaries. And, he was a con man, he had a charming side to him. But he was like a jailbird, definitely was like a jailbird. He'd probably been to prison. That night, he had said, "Oh, I'm going to test some stuff." And he's up on top of all the pallets, and up over the area over my office where no one ever went. There was just a lot of junk and some lumber, and old swing set that belonged to my daughter, just junk I had up there. There was no reason for anyone to be up there at all. He wasn't testing anything. Nothing was getting tested. So, I heard him out there, and I already knew what was going on. I just didn't care because I knew he wasn't going to find it. I thought, let him waste his time. I had it where they could never find it.

It's like two in the morning. Nobody slept around there. And there he was, moving everything, searching... At that point, maybe he didn't realize I was still in my office. Sometimes I would leave when someone was still there working. I wasn't always there late. So, he was searching ferociously, he was going to find that thing, man. And the other guys that worked for me, who were definite characters, some of them, who brought him in out of the blue. They had said, "Oh, this is so and so, and he knows all about how to break stuff down." And the guy had some good ability. They put him up to it. You know, they were all conspiring to get that Apple-1. Yeah, they thought they could get twenty grand or something like that.

Since the guy had come in offering to sell the Apple-1, everybody knew about it. So, I figure a plan was hatched immediately, 'Oh, forget about the *Abode Illustrator* disks and the *Word Perfect* disks, and this and that and that other rare art package. Let's go big time. Let's get that Apple-1.'

And he was too dangerous to confront. I just got him out of there. Actually, he got arrested. Something happened, he got arrested. I did sweep the warehouse clean, I fired everyone.
And I proceeded to find out what to do with the Apple-1. How to sell the Apple-1?

I contacted Southerbee's *(sic)*, a famous auction house in San Francisco, but they did not handle such items. (Neil means Sotheby's, but

353

the other famous San Francisco auction house was Butterfield's, so he may have the two confused.)

I had heard that Apple Computers had a museum. Maybe they would buy it. I decided it would be best if I could speak directly with Steve Jobs, but how? I did say, "Magical and amazing..."

Somehow, a delivery man was at the Computer Jones store and mentioned that he made deliveries to Steve Job's house, and that he saw him often. I explained the situation to him, and asked if he would do me the great favor of informing Steve Jobs about the Apple-1. The delivery man was glad to help. I gave him a packet of photos of the Apple-1 and copies of the original checks, and my phone number.

About a week went by, and one day I answered a call at the Computer Jones warehouse.

"Is this Brian Thomas?"

"Yes," I replied.

"Please hold for Mr. Jobs."

Steve Jobs came on the line and said hello. I started off telling him that it was an honor to speak with him and I meant it. Because of how he had come back and took hold of Apple, and what he had originally started. And what he was doing again. I was honored to talk to him, but I wasn't all shook up or anything.

We started discussing the Apple-1, and Steve said that he remembered the machine and the man who had bought it from him. Steve Jobs then offered me five thousand dollars for my Apple-1. I told him I had heard they were worth about thirty thousand dollars. Steve Jobs laughed a full, robust, "*Ho ho ho*," and said, "I rather doubt that."

I then asked him what they were working then at Apple and Pixar. He told me they were doing the animations for the new *Toy Shop* (*sic*) movie. There was my opportunity! I should have immediately told him about the *Archie's* TV music I had written, arranged and produced, and perhaps found an open door for what I was best at ...as well as one of

354

the best at. Writing catchy and clever little songs for kids. Instead, I blurted out, "I have some good music that would go well with that,"or some such amateur-sounding drivel. Steve Jobs seemed to take a deep gulp and said, "Uh, let me know if you want to sell the Apple-1 for five thousand dollars." I said, "Thanks for calling," and that was it. Steve Jobs definitely wanted it. But he wanted it for five thousand dollars. I knew it was worth more than that.

Chapter 39

Little Hat with a Pointed Top

Neil Brian Goldberg - Well, I didn't know what to do with it. And so Sotheby's said no, and I realized most auction houses, they're selling fine antique chandeliers, and whatever. They weren't going to want to mess with it. So, I looked in the phone book, called a few places, and a high-ranking San Francisco auction house took interest, and I decided to go with an auction. A very dapper, nice gentleman by the name of Jack Sacks came down. He was an Englishman, with a very impressive accent.

I had told him I had a few other machines. I had a KLM which Apple had never released, and that was pretty rare too. Stuff by the truckload came in all the time. I even found weapons sometimes, mixed in with the load. A whole truckload would come in, and I'd find all kinds of stuff.

So I decided to combine the Apple-1 with an Apple Lisa prototype, and the KLM prototype. It was an impressive lot of stuff. The auction house was able to get write-ups in the best papers, and some clumsy Internet promotion, along with a mail campaign.

I didn't attend the auction. It was too much for me. I had too much going on. I had trouble at the warehouse, with the help. I thought, 'It'll sell or it won't. They didn't need me there.

The auction came and went. Many people showed up. I know they didn't have any bids on the Apple-1 or the other ones. The auction company told me that they arranged to have a bid come in from some associate to save face, for like seventeen or eighteen thousand. I had a large reserve on the items, so I was able to take them back.

I drove all the way up to San Francisco again, through bad traffic, and all the way back. And I finally followed my wife's advice. "Why don't you just list it on *eBay*?" she kept saying. I had already been selling copies of the front page of the manual, the checks to Apple, and pictures of the rare bird; for fifteen dollars a packet on *eBay*, so I had, without

356

realizing it, already begun to promote the big auction, about to rock the computer world.

As I prepared to list the Apple-1 on *eBay*, I began to see a TV movie, which was showing over and over, just at that time. It was called *The Pirates of Silicon Valley*. What timing!

The Pirates of Silicon Valley was the story of Bill Gates, Steve Jobs, and the birth of the Microsoft and Apple computer empires. In the story, the very garage where Steve Jobs began Apple Computer, and where my Apple-1 was designed and built, was shown and talked about. All I had to do was carefully describe the great package I was offering, and then mention that this computer was built and sold from the very garage featured in the movie *The Pirates of Silicon Valley*.

I listed the auction on *eBay* with a five thousand dollar first bid, and a sixty thousand dollars reserve, meaning that if the final bid was below the sixty thousand dollars reserve, I did not have to sell it. The bidding began, and before I knew it, the price was up to ten thousand dollars. It then edged up to twelve thousand dollars. But then it stayed there for a couple days. I began to worry. What if it did not move? What if it stayed there? The value would be established as only twelve thousand dollars.

Then it went to thirteen thousand dollars. Then it went up to eighteen, nineteen, twenty-one, twenty-three, and then twenty-seven thousand dollars. But then, again, it stayed there for quite a while. I was still not happy. I was hoping for a much bigger auction. As the final days of the auction wound down, the price spurted up to thirty-five thousand, five hundred dollars, and that's where it stayed as the auction closed. I had no way of knowing who was bidding.

I still believed that this rare machine, and the even rarer docs that came with it, could command a higher price. I e-mailed all of my bidders that the reserve on the Apple-1 *eBay* listing had been sixty thousand dollars, but that we would be selling it at this time. I told them all that whoever came in with the highest bid, between thirty-five thousand five hundred dollars and sixty thousand dollars, would get the Apple-1.

There was no response from any of the bidders, but an email came flying in from nowhere. The man, not even one of the original bidders, had gotten my email address from a friend, and asked to see a picture of it. I didn't know how to upload pics, so the eBay auction had been run with no photos.

So I zapped him a few photos, and sent him the same message as I had sent to the others, except I added one extra line to his email. "If you say sixty thousand dollars now, you will probably get the machine."

And he came right back. Within a minute, within thirty seconds, maybe. He came right back and said, "Okay, I'll take it." I carefully emailed him back, asking, "When you say, 'I'll take it', does that mean you will pay sixty thousand dollars?" And that's when he came back immediately, *zoom*. "Yes, I'll pay sixty thousand dollars." he replied. *Kaboom*. Done.

You know, to me, I was never a big money guy. Sixty thousand dollars was a big deal.

The buyer was in Virginia or West Virginia. I wondered if it was Steve Jobs or someone working for him. I didn't know. I never knew for sure. I always wondered. My wife thought maybe they were going to put it in a museum in Washington, DC. I didn't know. I thought maybe it was Steve Jobs because he wanted it. I can't believe that he didn't. If he had offered me twenty thousand, I probably would have done it.

I remember the buyer by his initials, BMW. Bruce Waldack. I thought maybe he was part owner of BMW or something. So I was impressed.

We began to make arrangements, and he wired the sixty thousand dollars directly into my bank account. He was going to fly down in his private jet to pick it up. I said "Good." Then he called back and

358

said, "No, better just send it. Send it overnight, and insure it." I spoke with him on the phone, very decent guy, nice guy, very understanding. Didn't try to take advantage of me, he was very nice. I liked him.

They would only insure it up to about fifty thousand dollars, I think. And that was five hundred bucks. And then it was an oversized package because I took it to this Japanese UPS store, and the guy packed it like was war time, and I said, "Nothing can happen to this." He made like a little hat with a pointed roof over it, and I mean you could have hit that package with a sledgehammer. Man, that thing... I stood there and watched the guy spend over an hour packaging it. Every little detail. Very Japanese. All the tape, you know, worked down. Here it was an oversized package, overnight delivery, on a Saturday. So, the shipping wound up being like a thousand dollars, eleven hundred, something like that. So afterwards the buyer called me and complained about the price of the shipping. I said five hundred of it was insurance. It was UPS. I had followed his instructions, and that was the honest price to pack, ship and insure it. It was the way and at the speed he wanted.

He did, however, say that he was very happy with the Apple-1, and the deal. He was just a little shocked about the shipping costs. I don't think that he realized how much of that cost was actually insurance, which he wanted.

So the Apple-1 deal was done. I did put in a call to Steve Jobs and left a message on his voice-mail that the Apple-1 had sold for sixty thousand dollars, and though I had no animosity toward Mr. Jobs, it felt good. He was a nice man. Years later, I was sorry to hear he was ill, and of his passing. I prayed for him.

It was good for me because I wound up getting some good money for it. It meant a lot. And I did pay taxes on it. I did declare it.

Chapter 40

Printing Presses

On June 15th, 2012, Sotheby's offered an Apple-1 computer at auction in New York. It was described as having the accessory Apple-1 Cassette Interface, a rare item itself. It also came with the original owners' manual, which Sotheby's said had a tear along the fold and light staining.

Sotheby's had set a pre-sale estimate of one hundred twenty thousand dollars to one hundred eighty thousand dollars. The computer saw brisk and active bidding, and was knocked down as sold for three hundred seventy-four thousand five hundred dollars.

Five months later, on November 24th, Team Breker offered another Apple-1 at auction. Breker is a specialty auction house with international clientele, located in Koln, Germany. They specialize in antique technology and fine historic toys. The Apple-1 sold for a world record price of six hundred forty thousand dollars. This particular example was well-accessorized, including a vintage monitor. The owner's manual, though carrying an autograph of Steve Wozniak, was a reproduction.

In May of 2013, Team Breker offered another Apple-1 at public auction. I attended the auction at their galleries in Koln. Mr. Uwe Breker personally has one of the world's finest collections of mechanical collectibles, all housed in his auction gallery building. As you enter the front door, there are display rooms and the auction room on the first floor. On the second floor, behind a locked glass entryway, there's an entire wing filled with his collections. His museum-like office is situated there, amongst some of the finest treasure. I found it amusing to visit his wife's office, hidden away on the first floor, and clearly the center of finance for the business. Her office is stark white and minimalist, with not one decoration in sight. In the basement is what are probably the most extreme items in his collection; there must be forty large, early printing presses. Each is lovingly restored, and and would require a car trailer to move it. The presses are evidence that it's not all business for Mr. Breker, but very much a labor of love. There can't be much of a market for something so massive. But he recognizes their importance in history.

At the Breker auction, the Apple-1 sold for a world record price of six hundred seventy-one thousand dollars. It was sold to a phone bidder.

Just as this book was going to press, Christie's sold an Apple-1 (July 2013) for three hundred eighty thousand dollars. A friend of mine emailed me to suggest that I hurry up and sell mine...since the prices are going down! Actually, it wasn't that long ago that some were selling for twenty thousand or so, and then in the fifty thousand to seventy-five thousand dollar range. So, I'd suggest that nothing goes up in a straight line. It doesn't happen with paintings or antiques. But if you graph the sale prices, we're seeing a continued incline in valuations.

When *eBay* first became popular, the marketplace saw some prices of collectibles go down over time. That's because we now had a much more efficient way to sell antiques that were sitting up in the attic. However, some prices went down over time; lots of attics full of antiques, and the popularity and ease-of-use of *eBay* meant that, in many categories, supply soon caught up with demand. This won't happen with the Apple-1, because there is such a small supply of them; with this item we know there were only ever two hundred. As of today, *The Registry* identifies forty-eight surviving. Well, some of those are listed as "current whereabouts unknown," so it's possible that the full count of forty-eight don't really exist. But, no doubt, some will still come out of hiding in attics and closets. The machine that just sold for three hundred eighty thousand dollars was not on *The Registry*, so that's one that most of us didn't know existed. And there will be others (but only so many). Also, more and more seem to be going into museums. The odds are against them ever going on the market again. So all things considered, I think we'll see prices stay up there, or continue to climb.

As we see the market evolve and mature, I believe collectors will start looking even closer at each machine that comes to market. Originality, provenance and condition will help differentiate one machine from another. And 'the story' that goes along with an object can also be a big factor in its value and desirability.

Epilogue

I first read, in an old *Wired Magazine* article from 1999, that the Ricketts family relatives had consigned their Apple-1 to the LaSalle Gallery. If it had been Charles Ricketts' family that consigned it to auction, that might be an indication that he was deceased. Since Jef Raskin, a prominent Apple engineer, also had vintage Apple computers in the same auction, my guess was there might have been a connection between Raskin and Ricketts. Maybe they were friends. Maybe Raskin advised Ricketts' family to consign the computer to the auction, as part of clearing up the estate. Raskin died in 2005, six years after the 1999 auction, so I couldn't ask him. I contacted his son and his widow, but the effort was inconclusive.

Later, when I learned that Neil had consigned it, the Raskin-Ricketts connection went out the window. I still wonder how a tiny auction house, with a new owner who was not from the U.S., came to consign vintage Apples from both Neil *and* Raskin. That is curious.

We know Ricketts' Apple did not sell at LaSalle, and was returned to its consignor. It seems LaSalle desired to make the auction look successful, and the management roped O'Mahony in on the story. An eighteen thousand dollar sale did seem low, and Neil's *eBay* bidder results and subsequent sale support that. Captain Owen O'Mahony would make a great name for a character in a Roald Dahl children's book, but maybe it's a more common name in his country than in mine. The story of the Captain making the purchase was always puzzling, if for no other reason than he wasn't known to me as a collector. There are many *quiet* and private buyers of valuable items at auction, but usually their names are still recognizable because they've previously made auction purchases.

When I found that Owen O'Mahony really existed, and that he'd been the private pilot of Ayrton Senna, that led to the theory that maybe he was also the private pilot for Bruce Waldack's jet. But when I finally spoke with Owen, he shot down that theory.

From the beginning, it was murky as to why Bruce Waldack had fled the U.S. His brother David answered those questions, sadly. And the picture of Bruce that was painted by David, comments posted online when he passed away, and what was shared by Bruce's Argentinian-based friend Federico Ini went a long way in helping me understand why he died so young.

In February 2013, I was walking down Madison Avenue in New York City. I passed a shop called Macklowe Gallery. Inside the front window were three Tiffany lamps, and they had the look of the real thing. I rang the doorbell, and stepped into the shop. Seeing the lamps and further in back the display cases lined with Tiffany vases, I started to share the story of Bruce Waldack and his Tiffany collection. The proprietor of the store invited me downstairs, where he displayed what must be the world's finest collection of original Tiffany lamps. David Waldack told me that Bruce had a Drophead Dragonfly lamp, and I could see several of those in this room. As I was parting at the front door, I wondered aloud if Bruce might have been a client. He went over to his computer and typed in his name. Sure enough, there it was, the name Bruce Waldack on the screen. His co-worker in the shop asked the proprietor if he recalled Bruce. "That was in 2002. That's a long time ago to remember."

Finding and meeting Neil Brian Goldberg was the most instrumental aspect of learning the story of my Apple-1. But I almost missed him. And it took a mental review of comments I'd heard over time for it to occur to me to go back to Dave Larsen and ask who the broker was that he'd almost done a deal with. That led me to Sellam Ismail, who graciously shared his stories. And Sellam gave me enough hints to be able to find Neil.

Through Neil I learned that Charles' son had come to Neil's store, that there had been an attempt to steal the Apple-1, and that Steve Jobs offered to buy it. Neil shared the story of his consignment to LaSalle, and then taking his wife's advice and trying *eBay*. Only because of Neil did we know what he and Bruce discussed and about the deal they'd made.

As Neil and I sat on the patio of Dharma's Restaurant in Santa Cruz on a sparkling summer day in August 2012, Neil came up with an extra tidbit. Somehow the conversation came around to Sellam, and clearly there was no love lost between the two. But then Neil remembered something. He shared that Bruce Waldack told him that he had found out about Neil's Apple-1—my Apple-1—because Sellam directed him to Neil. I don't think that Sellam ever knew that. Sellam must have spoken with Bruce, who might have been looking for an Apple-1 because Sellam was known to have sold Apple-1's, and to have run the Vintage Computer Festivals. Somehow Bruce found Neil because of Sellam. But I don't think that's something Sellam was ever told. He probably never knew that the guy 'Bruce from the East Coast,' ended up buying an Apple-1 because of his referral.

Finding the Stanford University Apple archive was dumb luck. I'd owned the Apple-1 for a few years, and one day I did a *different* search than I'd ever done on Google. That was truly like opening up Aladdin's cave. And it had been sitting there all along, indexed on Google, just waiting for me to find it. No one I've spoken to—and I've asked many people—seems to know definitively why that check copy is in there. The only check. Cut down to size. At the very front of a chronologically-ordered archive. As Steve Wozniak once said to me, "Steve would know."

Footnote List

2.0 life – Indicates the second wave of Internet culture, in which interactivity is a major feature of the technology. [Ini]

6502 Manual – The instructional guide that outlines the design architecture of the 6502 series of microprocessors.

6502/6800 Processor – The budding engineers of the microcomputer revolution had to scrounge for components and parts; the desired tech equipment was highly specialized in nature, and costly relative to their lack of resources, and thus normally unavailable to them. The Motorola 6800 microprocessor was the industry standard, and as dauntingly expensive as it was powerful. Simply put, Motorola consolidated their technology and design programs to create a more accessible family of tech tools. Affordable knockoffs resulted, and young engineers had access to this scaled-down, but fully-compatible, generation of processors.

9-D – A branch of physics as applied to engineering. [Kottke]

Alan Turing – Turing was a mathematician cited as the father of modern computing. During WWII, Turing—who was British—was responsible for

366

decoding the encrypted messages of the German Enigma machine, an act that turned the tide for Allied intelligence.

Jim Alinksy – Indiana-based Apple enthusiast who assembled four mounted, framed Apple-1 boards.

Altair – A microprocessor from 1975, by MITS (**M**icro **I**nstrumental **T**elemetry **S**ystems) in Albuquerque, NM, the original consumer breakthrough of the PC world. The name itself is a *Star Trek* reference—Altair is a planetary system—and that (along with the recurrence of *Star Trek*-themed games,) indicates the extent of the impact of *Star Trek* on computer culture, and by broad extension, the influence of science fiction upon science fact.

Apartheid – Formally institutionalized racial separation and political exclusion of *Colored*, as opposed to White, South Africans (1948 – 1994). [O'Mahony]

Apple-1 Registry – While there's no definitive record of the Apple-1's still in existence, (certainly not within the official Apple domain) vintage tech enthusiast and replica designer Mike Willegal maintains an Internet registry of all known and possible machines.

Apple Glasses – a pair of novelty eyeglasses in which the lenses are shaped and colored like the original six-color rainbow spectrum Apple logo. [Huston]

Apple][, Apple][c – The Apple][(pronounced 'Apple two') was, of course, the breakthrough microprocessor of the PC revolution (which incorporated and improved upon aspects of the Apple-1), and Apple subsequently produced a number of derivations of the basic model over the course of the '80s. The Apple][c, the forth of these derivations, was Apple's first attempt to market a portable, ready-out-the-box machine.

ARPANET – The **A**dvanced **R**esearch **P**rojects **A**gency **Net**work, a precursor to the Internet, established by the Department of Defense as a private "intranet" web that connected a national network of universities, research laboratories, and facilities. As opposed to a single terminal hooked up to another single, remote terminal, it allowed for a central location to speak to all other networked sites.

Assembler – a program that interprets input and converts it into a bit-pattern—an assembly code—to enhance processing speed and efficacy.

Atlantis – Bahamas resort & casino complex, with it's centerpiece of two high rise buildings connected by an elevated walkway. [Ini]

Bandley – The Bandley location, in 1978, was the company's most formal-seeming industrial/office space, essentially a warehouse space divided into suites, and was the setting for Apple's post-Apple][growth.

BASIC – an acronym for **B**eginner's **A**ll Purpose **S**ymbolic **I**nstruction **C**ode, *BASIC* is a broad label for the assortment of highly accessible-to-the-user programming languages; the foundation for PC software. The *BASIC* template was adapted throughout the microcomputer industry; each major brand developed a proprietary version.

BASIC & Cassettes – Software programs must have a medium that allows the user to save their work. Through the '70s, that vehicle was cassette tape, which stored considerably more information electromagnetically than the previous generation technologies of perforated punch cards and paper ribbons.

Bits – In programming basics terms, a bit (as in **bi**nary dig**it**) is the smallest unit of information, either a "0" or a "1". Combinations of bits are strung together (eight of them in a row are a *byte*) to create a file.

Bitmapped Screen – A hardware application that enables a *bit* of computer memory to be displayed by a corresponding pixel seen on the monitor, which is what constructs the graphic image. [Kottke]

Blackjack team – Wozniak and Sokol were certainly not the first to attempt to game the system in Blackjack; the game has long been a target for gaming strategists. As of the late seventies, as one example, the MIT Blackjack team, students from MIT, Harvard, and the Harvard Business School rigorously coordinated interactions within an ensemble of bettors, using card-counting techniques and other odds-prediction schemes to legally outwit gambling establishments.

Blue Box –A device used by phone hackers—in the '70s, when the expense involved in long distance calling was truly onerous—that bypassed the exchange circuitry by emitting a tone that duplicated call frequencies; this was after it was discovered that a cereal premium whistle from a box of Cap'n Crunch produced the effect. The person most notorious for the Blue Box was Call Computer employee, and later Wozniak prankster-mentor, John Draper, aka "Cap'n Crunch."

BNC Connector – Specialty threaded input plug, used to connect other components to a television.

Breakout – *Breakout* was Atari's intended successor to the wildly popular 1976 game *Pong*. While *Pong* slid a cursor vertically upon its virtual *Ping-Pong* table layout, *Breakout* employed a horizontally-oriented paddle/cursor to control a zig-zagging projectile tasked with breaking down a wall of bricks. Steve Jobs was assigned a role in its development, and looking to skim on chips, farmed out its engineering design to Steve Wozniak.

Bytes – (See Bits) Eight bits form a byte (or **binary term**).

CAD – Computer-Aided Design, a software application; an electronic means of creating mechanical drawings.

Call Computer - an agency that supplied time-share use of a remote, or *dumb* terminal, a terminal helpless to respond to commands, or process input, since it's merely attached to a remote master computer. This was one solution to the formerly common too-few-computers-to-users ratio.

Cassette I-O Board – A cassette board houses cassettes for information storage on a vintage computer. The "I/O" stands for "input/output," which, in engineering terms, has to do with the boundary between the machine and the human user, sometimes also known as the "user-interface." It's basically an expression of how the machine interacts with the user and vice-versa, and how that relationship affects design criterion. In physical terms, it refers to the input holes for ports and pins that dot a circuit board.

Cassette Tape Interface – The pre-digital, analogue means of uploading software programs, or storing work within a program.

Chip - A small electronic circuit, also known as an integrated circuit.

Clock Driver – In processor design, a circuit that paces the timing signals that allow advanced processes to play out.

Commodore – Radio Shack's entry in the microcomputer stakes; the first reliable, cheap, all-in-one system that helped initiate the microprocessor age.

CPUs – Central Processing Unit, the main component powering an electronic device.

Cromenco Dazzler Card – To quote the 1976 ad from Cromenco, Los Altos "Specialists in Computer Peripherals," the Dazzler Card provided a "computer/TV interface circuit" that "lets you have a full-color computer display terminal for little more than a black & white terminal." It transferred the image that would have appeared on the computer, and rendered it to appear on a color television set.

Cyber 74 – One model of a family of supercomputers from Control Data Corporation, from the '70s and '80s. [Mimms]

Developer – Roughly, a programmer using any existing tech framework to create specialized applications or variations.

Disassembler – reverses and unravels the process as outlined in the Assembler; the binary pattern is converted back into the original assembly code.

DRAM/bipolar DRAM - **D**ynamic **R**andom **A**ccess **M**emory, a form of memory storage in integrated circuitry. Bipolar DRAMs additionally feature a switching mechanism, which is a means of extending the memory storage capabilities and reducing the limitations of processor technology.

John Draper – AKA Cap'n Crunch. (See: **Blue Box**) An original tech revolutionary, hacker, and phone phreaker. From pirate radio, to illicit phone activities, to computers, a man who's always been outside the confines of the law.

EEG – Acronym for Electroencephalogram, which is a device that, when affixed to the scalp, monitors the electrical activity of the brain. [Kottke]

Electronic Music Synthesizer –(see Moog). [Kottke]

EMI – Electromagnetic Interference.

ENIAC – **E**lectronic **N**umerical **I**ntegrator and **C**omputer, the original functional computer, from back in the day when computation was the bailiwick of scientific and mathematics professionals.

FABLINE – A quality control and analytic mechanism in the semiconductor industry that takes into account and compensates for component shrinkage. [Sander]

Lee Feldenstein – Feldenstein built a video application for the Altair, among his other works, while he was affiliated with Processer Technology. He's more pertinent to this narrative for conducting the Homebrew Club meetings at the Stanford Linear Accelerator venue. That means (according to Dan Sokol) that he was the Type A guy with the loudest voice. Feldenstein was multifaceted: his activities alternated between the Northern California tech community, and the counterculture. He earned a Bachelor of Science from UC, Berkeley, or was a tech school dropout (depending on the info source), and, when not in school, contributed to the underground press and war protest demonstrations.

Floating Point (version of *BASIC*) – In this form of BASIC programming, the *point* referred to in Floating Point is the decimal point, which can *float*, or be repositioned, thus affecting the value of the input contained in the numeric field. [Sander]

FORTRAN – FORTRAN is an early higher-level programming language; its name was derived from the IBM **For**mula **Tran**slating System, one iteration of which—Fortran II—was influential on the development of *BASIC*.

Robert Friedland – Steve Jobs' Reed College friend and mentor, engaged in the spiritual questing of the time which was philosophically manifested by reading about Eastern religious practices, and physically expressed through experimentation with natural foods. He's credited with the psyche-out techniques and mind-games that were a part of Jobs' arsenal. [Elizabeth Holmes]

Good Earth – The first official—as in *non-residential*—Apple office location, named after an organic health food restaurant frequented by Steve Jobs, located right on the same strip.

Gruds in Space – A 1983 computer game by Chuck Sommerville and Joseph Dudar, and published by Sirius Software, the player portrays a space captain running a rescue mission, the object of which is to fuel a ship stranded on Pluto. According to *Apple2games.com*, "At the heart of the game is a weird quirkiness that other adventures didn't seem to have."

GUI - **G**raphic **U**ser **I**nterface, or "Gooey": this refers to all of the graphic features intended to make computing accessible to the average user, as opposed an electrical engineer or other specialist. Features include the mobile pop-up window (or window*s*) that appear within the overall frame of the screen, icons, and other design elements that visually represent all the various basic files and locations.

Hole in the Wall – Computer education initiative, founded by Sugata Mitra, for kids without access to classroom resources. [Loop]

Hex code – Refers to *Hexidecimal* code, or, in other words, a framework for tying memory integers to location. It's a set of calculations used to arrange HTML, and etc. An example of one purpose of Hex is to colorize HTML programming content.

Hunt Brothers – Billionaire Texan oil barons who cornered the world market in silver in the '70s, until market corrections were set in place to offset inflation. [Bob & silver passage]

IMSAI – A notable rival of the Altair, manufactured by IMS Associates, Inc., intended for small business data processing and data-entry.

Integrated Circuits – These days, the electronics consumer is accustomed to extremely compact devices, even though only since the late '50s has it been possible to compute on anything smaller than a house. How has this development become possible? The use of transistors, as opposed to vacuum tubes, was one step towards miniaturization. But transistors and the other wiring and mechanisms involved in circuitry still need a certain allowance of space. The solution was to bundle the capacitors and resistors of a circuit into a single chip, which offers maximum compression.

Intel Intellect – **I**ntegrated **E**lectronics was founded in 1978, and is a highly influential semiconductor builder and pioneered in memory chip development, thus spearheading the microprocessor revolution. [Larsen]

Interpreter – A program that translates an instruction into computer language.

Janky – A disreputable, or low-quality item. [Ini]

Kenback-1 – The first ever commercially available PC, pre-microprocessor era, from 1971.

Mac OS X – Mac operating system with graphical user interface.

Memory – electronic data storage.

Memory Cards – physical means of data storage.

Mike Murray – Apple marketer responsible for overseeing the seminal 1984 Super Bowl commercial, and, with Jobs, partnered with Adobe to create desktop publishing. In the context of Solomonson's anecdote, Murray was acting as Jobs' traveling secretary. [Solomonson]

MITS – Stands for **M**icro **I**nstrumentation **T**elemetry **S**ystems, based in Albuquerque, NM. The producers of the Altair (1975), among the very first fully-functioning microprocessors, or personal computers, to enter the market.

Moog Synthesizer – An electronic musical device that merged the computer and the keyboard, the Moog occupied the next evolutionary stage after the Theremin, (the soundtrack instrument of choice for '50s sci-fi films,) which was basically a box and wand that emitted alterable sonic waves. Robert Moog used principles of the Theremin to develop the Moog Synthesizer, which processed tones formatted through a switchboard console. Moog later responded to musicians' desire for keyboard touch-sensitivity and the ability to tone shift, which allowed the instrument became less robotic and capable of nuanced musical expression.

Nand Gates – Having to do with both binary code and circuitry paths, according to Allen Baum, *nand* represents "*not and*," as in, "mathematically: not A & B." That is, the input/output can either only one or the other, hence the binary part. The *gates* have to do with electronic circuitry pathways.

Mnemonics – A computer language assembly code similar to standard mnemonics in the respect that it uses the first letters of a word to compose an acronym. An example would be *Software as a Service*: SaaS. [Sokol]

OHM – A unit of electrical voltage as named after German physicist Georg Ohm.

Operand – In computer terms, this refers to either specifically the data being used or the management of the data. [Kottke]

People's Computer Company – Specifically, a storefront in Menlo Park that hosted a time sharing terminal, and later (by 1973) was stocked with public-access microprocessors. More generally, the PCC was a computer collective formed with the intent of leveling the data playing field by taking information technology—pretty much solely in the hands of the engineering class and other technocrats—to the masses.

Phreaking – Hackers who, by use of inside information, or knowledge of a range of systemic technologic vulnerabilities, specialized in high-jacking national and international phone lines for fun, or as a means to strike a blow against the establishment.

Pong game – *Pong* was Atari's first major hit, and launched the era of computer games. In its day, it fascinated players with the steady pulse of its motion-element, and the challenge of having to anticipate the virtual paddle placement relative to that of the moving projectile. [Sokol]

Punch Sorter – Data storage has gone through many iterations. A primary means of recording and interpreting information through the '50s and '60s was by means of punched or perforated cards—the holes corresponding to selections on a form—which were then fed into a machine to be tabulated.

RAM – Random access memory. Since memory is structured on a two-dimensional grid, a memory cell is similar to a grid cell on an Excel spreadsheet. If you know the column and row, you can find and access the information in any cell. The 'Random Access' part is that broad flexibility of access.

Read-Write Capability – A *capability* is like a password that allows access to a program, by, for instance, skirting a firewall. Its purpose is to allow or disallow a user to complete an operation. In this example, the operation is the ability to read or write within the program.

Reality Distortion Field – It's not unusual for management to overreach. During its formative years, Jobs became known, by the developers on various projects, for his irrational expectations in regards to the humanly possible in terms of project deadlines and/or outcomes. He could be very persuasive. When making some clearly impossible assertion, those who didn't know better were taken in, and the justifiably skeptical could often be inspired to fulfill his unreasonable expectations. The term Reality Distortion Field was coined by , to refer to this phenomenon.

Resistors – Resistors dampen or channel electric current within a circuit.

ROM – Read-only Memory. An integrated circuit containing pre-programmed information.

Semiconductor – The semiconductor industry considerably pre-dates the microcomputer. PCs may seem to be the essence of Silicon Valley production, but the *silicon* of the term is the sealant used to ensure reliability in semiconductor assembly. Semiconductors were the electronic bits and pieces at the heart of vintage tech components; refrigerators, air conditioners... and really, too many items or products to name.

SLAC (Stanford Linear Accelerator Center): Stanford, at the behest of/or in partnership with the Department of Energy, constructed the world's largest particle accelerator facility, beginning in 1962. Particle acceleration is — very roughly—a means for physicists to replicate the dynamics of electrons, and other volatile subatomic elements, within a wide range of experimental variables and under controlled conditions. The center houses an active lecture hall, and The Homebrew Computer Club, after outgrowing other venues, was permitted to use the auditorium for its gatherings.

Snake Byte – In Snake Byte, the player manipulates the snake towards apples that pop up on the screen. Snake eats apple, grows larger, and so on. As the cycle continues, it becomes more challenging to maintain the apple-to-snake ratio. [Mimms]

Star Raiders – This simulation-style game wrings maximum excitement out of the rudimentary graphics and sound of the early Atari aesthetic. The graphics are composed of really large-scale pixels, and the robotic arcade audio scheme—swooshes, bleeps and etcetera—sets off the action convincingly. And action is the point of *Star Raider's* appeal. From the vantage of a pilot looking out at a star field, the *ship* advances, lunging and swerving into space, ducking photon torpedoes. The animation is highly evolved in comparison to the bold, yet lacking-in-all-detail graphics. [Copson]

Static RAMs, Dynamic RAMs – A variation of formats of memory. (See RAM.) Static RAM is the fast, expensive kind, since each chip contains less memory overall. Dynamic RAM is the slow, cheap kind, with more capacity.

Steve Dompier; Dompier Music – Steven Dompier was a founding member of the Homebrew Computer Club. Dompier Music refers to his adaptation of the Altair computer, which allowed it to play simple pre-programmed melodic tones.

Stevens Creek – Transitional location of the early phase of Apple office facility locations.

PARC Research – PARC stands for **P**alo **A**lto **R**esearch **C**enter. [Larsen]

Retiro – The surging, high-density transportation hub of the region, Retiro is known for both high-end, swanky retail, and for an intensive underworld presence. [Ini]

The Lisa – Successor to the Apple][, named for Steve Jobs' illegitimate daughter, apparently as a means of accepting his paternity.

Texas Instruments versus Intel –Lawsuit to determine which rival company was the first to produce and market a working semiconductor chip, and thus which company possessed a valid patent. [Larsen]

Trojan Horse – The full title is, *Behold the Trojan Horse: Instructional vs. Productivity Computing in the Classroom*, a paper for an educational symposium, dealing with computers as a tool for, or a subject of, learning. [Loop]

UNITA – An acronym for the Portuguese translation for National Front for Total Independence of Angola, with translates in Portuguese to **U**nião **N**acional para a **I**ndependência **T**otal de **A**ngola. The organization emerged from earlier factions, but the entity presided over by Jonas Savimbe pitted conservative Portuguese factions against communist Soviet influence. [O'Mahony]

Vax Server – Vax stands for **V**irtual **A**ddress E**x**tension, which was a Digital Equipment Corporation server from the late '70s. [Sams]

VisiCalc – the first computational spreadsheet program, a game-changer for the business world, designed by Dan Bricklin and Bob Frankson. [Sokol]

West Coast Computer Faire – Established in 1977, and held annually in and around the in San Francisco area, the Faire was a trade show that coincided with the emergence of the microcomputer, and the setting for more established companies, and bootstrap startups.

Xerox Star – The Star was Xerox's microcomputer which introduced several elements, such as screen icons and the mouse, that would inform Apple's development of the Lisa, and the Mac.

FOOTNOTE citations

9-D:

    http://admissions.ucdavis.edu/admission/transfers/trfr_stmr_ce.cfm

Jim Alinsky:

    http://mirrors.apple2.org.za/Apple%20II%20Documentation%20Project/Books
    /W.%20Gayler%20-%20The%20Apple%20II%20Circuit%20Description.pdf

    http://www.solomonson.net/Calculatorhtml/MIC.Apple1.Jim.html

Apple][, Apple][c:

    http://en.wikipedia.org/wiki/Apple_II_series

Apple computer models:

    http://www.webdesignerdepot.com/2009/01/the-evolution-of-apple-design-
    between-1977-2008/

    Apple Confidential, Owen Linzmayer (get publishers info) quoted in Chapter 9

Assembler:

    http://cnettv.cnet.com/wozniak-demon-typist/9742-1_53-29921.html (video)

Atlantic City Personal Computer Festival:

    http://allaboutstevejobs.com/bio/timeline.php

Atlantis:

    http://www.familyfunatatlantis.com/?gclid=CPjNmZyU_7UCFcqd4AodiAMAaQ

Bits:

    http://www.webopedia.com/TERM/B/bit.html

    http://computer.howstuffworks.com/bytes.htm

Bipolar DRAM:

    http://www.google.com/patents/US5262670

Bitmapped Screen:

    http://encyclopedia2.thefreedictionary.com/bitmap+display

Cassette tape memory storage:

    http://www.maximumpc.com/article/news/computer_data_storage_through
_ages

Chip:

    http://www.wisegeek.com/what-is-a-computer-chip.htm

Clock Driver:

    http://doc.ntp.org/4.1.1/refclock.htm

    http://bwrcs.eecs.berkeley.edu/IcBook/Projects/ClockDriver.pdf

Cyber 74:

    http://chessprogramming.wikispaces.com/CDC+Cyber

Disassemblers:

    http://en.wikibooks.org/wiki/X86_Disassembly/Disassemblers_and_Decompil
ers

EEG:

    http://www.nlm.nih.gov/medlineplus/ency/article/003931.htm

FABLINE:

    http://www.bruker.com/en/products/x-ray-diffraction-and-elemental-
analysis/x-ray-metrology/d8-fabline/overview.html

    http://www.thefreedictionary.com/metrology

Floating Point:

    http://support.esri.com/en/knowledgebase/GISDictionary/term/floating%20p
oint

Gruds in Space:

    http://www.apple2games.com/wiki/Gruds_in_Space

GUI:

    http://www.linfo.org/gui.html

Hunt Brothers:

    http://www.traderslog.com/hunt-brothers-silver/

Integrated Circuits:

    http://www.pbs.org/transistor/background1/events/icinv.html

Intel Intellect:

    http://www.telegraph.co.uk/finance/personalfinance/comment/4459475/Silic
on-Giants-Intels-intellect.html#mm_hash

Interpreter:

    http://www.merriam-webster.com/dictionary/interpreter

377

http://www.webopedia.com/TERM/I/interpreter.html

Janky:

https://www.google.com/url?sa=t&rct=j&q=&esrc=s&source=web&cd=1&cad
=rja&ved=0CDlQFjAA&url=http%3A%2F%2Fwww.urbandictionary.com%2Fdefine.php%
3Fterm%3DJanky&ei=XWBkUZzUKdXF4AOLn4DADg&usg=AFQjCNHz_TRXMULMTeBWTP
cuDcby4csIFA

Kenback-1:

http://www.kenbak-1.net/index.htm

Mac OS X:

http://www.howstuffworks.com/macs/mac-os-x.htm

Mike Murray:

www.deseretnews.com/article/print/705392073/1984-Apple-marketer-
remembers-Jobs-early-years.html

Mnemonics:

http://whatis.techtarget.com/definition/mnemonic

Nand Gates:

Allen Baum email

OHM:

http://www.merriam-webster.com/dictionary/ohm

Punch Card Sorter:

http://news.cnet.com/2300-13510_3-10002872.html

RAM:

http://computer.howstuffworks.com/ram.htm

Read/Write Capability:

http://www.eros-os.org/essays/capintro.html

Resistors:

kpsec.freeuk.com

Retiro:

http://en.wikipedia.org/wiki/Retiro,_Buenos_Aires

http://www.tripadvisor.com/Attraction_Review-g312741-d642258-Reviews-
Retiro-Buenos_Aires_Capital_Federal_District.html

Snake Byte:

http://www.vizzed.com/playonlinegames/game.php?id=29670

Sol-20:

http://www.sol20.org/

Resistors:

http://www.kpsec.freeuk.com/components/resist.htm#real

Robert Friedland:

Jobs bio, Walter Isaacson

ROM:

http://computer.howstuffworks.com/rom.htm

UNITA:

378

http://www.britannica.com/EBchecked/topic/405514/UNITA

VisiCalc:

http://www.bricklin.com/visicalc.htm

West Coast Computer Faire:

http://www.atariarchives.org/bcc3/showpage.php?page=98

Xerox Star, PARC:

http://xeroxstar.tripod.com/

The New Yorker, "Annals of Technology, The Tweaker," Malcolm Gladwell, November 14th, 2011.